THE COMPLETE IDIOT'S GUIDE® TO

2012

by Synthia Andrews and Colin Andrews

ALPHA

A member of Penguin Group (USA) Inc.

We would like to dedicate this book to all the ancestors; specifically our own, Mr. and Mrs. Gordon Andrews, and Dr. Gale Russel Ramsby.

ALPHA BOOKS

Published by the Penguin Group

Penguin Group (USA) Inc., 375 Hudson Street, New York, New York 10014, USA

Penguin Group (Canada), 90 Eglinton Avenue East, Suite 700, Toronto, Ontario M4P 2Y3, Canada (a division of Pearson Penguin Canada Inc.)

Penguin Books Ltd, 80 Strand, London WC2R 0RL, England

Penguin Ireland, 25 St. Stephen's Green, Dublin 2, Ireland (a division of Penguin Books Ltd.)

Penguin Group (Australia), 250 Camberwell Road, Camberwell, Victoria 3124, Australia (a division of Pearson Australia Group Pty. Ltd.)

Penguin Books India Pvt. Ltd., 11 Community Centre, Panchsheel Park, New Delhi—110 017, India

Penguin Group (NZ), 67 Apollo Drive, Rosedale, North Shore, Auckland 1311, New Zealand (a division of Pearson New Zealand Ltd.)

Penguin Books (South Africa) (Pty.) Ltd, 24 Sturdee Avenue, Rosebank, Johannesburg 2196, South Africa

Penguin Books Ltd., Registered Offices: 80 Strand, London WC2R 0RL, England

Publisher: *Marie Butler-Knight*
Editorial Director: *Mike Sanders*
Senior Managing Editor: *Billy Fields*
Executive Editor: *Randy Ladenheim-Gil*
Development Editor: *Lynn Northrup*
Production Editor: *Megan Douglass*
Copy Editor: *Michael Dietsch*

Cartoonist: *Steve Barr*
Cover Designer: *Kurt Owens*
Book Designer: *Trina Wurst*
Indexer: *Celia McCoy*
Layout: *Brian Massey*
Proofreader: *John Etchison*

Contents at a Glance

Contents

Foreword

From snowstorms to drought, to the inexplicable loss of insect and animal life, it seems that we are entering a time of planetary change. Do the signs of climate change indicate the end of human life on earth as we know it? Did the Mayans have an in-depth prophetic knowledge through which they could determine our extinction almost a thousand years ago? *The Complete Idiot's Guide to 2012* is a provocative tool to what many around the world see as the groundbreaking, historic event that will take place in our immediate future. The interplay of history, anthropology, and planetary changes has captivated the imagination and skills of Synthia and Colin Andrews, two gifted writers who bring us meticulous insights into the prophetic Mayan calendar, specifically the awaited Long Count day of the Mayan calendar: December 21, 2012.

Why were the Mayans looking so far into the future? The authors have provided us with a thorough examination of the prophetic timeline past, present, and future. Some of their research includes the strange disappearance of the ancient Mayans in Central America, the five ages of the Aztec culture, the present knowledge of pyramid power, the recent UN report on climate change, as well as future possibilities of stronger sun-spot cycles, a magnetic field reversal, increased gamma waves, and other astronomical events that can severely affect both our Sun and Earth.

With a comprehension of the possibilities of what 2012 has in store for us, the reader moves from the unknown to the known. The authors have provided a clear and insightful guide regarding the vast possibilities that are before us. In so doing, they also bring forth a hidden road map of positive solutions for changing our course of action that would activate a global emergence of humanity with greater dynamics of consciousness, recognizing our place in a vast and awesome universe. Thus, this book is a type of formula or Rosetta stone to alleviate our own lack of awareness and lead us step-by-step into a greater awakening so we can establish a positive side to global change.

There is a growing recognition that we are now entering an age of vast planetary change. The United Nations leaders connected with the Intergovernmental Panel on Climate Change (IPCC) are now telling us that we have only ten years to reduce our production of greenhouse gas emissions or face the extinction of many species worldwide, on land and in our oceans. This dire prediction seems to coordinate our contemporary problems with the deciphered 2012 prophecy of the Mayans. Indeed, the anticipated extraordinary scientific findings and views have been brought together in this book at this critical time to challenge humanity to re-think its future in the twenty-first century.

Yet, prophecy should be thought of as a wake-up call and not a *fait accompli*. Let us see this prophecy as a way to change what we are doing both technologically and in our relations with one another. Let the Mayan prophecy of 2012 send a clear signal to the citizens of the world that planetary change on all levels (climate, food, water, etc.) can lead to our demise if we do not make the necessary changes. Solutions should be found that will prescribe new emissions reductions, climate-friendly technologies, as well as establish the psychological, spiritual, and consciousness balance critically needed to stabilize and harmonize planet Earth.

In reading this book, we need to ask ourselves two important questions: How can these insights for both survival and transformation be applied by me to strengthen my understanding of the larger road map of life? Am I willing to be a partner in cooperation toward positive change in my contract with all peoples on Mother Earth?

This book is a guide to the wise to emphasize the positive possibilities that can come forth from our present planetary crisis and upheavals. The time is ripe to build on the momentum that is being forged by the Armageddon scenarios depicting our immediate future. Our soul searching to find answers should necessitate and inspire us to change and take the upward path and be part of the culture of peace and goodwill that will surely follow!

—James J. Hurtak, Ph.D., Founder and President of the Academy for Future Science, an international NGO in special consultative status with the United Nations Economic and Social Council

Introduction

You've heard of the enigmatic date of December 21, 2012, or you wouldn't have picked up this book. You may even have heard that on this date the world will come to an end. Who decided this and why? Images of volcanoes, floods, and giant storms have swamped the bookshelves relating to coming events of this date. Is this really what is foretold, and why should you believe it?

To answer these questions let your mind journey back 2,000 years to the Yucatán peninsula. A civilization is flourishing in the jungle, as highly developed as the most advanced Western civilization of the time. This is the empire of the Maya. They live in urban communities with plazas and marketplaces overshadowed by commanding step pyramids and imposing palaces. Hieroglyphic writing graces steles, monuments telling of the victories and history of their society. Along with written language and developed mathematics, the Maya have done what no other culture of their time has done: created a calendar that covers the span of 5,126 years with nearly the same accuracy as the atomic clock of today.

At a time when London was a lonely Roman outpost amidst Celtic warlords, when Europeans still believed the sun revolved around the earth, the Maya had made tremendous astronomical advances. Without telescopes or modern equipment they deciphered the night sky. They understood advanced astronomical concepts; tracked the movements of stars, planets, and the Milky Way galaxy; charted celestial alignments and calculated celestial events over epic spans of time. Without any way of confirming it, they knew through calculation that a full cycle through the precession of the equinoxes took approximately 26,000 years!

One way the Maya used their astronomical calculations was to observe repeating cycles and make predictions. Many of the predictions recorded in early codices, or books of knowledge, are only now unfolding and are being confirmed by today's NASA science.

The date of 2012 comes from modern interpretation of the Maya Long Count calendar. Beliefs about what will happen in this time frame range from catastrophe to transformation and evolution into a higher spiritual reality. Some predictions are foretold in Mayan holy books such as the *Popol Vuh* and *Chilam Balam*. However, current understanding of the books of the Maya are colored by our own cultural biases. No one can speak for the Maya except the Maya Elders, and only a few of the Elders are talking at this time.

The year 2012 has become the focus of many end-of-the-world predictions. These predictions eerily match many of the trends of the times we're in. This book will explain the predictions, the controversies, and the hope of the changing of the ages. Shall we take a journey back to the times of the Maya?

How to Use This Book

This book is divided into six parts. Each part provides vital insights preparing you for the next part. Consider you are starting on a journey into the land and mind of the Maya. Let your imagination embrace the many concepts you will encounter.

Part 1, "The Timekeepers," introduces you to the history, beliefs, and sacred texts of the Maya. It takes you through the development of their math and astronomy and into the creation of the calendars. It provides the essential foundation for understanding how the predictions work and why they're so intricate and exact.

Part 2, "Cosmic Treasure Hunt," takes you into the mystical workings of the Mayan calendars, through the movements of celestial alignments, and into the codes within the Mayan pyramids. It provides the answers to why December 21, 2012, is the end date, what astronomical changes could happen, and what the significance of a changing age is.

Part 3, "Predications of 2012," takes you into the predictions themselves. What will happen in 2012? Will the world end? The actual calendar predictions and Mayan prophecies are revealed. They are compared to other end-time predictions from the Bible, the Hopi, Nostradamus, Edgar Cayce, and New Age visionaries. Past prophecies are examined for accuracy and incongruence. This part ends with the perspective expressed by different Mayan Elders of today.

Part 4, "2012: Signs of Change," looks at the world today for evidence of the fulfilling predictions. World events, climate change, and changes in people's awareness are examined in the light of 2012. You might be surprised at what this part reveals.

Part 5, "Transition," helps prepare you for the challenges of what's to come. You'll learn how to identify the changing times in your personal life; simple preparedness for storms and crises; and skills for inner empowerment. This part supports an easy and graceful transition.

Part 6, "After 2012," explores the awakening the Mayans predict for the coming golden age. It lets you see what the future may hold for you. Is there another calendar cycle? What do the prophecies say about it?

More Mayan Magic

Throughout this book we add four types of sidebars to help enhance your understanding of the text:

Celestial Connection
Check these boxes for intriguing links to different cultures, scientific facts, or interesting insights.

 Codex Cues

These boxes give you a little extra direction into interesting ideas.

 Cosmic Caution

These boxes contain cautions for when taking something too far could be dangerous, as well as common misconceptions.

def•i•ni•tion

Check these boxes for definitions of unusual or unfamiliar terms and expressions.

Acknowledgments

First and foremost we would like to thank the Mayan Elders who have held the ancient traditions that mean so much to the world today. We are also grateful to the archeologists, astronomers, and writers who have put their reputations on the line to uncover and report alternate information. Many people have contributed time, information, and insight to this book, and we thank them all! Special thanks to the following:

Dr. Jean-Noel Aubrun, physicist and engineer, founder of the Marjan Research Company, contractor at NASA and the Ames National Aeronautical Research Center.

Dr. Melih Arici

Drunvalo Melchizedek, founder of the Flower of Life Workshop and a respected futurist.

Dr. James Hurtak and Dr. Desiree Hurtak, founders of the Academy for Future Science (AFFS), an NGO in consultative status with the United Nations Economic and Social Council.

Dr. Simeon Hein, remote viewer, founder of Mount Baldy Press, and author of *Open Minds*.

Prof. Gerald Hawkins, Department of Astronomy, Boston University, and author of many books, including *Stonehenge Decoded.* He discovered diatonic ratios in crop circles while working on Colin's research data.

Bert Gunn, translator and envoy to Toltec Elder Tlakaelel.

Tlakaelel, Aztec, Mexica-Tolteca Elder, protector of the oral tradition of the Toltec indigenous knowledge.

Ellis Bradley, envoy to the Kogi tribe, Colombia.

Quinn Ramsby, biomedical engineer, MS.

Ron Russell, well-known visionary space artist, remote viewer, and crop circle researcher.

Laura Turlington and Luca DiMatteo, creators of One Community Programs.

Randy Ladenheim-Gil, executive editor, Alpha Books.

Lynn Northrup, development editor.

A very special thanks to our agent, **Marilyn Allen,** who dropped this golden opportunity into our laps, opening a magical door of synchronicity.

Trademarks

All terms mentioned in this book that are known to be or are suspected of being trademarks or service marks have been appropriately capitalized. Alpha Books and Penguin Group (USA) Inc. cannot attest to the accuracy of this information. Use of a term in this book should not be regarded as affecting the validity of any trademark or service mark.

Part 1

The Timekeepers

To fully appreciate the significance of 2012 and the Mayan calendar, you may want to know more about Mayan history and culture. Don't worry; we won't submerge you in too many facts and figures!

The hardest element for most people to grasp is the unique worldview of the Maya. They saw humans as an integral part of an interactive, living galaxy. This worldview was fertile ground for the development of hieroglyphic writing, mathematics, advanced architecture, and the formulation of prophecy. The accuracy of their prophecies allowed them to prepare for disasters such as the coming of the Spanish; to protect themselves and their holy records; and to plan for a future time when once again their knowledge would rise. That future time is now and their knowledge is again coming to the forefront.

The Mysterious Maya

In This Chapter

◆ The remnants of Mayan knowledge

◆ Origins of the ancient Maya

◆ The Mayan lifestyle

◆ Theories on why the Maya vanished

◆ Other people in the region

◆ The Maya among us

Prior to hearing about end-of-the-world predictions for 2012, how much did you know of the Mayan people? How much do you know now? Probably not a lot. You've almost certainly seen pictures of their pyramids and you might have heard something about their advanced mathematics and astronomy. However, for most of us, the Maya remain shrouded in romantic mystery.

There are many reasons for this mystique, not the least of which is our inability to entertain the advanced nature of their civilization. For example, it's hard for us to consider an ancient culture having a sophisticated concept of time, where time wasn't seen as an unchanging constant but was seen the same way modern-day quantum physics sees it—as a dimension whose properties can expand and contract. It was the Maya's fascination with time that opened the door to the insights for the 2012 predictions.

Lost Knowledge

Although the ancient Maya had a sophisticated writing system and kept records of historical events, religious practices, calendar interpretations, and more, we have almost no original books to learn from. They were lost along with many sacred items of the Maya when the Spanish arrived in the 1500s. Spanish conquistadores invading South America destroyed as many of the Mayan sacred books as they could find. Only three complete books and a fragment of a fourth were saved from the fires and have been available for study by Western scholars. For many years it was believed these books, called *codices*, were the only remnants of preconquest Maya knowledge. The truth is that many books were saved by the Mayan people and hidden for centuries by the elders and holy people.

def•i•ni•tion

The Maya recorded their history in books of paper made from the inner bark of wild fig trees. Mayan paper was developed around the same time as papyrus paper was developed in Rome. The books are called **codices** (or **codex,** singular) or folding books because of the way they were folded, wrapped in hides, and stored in record rooms. Modern excavations occasionally turn up more books, ruined by humidity and weather.

The loss of such valuable documents to Western study has made it hard to decipher the hieroglyphic language of the Maya, a feat still not fully accomplished. In fact, significant breakthroughs didn't occur until the 1970s, with major translations happening in the 1990s.

Also, Western scholars study ancient manuscripts with a biased eye. Everything we know is based on interpretation through the lens of our own culture. What the Maya mean and what we think they mean can be two very different things. It's good to keep this in mind when you read about Mayan mythology. The traditional interpretations may be far from the true Mayan meaning. Until the Maya elders themselves come forward to share their knowledge in the future, you and I will never truly know their history and depth.

So what do we know about ancient Mayan civilization? Who are these mysterious people?

The Ancient Maya

The ancient Maya lived in Central America, south of the Tropic of Cancer and north of the equator. The region they occupied is referred to as the Maya Area and is still inhabited by the Mayan people today. The Maya Area is loosely divided into three zones:

◆ Southern Maya highlands, including the mountain terrain of Guatemala and southern Mexico

◆ Southern (or central) Maya lowlands, which are north of the highlands and include parts of Mexico, northern Guatemala, Belize, Honduras, and El Salvador

◆ Northern Maya lowlands of the Yucatán peninsula

The land they inhabited ranged from fertile plains to the high mountain ranges of the Sierra Madre; from jungles and swamps to volcanic plateaus. Fragile ecosystems required advanced agricultural practice, and the key limiting natural resource was water.

Visitors today are struck by the presence of massive stone monuments rising out of the denseness of the misty forest, silent tributes to a lost civilization. In this place, time is said to move to a different rhythm and belong to a more complete reality. It's easy to get caught up in a mythical and magical view of these people, and yet they were not so different than we are today—occupied with farming, trading, and building intricate communities. They were involved with politics and wars, struggled to maintain good relationships with neighbors and fair systems of trade and government. People suffered loss and illness, death, and calamity; performed religious ritual; and labored to understand the complexity of the world they lived in.

The Maya Area included parts of Southern Mexico, the Yucatán, northern Guatemala, Belize, Honduras, and El Salvador.

Roots of the Mayan People

Even the origin of the Mayan people has an element of the mysterious. The first people to inhabit Central America were believed to have arrived around 10000 B.C.E. However, radiocarbon dating of bones found near Mexico City show that hunter-gatherers lived in the region as early as 21000 B.C.E. Anthropologists believe the tribes came from the north after crossing the Bering Strait land bridge between Siberia and Alaska. Settlements formed between 7000 and 5000 B.C.E. and farming of corn, squash, and other wild plants began. By 5000 B.C.E. selective breeding of corn had turned it into a staple crop, and by 2000 B.C.E. people lived in villages and cultivated cotton for clothing. In Europe at this time, people were also starting to live in villages and grow crops. Pottery was showing up worldwide. The first four classic civilizations appeared in Mesopotamia, Egypt, India, and China. It appears the Maya, although unknown, were the fifth of the "first civilizations."

Celestial Connection

Interestingly, the Mayan pyramids are older than the Egyptian pyramids, although people often think it's the other way around. Actually, Stonehenge was built in England in 2800 B.C.E., while the pyramid at Cuicuilco in Mexico was built in 2750 B.C.E. and the Great Pyramid in Egypt was built in 2560 B.C.E. It's amazing that early civilizations seemed to erupt all across the planet in the same general time period!

Indications of a single Mayan language, called Proto-Maya, existed at this time. Later this language would develop into several distinct dialects.

Let's explore some theories about the roots of the Maya.

The Maya and the Olmec

The Olmec are considered the first Mesoamerican civilization, followed closely by the Zapotec. Both are credited with developing the basics of writing and mathematics, which were later perfected by the Maya. However, there is substantial disagreement among historians.

Some argue the Maya arrived independently of the Olmec/Zapotec, developed side-by-side, and cross-fertilized culture, ideas, mathematics, and astronomy. This theory is based in part on the vast differences between the abilities, artwork, and traditions of the two cultures. If the Maya evolved from the Olmec, they underwent a huge leap forward with no known stimulus. Recent excavations at an early Mayan site called Cival suggest that Mayan civilization developed much earlier than previously thought and independently of the Olmec. The disagreement doesn't end there. Many alternative historians don't believe the Maya arrived by the Bering Strait land bridge at all.

Conquistadores' Theories

The Spanish conquistadores were the first to argue a more exotic origin. They were awed on their arrival at the Aztec city-state of Tenochtitlán, what is now Mexico City. Although amazed by the structures and the clearly advanced culture, they were truly stunned when further exploration revealed the more elaborate ruins of the Maya. They assumed the supremacy of the older Maya ruins, compared to later Aztec cities, indicated a slowly devolving society. Was there an earlier advanced culture that started Mesoamerican civilization? Did their knowledge slowly disappear with time? Searching for an explanation, they decided the Maya were one of the Lost Tribes of Israel.

Celestial Connection
Ten tribes of Israel were lost from Biblical record following the destruction of the Kingdom of Israel by Assyrians in 722 B.C.E. They were thought to be dispersed across the continents where they continued to keep and teach the tenants of Judaism. Of course, they could equally have been destroyed or absorbed into Assyrian culture. Theories as to where the Lost Tribes ended up are boundless. At different times Japanese, Celts, and Native Americans have been considered Lost Tribes. The Book of Mormon refers to Native Americans as one of the Lost Tribes despite the absence of connection between their languages, traditions, or genotype.

Mayan Legends

Another popular theory of the origin of the Maya comes from the Maya themselves. They refer to their arrival in Central America as the end of a migration from their destroyed homeland, named Aztlan. Could Aztlan be Plato's lost continent of Atlantis?

The origin of the story of Atlantis started with Plato between 350 and 300 B.C.E. He claimed the existence of a continent named Atlantis in the Atlantic Ocean off the Coast of Gibraltar. The inhabitants were an advanced civilization that dispersed when the continent was destroyed and sank under water. Many cultures around the world share this basic story. The legend survives in different forms with names such as Atalaya in the Canary Islands, Atlaintica in Spain, Attala in North Africa, Aztlan among the Maya, and Azatlan among North American Indigenous people.

The legend claims many Atlanteans escaped and colonized different civilizations. A theory that the Maya came from Atlantis was promoted by the famous prophet Edgar Cayce. While in a trance in April 1939, he claimed the breaking up of Atlantis resulted in the emigration of Atlanteans to colonize the Incas in Peru, the Maya in the Yucatan, as well as the Egyptians. (You'll learn more about Cayce and his predictions in Chapter 11.)

This theory is favored by those who are struck by the fact that these cultures developed advanced *hieroglyphic writing* styles and designed massive pyramid structures. Proponents remark on the ruins off the coast of the Bimini Islands as evidence of a network of past civilizations now underwater.

def•i•ni•tion

Hieroglyphic writing is a system of writing that uses pictures to represent words or concepts. A hieroglyph is a symbol used in hieroglyphic writing.

An Additional Theory

Theories on the connection between ancient Egypt and Mesoamerica were not limited to the Atlantis theory. Many alternative historians believe there were cultural dispersions from Egypt and other old-world communities to Central America. These historians believe that ancient Egyptians traveled by boat across the Atlantic Ocean, where they influenced the Mesoamerican cultural trends. This theory is a little hard to accept once you realize that the Mayan pyramids are older than the Egyptian pyramids.

The Life of the Maya

The history of the Maya remained hidden in the jungles for centuries. Abandoned ruins doled out their secrets slowly to dedicated explorers. Today advanced mapping and aerial surveillance allows discovery of lost structures previously concealed. Many new sites have been excavated in the last five to ten years. Two recent discoveries show pyramids, plazas, and complex writing much earlier than previously thought.

San Bartolo in northern Guatemala was discovered in 2001 by modern grave robbers and excavated in 2004. Cival, in the Peten basin of Guatemala, was discovered in the 1980s and excavated in 2001. These sites have helped reframe our understanding of the extent and completeness of the early Maya. Add to this the advances in deciphering the hieroglyphic language, and for the first time we begin to get a clearer picture of these ancient people.

Limited Sources

Regardless of the scientific advances, keep in mind the limited sources of information we have. In addition to the three surviving codices are two holy books translated into Spanish by Mayan scribes in the late 1500s. These books, the *Popol Vuh* and *Chilam Balam*, have been invaluable in understanding Mayan thought. However, a lot of what we know comes from inscriptions on monuments, funeral tombs, buildings, and murals in the temples. (See Chapter 2 for more on these books and the surviving codices.)

Imagine what would happen if all evidence of present-day American culture disappeared except for a couple of books and what was written on gravestones, public buildings, churches, shrines, and monuments. What would future explorers think excavating Washington, D.C., and deciphering the Jefferson and Lincoln Memorials, the lists of soldiers lost in World Wars I and II, Vietnam, and Korea? After reading our tombstones in Arlington Cemetery what would they think of our beliefs of the afterlife? We can all agree they would not have a complete view of our culture!

So what do we know about the ancient Maya? They farmed squash, corn, beans, cocoa, and other crops, which they both consumed and traded in the huge central plazas of their towns and cities. They grew cotton and developed a textile industry that spun and dyed thread used to weave clothing, bags, and ceremonial objects. They built elaborate roads, temples, astronomical observatories, and palaces.

They were both artists and scientists, but they never developed the wheel or used metal tools. They used obsidian, a very hard glass created from prehistoric volcanic lava, for spears and knifes. Even though they did not use metal tools, they mined copper, gold, silver, and jade, with which they made valuable art pieces and treasures. Mayan artwork is considered the most sophisticated in Mesoamerica.

Mayan Communities

The Maya lived in cities and villages that were related but there was no central government. Each region spoke its own dialect of the Mayan language. Every city was governed by a king who claimed descendance from a different god in the Mayan pantheon. Most of the time the kings were also shamans, or holy men, and served to open portals to the gods via ecstatic states (you'll learn more about portals in Chapters 2 and 3). The Maya still believe the material world is the result of spiritual forces, so the role of the king was essential. He not only had access to knowledge and wisdom for science but also was key to the survival and supremacy of the people. When things went wrong, there were no scapegoats; it was the king's responsibility to make things right.

Wealth was controlled by a powerful elite class and supported by the work of the peasantry. The Maya engaged in warfare as well as trade with neighboring city-states and other tribes. They were fierce in battle, as we know from the war monuments! Kings did not plan wars and send young men to battle. They led the battles themselves, and if they lost, they were sacrificed so the people could continue. It's also thought that the Maya settled disputes in the ball courts as an alternative to war. Ball courts were stadiums where ball games were played. At the end of the game, the losing (and occasionally, even the winning!) teammates were often sacrificed.

Mayan centers were large with huge populations. The Guatemalan ancient city of Tikal had an estimated population of well over 50,000 people. It covered six square miles and had more than 3,000 buildings. There were huge palaces boasting hundreds of rooms, multiple plazas, and miles of wooden huts. (And this at a time when London was a lonely outpost of the Roman Empire!)

As the population grew in the larger centers, producing enough food in the fragile thin soils became difficult. Extensive agricultural projects existed using terraced growing fields and advanced irrigation systems. Because of the fragility of food production, the Maya limited war activity to the dry seasons so agriculture would not be interrupted.

Historical Eras

Historians divide Mayan history into three eras:

- **Pre-classic (2000 B.C.E. to 250 C.E.).** The is the period of development when writing, ritual, astronomy, and architecture evolved. The calendars were designed in this period, recording events as far back as 600 B.C.E. Key archeological sites from this time period are Nakbe, El Mirada, Cival, and San Bartolo, all in the Peten region of Guatemala. This is considered the cradle of Mayan civilization and the center of the pre-classic era.

- **Classic (250 C.E. to 900 C.E.).** Mayan civilization reached its peak in this era. It was established as the dominant power in the region with advanced science, art, and architecture. The center of the civilization shifted north and the cities of Palenque, Tikal, and Calakmul were key centers of power. By 800 C.E. the lowland cities began to collapse, leading to the downfall of Mayan supremacy.

- **Post-classic (900 C.E. to 1521 C.E.).** By the beginning of this era the Maya were abandoning their cities in the southern lowlands. Chichen Itza in the Yucatán peninsula became the strongest Mayan center and ruled the northern regions, commanding many essential trade routes.

Vanishing Act

When the Spanish conquistadores explored the Maya Area looking for gold and treasure, they were disappointed. They describe entering massive cities, walking down paved streets alongside incredible temples and pyramids; all eerily empty. What happened? At first, famine or plague was assumed, but there were no vast gravesites or other signs of immediate, massive death. It was as if the people had simply disappeared.

Cosmic Caution

A common misconception is that the Mayan civilization was destroyed by the Spanish. Actually, Mayan centers were being abandoned 500 years before the Spanish arrived.

The exodus occurred during the last 100 years of the classic Maya period, around 800 C.E. It started with the collapse and abandonment of the southern lowland communities such as Tikal. Theories are grouped in three general camps: social/political upheaval, environmental collapse, and climate change. There is evidence to support all these theories, and the reality might be some combination of all.

Social/Political Upheaval

People may have voluntarily left the cities, perhaps due to information from the prophecies. Prophecies for this time period, as written in the *Chilam Balam*, describe a period of hardship when Mayan knowledge would need to be hidden. Many believe the Maya simply went underground to protect their culture from war or invasion with greater warrior societies like the Toltec.

Although destruction by warfare was a popular theory, there is no real evidence to support it. Usually victors take over and inhabit the cities they win in battle. This clearly did not happen here.

Another theory is revolution against the elite class, or even wars among the ruling class. At the end of the classic period, there was an unprecedented increase in urban construction followed by the complete cessation of building, then abandonment. Steles, the stone pillars with hieroglyphic inscriptions, and monuments were vandalized.

The theory is that social stress, increased war, and decreased trade along with a food shortage caused the ruling class to fight against each other and caused people to lose faith. If the king and his ruling class could no longer balance the universe, why build for them and work the fields? There is some evidence that after the ruling class was driven out, members of the population maintained the cities for a short period before they also abandoned them.

Environmental Collapse

The most accepted version is environmental. As the population in the great cities grew, it became harder and harder to provide food. The lands were overfarmed, deforestation occurred, and the depleted soils stopped producing. Add a little drought and the result is disaster. A 2004 NASA study seems to support this theory. NASA researchers studied the layers of sediment around major cities from the time of the abandonment. Pollen trapped in the sediment was from weeds only, indicating the trees were gone.

Climate Change

Finally, there was a substantial drought during this time period initiated by climate change. Water was already a limited commodity needing careful management. A series of droughts may well have been the turning point for the Maya.

We may never know the true circumstances, but the end result is that Mayan culture disappeared from the forefront of the Mesoamerican scene before the Spanish came in the 1500s.

Spanish Conquest

The Spanish conquest of the Americas rightly starts with Christopher Columbus. The stories he brought to Spain of the riches, animals, and resources in the "New World" sparked the imagination of Hernando Cortés Pizarro. Setting sail from Spain in 1505, Cortés landed in Hispaniola where he lived for several years. In 1519 he sailed to Cuba to claim it from the natives for Spain. In February 1519 he sailed for the coast of Yucatán. With 11 ships, approximately 500 to 600 soldiers, and 16 horses he landed at Tabasco on the northern coast of the Yucatán peninsula.

Celestial Connection

You probably know that Christopher Columbus was looking for a new trade route to India and Japan when he discovered the Americas in 1492. Instead of finding India, he found what are now the Bahamian Islands. He named the first island he landed on San Salvador, despite the fact that the inhabitants had already named it Guahanal. Columbus did not actually reach South America until his third voyage, in 1498. Many men from his first voyage stayed and settled throughout the islands. The main island inhabited by the Spanish was Hispaniola, now Santa Domingo.

Military Conquest

The remnants of the once mighty Maya lived primarily in the Yucatán. Their large cities like Chichen Itza and Mayapan had already fallen through warfare with neighboring tribes. The region was fragmented into 16 city-states, each independently governed although they shared the same belief systems. The Maya initially received Cortés with friendship and presented him with gifts, some freely and others to forestall conflict. One way or the other, Cortés received the gift of 20 women. He took one of them, named Malinche, to become both his mistress and interpreter. Malinche has been the subject of much dispute. Many see her as a traitor to her people. She was born into a noble Aztec family but when her father died she was put into slavery. She ended up a slave in the Yucatán, where she learned the Mayan language in several dialects. Her ability to interpret for Cortés allowed negotiation that saved thousands of lives, making her essential to the success of Cortés's campaign to conquer the Aztec. She eventually converted to Catholicism and gave birth to Cortés's son, the first "Mexican."

Codex Cues

It is said that the Aztec and Maya welcomed Cortés into their cities, believing him to be the return of the white god Quetzalcoatl, the Great Plumed Serpent God of Mesoamerica, whose return was anticipated. However, modern historians disagree. Documents that suggest this have been influenced by the Spanish and may even be entirely of Spanish origin.

In 1519, Cortés invaded the Aztec capitol of Tenochtitlán. He destroyed the city, rebuilding it as Mexico City in 1521. By the end of 1521, after many betrayals and brutal massacres, the Aztec empire fell.

Conquest of the Maya was more difficult because there was no single political center to overthrow. Each Mayan city-state fiercely resisted the Spanish and each had to be overcome one by one. In the end it was not Cortés who subjugated the Maya. A member of his original war party returned with his own army. He waged war with the Maya through three separate campaigns between 1527 and 1546. It would take over 150 years before Itza, the last Maya stronghold, fell in 1697.

Missionary Conquest

The worst damage to the Maya was done by the missionaries who traveled with the conquistadores. Diego de Landa, a Franciscan missionary, decreed the destruction of the Mayan holy books. Landa cared for the Mayan people and interceded on their behalf with the Spanish conquistadores. Unfortunately, he was convinced Mayan religious practices consisted of devil worship and he ordered the burning and destruction of all Mayan books and idols. The only known books that survived the destruction are the three and a half we mentioned earlier in this chapter.

In 1566, Landa wrote a book describing the customs, hieroglyphs, temples, religious practice, and history of the Maya, colored by his own religious bias. In addition, many Mayans learned Spanish and translated the creation stories and prophecies as well as some of the original codices. This was done to preserve them, as anything written in the Mayan language was sure to be destroyed. Two of these books, the *Popol Vuh* and *Chilam Balam*, have become cornerstones in understanding Mayan beliefs.

Some of the codices written in Spanish actually describe the Spanish conquest from the Aztec and Maya perspective. However, the accuracy of post-conquest codices and translations are questionable simply because the contents seem to have been tampered with by the missionaries. Undoubtedly the Maya wrote and hid books still to be revealed.

The Neighboring People

The Maya were not the only people living in the region. Mesoamerica was a richly populated place with many different tribes contributing to the greater culture of the region. The best-known friends, enemies, and relations to the Maya were the Olmec, Zapotec, Teotihuacanos, Toltec, and Aztec. Each group offered something unique to the whole of Mesoamerican culture—some good, some bad. They cross-fertilized each other with ideas, advances, tradition, and legends. The Olmec and Zapotec are credited with starting the style of hieroglyphic writing, astronomy, and even the calendars that the Maya later perfected. This, of course, is hotly disputed! Here is some brief info on these key cultures.

Olmec

The Olmec established the region's first major civilization. They lived along the central coast of the Gulf of Mexico, just west of the Yucatán Peninsula, in the swampy jungle river basins. Later they expanded into the highlands of Mexico, Mexico Valley, Oaxaca, and Guerrero. The height of their influence was between 1500 and 600 B.C.E. The Olmec used stone in sculpture and architecture, traveling to distant mountains to quarry it. Their colossal stone heads remain one of the mysteries of the ancient world. The male heads stand about nine feet high and weigh several tons. The Olmec may have developed the earliest known writing system in the Americas, but the symbols are not related to other hieroglyphic scripts like the Maya's, indicating other scripts derived separately.

Zapotec

The Zapotec lived in the highlands of Oaxaca, Mexico, and might have been the first to create a hieroglyphic writing system. The Zapotec language probably originated more than 6,000 years ago but is still spoken by approximately 300,000 people. They built the first plaster-style houses and created the first political system of the region. Their capital, Monte Alban, housed about 30,000 people at the height of its power. This was the first true city-state in Mesoamerica.

Teotihuacanos

Teotihuacanos are the people who inhabited the city of Teotihuacán, northeast of present-day Mexico City. The city was founded in 200 B.C.E., although it was built on a site inhabited since 1000 B.C.E. The Teotihuacanos had close contacts with the Maya during the early classic period (about 300 to 900 C.E.), especially at Tikal in Guatemala. At its peak in 600 B.C.E., Teotihuacán was one of the largest cities in the world. It covered an area of eight square miles and had a population of over 100,000 people! It had two great pyramids, the Pyramid of the Sun and the Pyramid of the Moon, built between the first and second centuries C.E. The Pyramid of the Sun is one of the largest structures ever built by indigenous people.

Toltec

The Toltec arrived on the scene after the decline of some the great cities like Teotihuacán. They established their empire in the central valley around 900 C.E. They brought the rise of militarism to Mesoamerica, using their superior military force to dominate the neighborhood. Their capital city was Tollan (also known as Tula), northeast of Mexico City.

Tollan had three large pyramids, one dedicated to Quetzalcoatl. However, the story goes that Quetzalcoatl became fed up with their bloodthirsty ways and abandoned the city, taking his followers to Chichen Itza. Chichen Itza then emerged as the power in the north. The Toltec declined in the 1100s as northern tribes invaded the central valley and eventually sacked Tollan.

Aztec

The Aztec empire was founded by the Tenocha, the Nahuatl-speaking people of the Valley of Mexico. They built great cities with complex social, political, and religious structures. Their capital, Tenochtitlán, was an island city built on reclaimed swampland. It is the site of present-day Mexico City. Tenochtitlán was possibly the largest city in the world at the time of the Spanish conquest. It featured a huge temple complex, a royal palace, and numerous canals. The name Aztec derives from the name Aztlan, the legendary Atlantean homeland of the Mesoamerican people.

The Maya of Today

Despite the long campaign against them, the Maya did not disappear. Although there are few full-blooded Maya left, many Mayan descendents still live in the same villages and cities of the original Maya Area. Some still practice the old beliefs, although most do not. Most practice a blend of their older beliefs with Catholicism. Although everyone speaks Spanish, many still know the original Mayan language, including the elders who hold the Mayan knowledge.

Elders still follow the teachings of the past. There are 440 tribes within the Maya, and each one has an elder. These 440 elders make up the Mayan Council. The elected president of the Mayan Council is Grandfather Alexhandro Cililo. The prophecy of the Maya exists in the form of calendars that record cycles of time.

> **Celestial Connection**
>
> The Maya of today are doctors, lawyers, farmers, architects, artists, and more, and in general occupy all levels of the social strata.

In the Mayan prophecies, it is said that the Mayan knowledge would have to be hidden during a time of suppression. Then a time will come when the knowledge will be revealed to restore balance on Earth. There are still five prophetic calendars that have only been seen by the Mayan people. Elders who hold these sacred documents meet each year to determine when and what should be revealed. The next revelation about the Mayan prophecy will be told by the Mayan elders in a planned release in the near future. You'll hear more from the Mayan elders in Chapter 14.

The Least You Need to Know

- Destruction of the Mayan codices, or books, limits our knowledge of their culture.

- The origin of the ancient Maya is steeped in mystery.

- The Maya were an advanced society in Central America with highly developed language, writing, architecture, and astronomy. Their culture thrived from 200 B.C.E. to 900 C.E.

◆ Historians believe the Maya vanished due to social/political upheaval, environmental collapse, climate change, or a combination of all three.

◆ Neighboring people to the Maya were the Olmec, Zapotec, Teotihuacanos, Toltec, and Aztec.

◆ The Maya people have not disappeared; many descendents still live in the original Maya Area, and some still practice the old beliefs.

Chapter 2

Maya Worldview

In This Chapter

- ◆ The life force that is k'ul
- ◆ Our connection to the cosmos
- ◆ The holy codices of the Maya
- ◆ The three realms
- ◆ Mayan mythology
- ◆ Mayan understanding of time and other concepts

When you look at the world, do you see rocks and trees, the sky, clouds, grass, birds, and so on, or do you see the essence behind them? For the Maya, the most real part of the universe was the spiritual essence behind it. They believed everything is filled with a divine essence, an unseen power they called k'ul (ch'ul in the highland dialect).

In the Maya worldview (what we'll call the Maya-view), there were two key beliefs that determined how they related to the world. The first is the belief in k'ul. The second is how they viewed time. This may be a strange thought, but the calendar you use influences how you think. The Gregorian calendar measures days that turn into years. Using this calendar you are sure to see time as a straight line, a linear progression into the future and away from the past. The Mayan calendar measures cycles. In Maya-view, cycles don't measure the passage of time as much as they measure the quality of time periods.

As you'll see, the Maya culture reflects these two key beliefs at all levels.

The Sea of K'ul

In Maya-view, there is no separation between the seen and the unseen worlds, between what is material and the forces that move through the material. The world is alive, all parts of it; animate parts like plants and animals as well as inanimate parts like rocks, water, the earth, and all the celestial bodies. The study of the ebb and flow of *k'ul* was the domain of the shamans and priests. To ensure the safety of the community, they needed to understand the cycles, rhythms, and expressions of k'ul. The world needed to be kept in balance to prevent disaster. Ceremonies were performed to keep harmony between the material and spiritual worlds.

def•i•ni•tion

> The root word of k'ul is k'u, which means "sacred entity" or "god." "L" is the contraction of *lil*, which means "vibration." So we can roughly translate **k'ul** to mean "the sacred vibration of God." This vibration is considered the vital life force that animates all matter.

Sacred Sites

The k'ul (vital life force) that fills the earth concentrates at certain points, which are known as sacred sites. The Maya believed that sacred sites were connected to each other by flows of k'ul. Shamans studied the patterns between sacred sites and the grid they formed. Movement of energy along this grid was influenced by the movement and alignment of planets, stars, and other celestial bodies. Additionally, shamans and priests influenced the movement of k'ul through ceremony and ritual.

Moving K'ul

You may wonder why the Maya wanted to manipulate the movement of k'ul. If it's a sacred essence, why not just let it do its thing? Bottom line, not everything has the same amount of k'ul. Much of Mayan tradition and ritual was based on finding ways to gain and direct larger amounts of k'ul to influence the outcome of earthly affairs. Shamans manipulated the flow of energy to create portals through which they had direct access to the sacred spirit.

Of course, since k'ul is very powerful, too much could be harmful—especially if it was chaotic and out of balance. It could also create harm if it was collected in a person, object, or place that was not strong enough to hold it. You need to have a worthy vessel. The need to control both the positive and negative aspects of k'ul, and to be worthy of it, guided much of Mayan life. It directed how and where they built their houses, determined the structure of their cities and temples, and established how they worshipped.

Celestial Connection

Many ancient cultures believed in spiritual energy that flowed through the earth accumulating at sacred sites. The many megalithic stone circles in England, Wales, Scotland, and Ireland, such as Stonehenge and Avebury in England, are thought to be energy accumulators at sacred sites. Many believe the sites are connected to each other in a grid-work matrix. Ancient ritual in the circles utilized the energy for fertility, to increase crop harvest, and to create sacred space in which ancients could communicate with the gods. It is thought by some that the appearance of crop circles near sacred sites is a modern-day reflection of ancient energy grids and man's interaction with them.

Human Connection to the Cosmos

Humans are part of an interactive galaxy. In Maya-view, you have many connections to the universe through your own body. Areas of your body relate to areas of the galaxy, and at the time of your birth these connections are solidified. The relationship between the galaxy and your body is reflected in the Maya numbering system and the calendars. You'll learn more about this in Chapter 4. For the Maya, everything was based on relationship.

Suspended by K'ul

In Maya-view, people are directly connected to the heavenly cosmos by the energy running through them. Your fingers, pointing to heaven, connect you to the celestial realms, and your toes on the earth connect you to the underworlds. This creates a flow that runs through your body. In addition to being suspended on k'ul between heaven and Earth, points in your body are associated with different parts of the galaxy. You have thirteen key jointed areas (your neck, two shoulders, two elbows, two wrists, two hips, two knees, and two ankles) that reflect thirteen key points in the galaxy. As above, so below: each is a reflection of the other, and movement in one affects the other. In short, the Maya seemed to understand the concept of a hologram: that all parts of the whole are evident in each part of the whole.

Numbers and Cycles

The relationship between the body and the cosmos is reflected in the Mayan numbering system. The numbering system in modern use is based on units of 10. The Mayan base is units of 20; the number of your fingers and toes. Twenty is also the number of days in the months of the Mayan Long Count Calendar, one of the most important of the Mayan cycles.

Thirteen, the number of your joint areas, is a sacred number also. In the Calendar Round, 13 times 20 is a key time cycle still celebrated today. It becomes very clear that Maya saw everything in terms of numbers and cycles.

Celestial Connection

Chinese medicine believes that humans are suspended between heaven and earth through energy points in the fingers and toes. The points are the starting and ending points of the 12 pairs of meridians, or energy channels in the human body. They are referred to as the "warp" points on the "loom of the universe." Humans are the tapestry being woven.

Wayebs

Another human connection between the seen and unseen realms is the existence of an entity called a *Wayeb* (pronounced *Why-eb*). The Wayeb, or Way, is a spirit companion. Every person, including you, has a personal Wayeb. They are often referred to as spiritual doubles, or co-essences. Yours takes care of your needs on a spiritual level, but it's not a one-way street. You take care of your Wayeb's needs on a material level. For example, if you want to understand something about the unseen forces, you might call on your Wayeb for insight. On the other hand, if your Wayeb wants to open a door to let an unseen force act on earth, it might call on you to perform a ritual or open a portal. Each person's destiny is intertwined with the destiny of their Wayeb. For you

def•i•ni•tion

A **Wayeb**, also called a Way, is a spirit companion. Every person has one and as you grow and develop, your spirit companion does, too.

to meet your goals and objectives, your Wayeb has to meet its goals and objectives as well. Pretty cool stuff. Spirit companions weren't limited to humans. Mayan deities had their own Wayebs, too!

Another way of viewing the Wayeb is as the spiritual counterpart to your self. Not an individual, but your own double in the spirit world.

Material Manifestation

Wayebs usually inhabit the invisible realms, but they can manifest in the material world if needed. They show up in animal-like or human-like form. This is similar to the animal totems of North American tribes. Just like people are not all the same, not all Wayebs have the same amount of k'ul. The most powerful spirit companions were associated with the deities who controlled aspects of the universe. So the sun god, for instance, must have had a pretty strong Wayeb.

Meeting Your Wayeb

The Maya today continue to believe each person has a spirit companion. The easiest place for you to meet your Wayeb is in your dreams. In Maya-view, dream time is the meeting place between the seen and unseen realms; the place where both you and your Wayeb can show up. So pay attention! If you want to get to know your spirit companion, invite your Wayeb to a dream meeting and start writing your dreams down. Pay attention especially to the animals in your dreams and see if one type of animal shows up over and over.

Holy Books of the Maya: Codices

You may be wondering how we know about the Mayan spiritual practice. As you know from Chapter 1, the information we have about the Maya-view comes mostly from three and a half surviving pre-Columbus codices. These were the books that survived destruction at the hands of the zealous missionaries. They are the only known unadulterated record of the knowledge and culture of the ancient Maya. In addition, there are two other books that are invaluable in understanding the realm of Maya spiritual practice: the *Popol Vuh* and the *Chilam Balam*.

Dresden Codex

The Dresden Codex is the most elaborate of the codices. It contains information about astronomical events. It has a large focus on Venus and the cycles of Venus that were used to predict outcomes of war. It was smuggled out of Mesoamerica in the 1600s, making its way to the royal courts of Saxony in Dresden.

Madrid Codex

The Madrid Codex was sent to the royal courts of Spain by Cortés. It was split into two codices that traveled separately until 1880 when it was reunited. The Madrid Codex contains descriptions of the rituals and divinities associated with each day of the 260-day Mesoamerican sacred calendar, the Tzolk'in. It may have been written post-conquest.

def•i•ni•tion

The **ecliptic** is the path the sun, planets, and constellations travel across the sky.

Paris Codex

The Paris Codex is similar to the *Chilam Balam* and relates prophetic events for the Mayan calendars and zodiac. It includes what appears to be a Maya zodiac of the constellations traversing a path along the *ecliptic*.

Grolier Codex

The Grolier Codex is a fragment of 11 pages that didn't surface until the 1970s. Not everyone is convinced of its authenticity.

Chilam Balam and *Popol Vuh*

In the 1500s and 1600s, many Mayan records were transcribed from hieroglyphics by the Mayan people and written down in Spanish or Latin to preserve them. Although most were influenced by the missionaries and don't offer an accurate report, the *Popol Vuh* and *Chilam Balam* are considered relatively free of influence and are rich resources for understanding Mayan spirituality. The *Popol Vuh* is the Quiche Mayan book of creation. The Quiche Maya live in the highlands of Guatemala.

The *Chilam Balam* is a historical record and includes prophecy and predictions from the calendars. In the *Chilam Balam* there are references to the dark time coming for the Maya people with the arrival of white people from the east.

Both books are extremely important because the content has been verified through hieroglyphic stories found on murals in caves and newly discovered ruins. The murals in the ruins at San Bartolo in Guatemala recreate the creation story as recorded in the *Popol Vuh*.

New Revelations

There are many other codices that were transcribed in the 1500s and 1600s, some of which have come to light only recently and are changing ideas about Mayan history. For example, you probably were told that the Aztec welcomed Cortés because they believed he was the return of Quetzalcoatl. Quetzalcoatl, or Kukulkan in Mayan, was a god who appeared in human form as a white man with a black beard and brought wisdom to the Maya. The legends say he left in a boat proclaiming he would return to bring prosperity and peace. The newly found codices say that Cortés learned of the legend and was taken with the idea that he was Quetzalcoatl. He began to call himself Quetzalcoatl, the return of the plumed serpent. Well, that's a switch!

Cosmic Caution

A lot of history is written about conquest of one people over another. It's a good idea to remember that history is written by the victors and reflects only their side of the story. Not everything we think we know about the ancient Maya is true.

Centering the World

Maya-view does not separate natural and supernatural realms. As with Christianity, they believe in three realms: the underworld, the realm we live in, and the heavens or celestial realms. However, these are not separate domains; they are interconnected, as expressed in the *Chilam Balam*.

Each realm has different levels, which are ruled by different deities:

- ◆ The underworld is called Xibalba and has nine levels and nine ruling deities, called the Bolontik'u gods. (Unlike the Christian view, the underworlds are not necessarily bad. They are where the dead live before being reborn. The Maya believed in reincarnation into the earth realm.)

- ◆ The Earth realm that we live in. This realm has only one level, the one we are in.

- ◆ The heavens have thirteen levels and thirteen ruling deities, called the Oxalhuntik'u gods.

Tree of Life

The realms are interconnected through the Tree of Life, the Yaxche tree in Maya. The Tree of Life is one of the most sacred concepts of Mesoamerica. It's represented by a vertical line that goes through all three realms. Imagine the realms to be spinning like a top; the vertical line is the axis they spin around. The roots are in the underworld, the trunk is in the earth realm, and the branches are in the heavens, supporting the sky. The axis is called the navel of the world.

Codex Cues

The tree of life is a sacred symbol in many cultures including, to name a few, the Celtic Tree of Life, the Hebrew Tree of Life, and the yogi Tree of Life.

The Tree of Life symbolism acknowledges that all levels of the universe are important. The underworld provides the nourishment for the roots of the tree. The trunk provides life for the middle realm, which developed from the underworld. The branches support the sky. Without all three, the universe would collapse. The Tree of Life is represented in the cosmos as the Milky Way.

Depicting the Earth

The earth is described as a flat land between the two invisible realms. It was often portrayed as the back of a crocodile or turtle. The tree of life separates the realms in the center, anchoring on the North Star. The corners of the world are held up by the gods of the four directions.

Many scholars believe this symbolism means the ancient Maya thought the earth was flat. Remember the problem of the biased eye! Scholars often missed the richness of the symbolism. The Maya, who understood advanced astronomy, most certainly knew the earth was a sphere.

The Bacabs

The Bacabs are the gods that hold up the corners of the world in the four directions. Each direction represents a quality of spiritual inspiration expressed by its Bacab and is associated with a specific color. When the wind blows, it carries the quality of the Bacab from that direction.

Different time periods are also governed by the Bacabs; some time periods will be red times, some white times, and so on. Each period of time will reflect the spiritual quality of its overseeing deity.

- *East* is the direction of sun being reborn each morning and its color is red. It is ruled by the Bacab Kan.

- *West* is the dying sun falling into Xibalba and its color is black. It is ruled by the Bacab Ix.

- *North* points to the zenith, the direction of the sun at noon, and its color is white. It represents the fullness of life in the sky, and the ruling Bacab is Mulac.

- *South* points to the nadir, the direction of the dead sun that battles the underworld to be reborn each day, and its color is yellow. Its ruling Bacab is Cauac.

There are actually five directions: north, south, east, west, which are the corners of the world, and the fifth direction, the center symbolized by the Tree of Life, or the axis of the earth. Green is the color of the center.

The Tree of Life is not a specific axis through the earth. It doesn't correspond to the magnetic axis or the North Pole axis or anything else. It is the *axis mundi*, the stable world center. It is established wherever it is envisioned. Each house was organized to create a central axis, as was each city, each temple, each ball court. The Maya used their knowledge of the tree of life and the directions to enrich all aspects of life.

Mayan Mythology

Mayan mythology was incorporated into daily life. Mythological stories were reenacted in everyday rituals to keep the essence of the story alive and keep people connected to the gods. This ensured that people continued to evolve in consciousness.

The *Popol Vuh* begins with the creation myth of the Quiche Maya. All Mayan mythology expresses cosmological events. The creation story tells of the changing of the ages; each age is a new creation and expresses an evolutionary stage of development. There are five ages in creation; we are currently in the fourth or fifth age. The creation story is complex and confusing. Gods change identities, names, and qualities. It's hard to keep track of who's who. Following are some creation stories that will show up again later in this book.

Creation of the Previous Ages

The creation of man happened in four or five stages, depending on the translation. According to the story, two gods sat and meditated; whatever they put their thought to was manifested. Through their thoughts and words they brought into being the earth, mountains, trees, and animals. Then the gods decided to create a race of beings who could worship them. Unfortunately, the gods made several false starts in setting humanity on the earth path.

In the first attempt humans were made of clay, but they couldn't speak and worship so the gods destroyed them. Other gods were summoned to help the creation, and in the next attempt, humans were made of wood. Unfortunately, these humans had no soul and they forgot to worship, so naturally the gods "rained blackness on their heads" and "tore them apart." In the next creation, with the help of even more gods, the "true people" were formed out of mesa, or corn dough. As such, the ancient Maya believed that maize was not only the cornerstone of their diet, but was their material essence as well.

It's unclear how many ages have actually passed. Was the first age the age with minerals? Or the age with animals? Or did the ages start with the first people? Depending on interpretations, the current age could be the third, fourth, or fifth age. Researchers commonly consider it the fifth age as we approach the next change at 2012. However, modern Mayan elders consider it the fourth age.

The Hero Twins

The *Popol Vuh* follows the creation myth with the story of the Hero Twins. The Hero Twins are superior ball players and draw the attention of the gods. They're taken to the underworld to play a game against the gods. While trapped in the underworld they're given a set of five challenges that are meant to defeat them. Instead, the twins trick the gods, win the tests, and defeat death. Although they were born human, they become gods.

The story ends with the Hero Twins' ascension to the celestial realms, where they became Venus and the Sun. The disappearance of Venus as the evening star represents the descent into the underworld. The reemergence of Venus as the morning star represents the defeat of death. Also in the story of the Hero Twins we see the reinforcement of the creation story. There are five ages and five challenges or tests to overcome.

The story of the Hero Twins was also reenacted in the ball court game itself. The ball games were played in Mesoamerica for over 3,000 years. The games could be played on many levels. They might be played casually for fun between two people or community teams. They were also played as part of ritual to commemorate the cycles of death and rebirth. Ritual ball games usually involved human sacrifice.

At times, the games were played as proxy for war and the losing (and sometimes winning) team was sacrificed. The ball court was seen as the threshold between the earth and the underworld. To die on the ball court was to invite rebirth and was considered an honor and opportunity. Mayan kings who were sacrificed after losing a war were killed in the ball courts so they could join the lords of the underworld.

Cosmic Mythology

Every story of the Maya is an expression of a cosmological event. The Tree of Life, the creation story, the Hero Twins can all be found in the movement and drama of the celestial bodies. The bottom line is that for the Maya all things are connected. Daily life, the stars, the gods are all expressions of the same oneness. This can be a balanced perspective of integration, or it can be a constant battle to balance the forces through ritual and appeasement. At different times in Mayan history it has been both.

Cycles and Harmony

An important part of the Maya-view was based on their understanding of time. Time was cyclic, it breathed in and breathed out. It was alive, an outpouring of energy from the Bacab deity that governed each returning cycle. The calendar we use marks the passage of time, measuring the movement of days. In contrast, the Maya calendar marked the patterns of the emergence and disappearance of spiritual essence. For the Maya, each cycle of time was the expression of a certain spiritual quality that held specific lessons. Knowing which cycle was present guided decisions. Planting crops, going to war, building a temple—all were governed by the cycles of time.

Generational Qualities

Consider this thought in regard to the distinctiveness of different generations. The generation of the 1940s had a completely different "flavor" than the generation of the 1960s. From our modern-day worldview, changes in the way people think and behave, or changes in consciousness, create the generational flavor.

The Maya would say differently. They would say that each generation is governed by a different time cycle, a different Bacab with a different spiritual quality. The spiritual quality creates the flavor of the generation, which changes how people think and behave, guiding the evolution of consciousness.

Holy Time

Maya ritual and ceremony were woven into celestial and terrestrial cycles. Each cycle was inscribed into a calendar. The Maya priest had the job of interpreting these cycles and their interactions, and then giving a prophetic outlook on the future or past. The priest also had to determine if the "heavens" were in alignment with the performance of certain religious ceremonies.

The cycles of time interact with all the realms of the universe. They interact with the thirteen hierarchical levels of the heavens as well as the nine levels of the underworld. In a sense, time is the glue that holds the realms in relation to each other. It's hard for us to appreciate the complexity that was coded into the calendars. It requires a shift in thinking that few are prepared to make.

The power of time to create patterns influenced all of Mayan life. All buildings, marriages, births, contracts, wars, and so on were consecrated with a date that determined the spiritual quality that would be expressed in the endeavor. They lived in a universe of "holy time."

Maya Cosmovision

The term *Maya cosmovision* means the way in which the Maya see themselves in relation to the universe. In Maya-view, the universe is both alive and ordered. It's governed by spiritual forces or guiding principles. The most important point, however, is that humans can interact with these forces. In fact, humans have a "galactic resonance" based on the 13 intersection points between our bodies and the galaxy. These intersection points can act as portals to communicate with the gods and unseen realms. How well you use these portals may depend on many factors, including the spiritual quality expressed in the time of your birth, the amount of k'ul you can accumulate and direct in your body, and the cosmic alignment at any given time.

Codex Cues

Other cultures also believe the human body has energy centers that resonate with the cosmos. You might want to experience this by meditating with the chakras. There are many good tapes to guide you through. One of our favorites is *Chakra Meditation* by Layne Redmond, available at SoundsTrue.com.

Priests and Shamans

Shamans were holy men who communicated with deities and interpreted the universe. They also performed healing, divination, and ceremony. They tended to the needs of the common people. Priests emerged as society became more complex and worked for the elite class. In the early Mayan cities, the kings were shaman-kings; but as time went on, priests took on more and more of this role.

Shamans and priests dedicated their time to maximizing the synchronization between human activities and cosmic events. Rituals were utilized to accumulate k'ul in sacred sites so it could be accessed to empower human activity. You might call this the mechanisms of a blessing. Asking one of the gods to bless something is asking him or her to place their attention on a specific target. This naturally brings more energy to it and empowers its success.

A typical ritual began with purification. The people involved in the ceremony would often fast, and all the objects were purified with energy from the sun and moon. Music and processions followed, which helped elevate the participants to higher states of mind. The participants burned incense, usually a tree resin called *copal*. The copal cleared, purified, and uplifted the individual. After everyone was presentable to the gods, the gods were offered gifts of tobacco, corn, and food. For a very important ceremony, the god might have been offered blood. The blood could be collected from cutting someone, or in very important ceremonies, from sacrifices of animals or humans. The ceremony closed with dancing, feasting, and drinking.

The Life Span of Buildings

Mayan buildings and cities were designed to maximize the accumulation and movement of k'ul. Constructing a pyramid or temple, for instance, required matching the function of the structure with the specific time cycle it would be used in. The time cycle may have been a long galactic cycle, like the 26,000 years of the precession, or it might have been related to a shorter cycle. The building was "born" with initiation rituals before construction began. It would have a life span, during which time it had maximum flow of energy into it from both celestial and terrestrial realms. It acted as an accumulator of vital life force, or k'ul. The k'ul could then be used by the priests and shamans to bless human endeavors.

When the time cycle it was made for ended, the building would no longer be in sync with the new cycle. This means it would not be able to hold the energy of the new time. The temple was said to have died, would receive termination rites, and would be dismantled. Not wanting to lose the energy that had amassed at the site, the Maya built their new temples on the same sites as the old. The new building, in sync with the new cycle, was more powerful than the last as it magnified the energy from the past. As kings built and rebuilt on top of the old, sanctums became ever more sacred and established portals that allowed ancestors and gods to pass through.

This process was true of cities and private homes as well as temples and sacred places. The function of different buildings varied, so they would be geared to different cycles. When communities believed the power of their city was finished, they simply walked away. This may explain the many abandoned Mayan cities in 900 C.E. Could it be the cities were not in sync with the coming new time cycle and lost power, causing the people to leave? Maybe all the new construction prior to abandonment was a failed attempt to repower their structures.

Codex Cues

Feng shui is an ancient Chinese practice that seeks the proper placement of homes, objects, and space in order to increase the harmonious flow of *chi*. To see how proper alignment and energy flow can improve your life, pick up a book on feng shui principles and try them out! Our favorite is *The Complete Illustrated Guide to Feng Shui*, by Lillian Too (Element Books, 1996).

Sacred Design

Mayan buildings and cities reflected the Mayan cosmos. Every building and city created its own Tree of Life axis. Because the axis is not geographical, the center is wherever you are standing. You are always in the center of your world. The Tree of Life was re-created in every house with a central support pole and four outer corners. The corners were aligned with the directions. Once established, the axis could be activated by ritual. In the presence of a shaman, it could materialize a portal between the realms.

The center of most cities and villages had a Ceiba tree or Yaxche tree, representing the central axis, or Tree of Life. You might have seen pictures of one of these trees; they grow very large and are often featured in magazine articles. Ceiba trees have large roots, massive, straight trunks, and four main branches that spread in the four directions. The branches form a canopy overhead and house eagle nests. Openings in the trunks of older trees provide housing for bats, emissaries to the underworld.

Portals

You might be getting the idea that portals were an important part of the Maya-view. This is true. Interacting with the invisible realms was highly desired. Activating portals created a sacred space that allowed passage from one realm to the next. Ancestors, gods, and Wayebs could all pass through to the material realm, and humans could pass through to celestial realms. Keep this in mind in Chapter 3 when we discuss how the Maya knew about galactic time spans!

In addition to creating portals, there was security and safety in a properly ordered place. When the positions of buildings were aligned with the primary directions and anchored through the tree of life, the world was safer. It was protected by kings and deities alike. The king lived in the center of the city, the heart of the heavens; the city revolved around him.

Other Sacred Structures

The legend of the Hero Twins shows the sacredness of ball courts. They were also believed to be located at the intervening threshold between this world and the celestial world. Sacred ball games and sacrifices were conducted here to please and placate the gods.

Tombs were where rich people were buried and were built to mimic the function of caves. Temple doorways were symbolic of cave entrances that allowed kings and priests to enter the sacred mountain and communicate with the lords of Xibalba. The tops of temples were flat to allow the kings and priests to stand on top of the mountain, gaining access to both k'ul, the vital life force, and Hunab K'u, the highest god.

Gods of the Maya

The gods of the Maya could be confusing and overwhelming. One could turn into another; they had visible and invisible qualities and could transform themselves at will. They represented polarities, so their actions and functions seemed contradictory based on what side of the polarity they were expressing. They expressed different aspects based on the quality of the direction they were facing or the color they were wearing. These are not your Greek gods!

Some scholars think the Mayan gods were representations of the numbers and cycles on the calendars. Others say the numbers and cycles of the calendars were important because they reflected the myths and legends of the Mayan gods. In Maya-view, what is the difference? Matter is a reflection of the spiritual essence that flows through it ....

Monotheism

At first glance, it seems obvious that the Maya believed in polytheism, or more than one god. Have you learned by now that nothing with the Maya is obvious?

According to creation legends in the *Popol Vuh*, Hunab K'u is the supreme god. All other gods are said to be different faces of Hunab K'u; different expressions of one complex dude! In this sense the ancient Maya were monotheistic, worshipping one supreme god whose essence animates many lesser fragments of himself. Since everything is part of Hunab K'u, all of existence is a part of god. This is a common theme in Earth-based religions.

Abilities of the Gods

Each of the gods had separate traits and abilities. However, a good or evil trait expressed by a god is not necessarily a permanent part of its nature. Gods changed with changing cycles. Good was not always considered a "good" trait, either. What was inappropriate at one time might have been necessary in another. Since Mayan religious tradition was based on cycles, the gods behaved accordingly.

In general the gods expressed themselves invisibly, directing the movements of the universe, charting the course of the celestial bodies through the sky. When they chose, they could express themselves in material form as well. They usually appeared in animal form. Some animals, the jaguar and snake for example, had sacred status to the Maya and were common forms for the gods to take. The gods could also show up in dreams with messages, warnings, and inspiration.

There were hundreds of individual Mayan deities. Here are a few of the key ones you will see represented in the calendars and texts:

- ◆ *Hunab K'u* is the creator of the universe, the supreme god and creator of the Maya. This is the head honcho of the gods. He's responsible for rebuilding the world after the previous three ages.

- ◆ *Kukulkan* (also called Quetzalcoatl in Aztec) is known as the feathered serpent or plumed god. In some myths he is credited with developing the Mayan culture, bringing maize, and teaching the people to write and heal. In Quiche tradition, he is one of the three gods, including Hunab K'u, who created the world. He is master in many realms and governs the wind and rain.

◆ *Voltan* was born a man, a hero who was deified by the gods. He is known as the "heart of the cities" and is the patron god of the drum.

◆ *The Bacabs* are a group of four protective deities, giants who hold up the earth at the four cardinal directions. They are Kan (east, red); Ix (west, black); Mulac (north, white); and Cauac (south, yellow).

Changing of the Ages: The Significance of 2012

In the Mayan creation stories, three previous worlds, or ages, have been destroyed. According to current interpretations of the Mayan calendars, 2012 is the end of the present age. The calendars say this age will be destroyed by fire. However, the end of each age is the birth of the next age, and there is never complete destruction of the old. The parts of the old that don't work are destroyed, and the rest becomes the seeds of the new age. This makes the ending of the old age a time of purification, not destruction of the earth, and the beginning of the next age is a time of transformation.

Many people are focusing on the end of this age and losing sight of the transformation to come. Some Mayan elders are concerned 2012 is becoming a magnet for our fears. After all, this is an insecure time. You may be worried about your finances, about the degradation of the environment, about the state of social affairs, or terrorism. It's easy to start thinking that only bad things will happen as this date approaches.

Of course, we don't want to make this a self-fulfilling prophecy by creating what we're thinking about. Our minds and focus are powerful forces. They affect the flow of energy along the grid lines and they affect the circumstances of our lives. In Maya-view, this is the time to use ceremony to terminate the old and consecrate the building of the new. Ceremony can help smooth the shifting of the flow of k'ul and help every-one see the right path to take through the changes we face. 2012 is not the destruction of the earth; it's the destruction by fire of old ways that don't work.

To face the future with confidence, each of us must become a confident person. What do you need to become more confident? Now is the time to get what you need. Now is the time to embrace the possibilities of what the future can hold. This is the significance of the time leading toward 2012: that what we focus on becomes what is. Do you want to focus on destruction of the old or focus on creating the new cycle to come?

The Least You Need to Know

◆ K'ul is the life force that flows through and connects all things in the universe. It travels along planetary grids and collects in sacred sites.

◆ We are connected to the cosmos by k'ul that runs from the universe into channels within our bodies. We can influence k'ul in ourselves and the planet through ceremony and ritual.

◆ The Mayan codices are holy books that tell us the practices and beliefs of the ancient civilization.

◆ The Maya believed in three realms: the underworld, the earth realm, and the heavenly sky. All three worlds were interconnected by the Tree of Life.

◆ Mayan mythology and Mayan gods are reflections of celestial events in the night sky. These events are coded into the Mayan calendars and can be used to predict the future.

◆ The Maya see time as a cycle of qualities rather than a progression of events. Even though exact time doesn't repeat, the quality of a period repeats, allowing the Mayan priests and shamans to understand and predict the future.

Sky Watchers

In This Chapter

- ◆ Working with Mayan math
- ◆ Discovering astronomy techniques
- ◆ Coding the sky into buildings
- ◆ Mayan time and cosmic events

The Mayan calendars were coded with detailed astronomic information. This information was gained through continuous observation—endless hours spent tracking planets, stars, and constellations through the night sky. Days were spent recording these movements, searching for patterns, and seeking to make sense of the mountains of data. The Maya didn't keep track for a year, 10 years, or even 50 years. They kept track for centuries. By using an ingenious numbering system and applying advanced mathematics, they calculated the precision of cycles that were as long as 26,000 years. Without telescopes, calculators, or computers, how did they do it?

The calendars are not the only record of the Mayan astronomical feats. With extraordinary accuracy they coded information into their pyramids, temples, and city layouts. To an uneducated eye, Mayan temples are impressive for their size, architectural structure, and beauty. To the educated eye, they are impressive for the mathematics and astronomy they contain.

As always, everything in the Mayan world reflects the spiritual essence behind it. Numbers were no exception. Every number had a spiritual meaning that was expressed through all aspects of daily life. If you're like us, your head might start spinning when you see paragraphs full of numbers. Don't worry; we have simplified this to a level we can all digest!

Counting System

The Maya needed a counting system for more than just celestial data. They were also merchants, trading cotton, cocoa, corn, jade, obsidian, and other goods. An accurate and fast accounting system was essential and had to be shareable with neighboring traders. Some of the inscriptions depict sums being added, subtracted, and calculated in the order of hundreds and millions. The system they developed is ingenious in its simplicity and versatility.

Celestial data posed entirely different challenges. They had to keep track of changes in degrees of the planets rising, their movements, trajectories, etc. They had to be able to use that information to perform elaborate calculations for predicting eclipses and other celestial events. Most importantly, they had to use a base number in their counting system that fit the cycles in the sky. The Mayan calendars all fit together like cogs in wheels, and proportions were essential. You'll learn more about this in Chapter 4.

Vestigial System

The Maya and the rest of the Mesoamerican neighborhood devised a system based on the number of their vestiges, otherwise known as fingers and toes. In other words, it was based on a count of 20. You can ask any child what our current 10-digit system is based on: our 10 fingers!

Using a base of 20 and a base of 5, the Maya had almost everything they needed for advanced calculation. All that was missing was the concept of zero. In Mesoamerica, the concept of zero was first seen in the fourth century B.C.E. used by the Olmec. It was well in place in the Mayan calendar system by 36 B.C.E. Once zero was understood, the door was opened for advanced calculations.

Celestial Connection

The use of zero was first seen in Babylonian culture in 2000 B.C.E., but it was used only as a place marker. It had no numerical significance. While ancient Greek philosophers debated the ability to "have" nothing, the ancient Romans understood the concept of zero and were using it numerically by the fifth century B.C.E.

Keeping Track of Numbers

To record amounts, the Maya used a system of bars and dots. A dot stood for one and a bar stood for five. Zero was signified by a conch shell. Dots and bars were used to count to 20; large numbers were counted as powers of 20. We count in powers of 10. Any number under 20 would be written in combination of bars and dots as depicted in the following illustration.

🐚	•	• •	• • •	• • • •
0	**1**	**2**	**3**	**4**
▬	• ▬	• • ▬	• • • ▬	• • • • ▬
5	**6**	**7**	**8**	**9**
▬ ▬	• ▬ ▬	• • ▬ ▬	• • • ▬ ▬	• • • • ▬ ▬
10	**11**	**12**	**13**	**14**
▬ ▬ ▬	• ▬ ▬ ▬	• • ▬ ▬ ▬	• • • ▬ ▬ ▬	• • • • ▬ ▬ ▬
15	**16**	**17**	**18**	**19**

The dots stand for ones and the bars stand for five.

Numbers over 20 would be written as a combination of bars and dots that were either added to or multiplied by 20. For example, 53 would be expressed as 2 times 20 plus 13. When writing numbers, the Maya located the positions in columns rather than in rows as we do. When we write a three-digit number, such as four hundred fifty-one, we write 451. We know that the third position to the left stands for the hundreds (10×10), the second position for the tens, and the first position for the ones. To write higher numbers, we add positions to the left that stand for powers of 10 (1,000; 100,000; 1,000,000). In the Mayan system using powers of 20, the bottom position is for 0 to 20; the middle position is for multiples of 20 (1×20); and the top position is for the 400s (20×20). To write higher numbers, you would add positions to the top of the column that stand for higher powers of 20 (8,000, 160,000, 3,200,000). So 451 in Mayan columns would look like the following illustration.

The Mayan system easily handles large numbers in a similar manner to our own. The number in the top position is multiplied by 400, in this case 1×400; the number in the middle position is multiplied by 20, in this case 2×20; the number in the bottom position is not a multiple. So this represents 400 + 40 + 11 = 451.

Top position	●	(1 dot x 400 = 400)
Middle position	● ●	(2 dots x 20 = 40)
Botton position	● over 2 lines	(1 dot over 2 lines = 11)

Simple Math

Adding and subtracting was very easy with this system. It was only a matter of adding bars and dots located in the same column position. Just like we line up numbers and add the ones column first, then the tens, then the hundreds, it worked for the Mayan system in the same way. If it sounds complicated in words, take a minute to check out the following illustration, and with a little concentration you'll be surprised just how easy and accurate it is!

You can see how easy it is to add and subtract large numbers. It's also claimed that they multiplied and divided as well.

8,000's	●	+	●	+	● ●
	1x8,000=8,000		1x8,000=8,000		2x8,000=16,000
400's	● ●	+	▬		● ● over ▬
	2x400=800		5x400=2,000		7x400=2,800
20's	● ● over ▬	+	●	=	● ● ● over ▬
	7x20=140		1x20=20		8x20=160
1's	● ● ● over ▬	+	● over ▬	+	● ● ● ● over ▬▬
	8x1=8		6x1=6		14x1=14
	8,948	+	10,026	=	18,974

Although simple, you can see that this system can handle large numbers with relative ease. The main drawback is that they did not use fractions. When calculating astronomical cycles, this created a problem. The only way around it is to watch the sky for long periods of time for whole numbered cycles to repeat. The significance of this becomes apparent in Chapter 4.

Spiritual Qualities of Numbers

To the Maya, numbers were invested with specific spiritual qualities. Each of the 20 numbers was represented by a glyph and a name. When used in the calendars, they are called day-signs. Each day-sign represents an important theme in everyday Mayan life and suggested a progression of self-development. A day-sign signifies what the spiritual quality of the number will be that is expressed on a given day. Each month also had a spiritual quality, as did the year. Knowing the day's energy allowed the Maya to plan events.

For example, if you were a Maya, a 9 Muluc day, which emphasizes payments and the law of cause and effect, might be a good day for a ritual to appease the gods or to pay off your debts. On the other hand, you might not want to do these things on a 7 Manik day, which is more likely to manifest deception. You'll learn more in Chapter 5. For now it's enough to know that numbers had significance beyond keeping count of material objects or time periods, or to make calculations. They were spiritual expressions, as was everything else in the Mayan world!

Astronomical Feats

The Maya did not have telescopes, measuring devices, clocks, or even the use of fractions, and yet they were very accurate in determining astronomical constants. Much of what they knew about the sky was recorded in the form of myth and religious story.

The Tree of Life is thought to be a depiction of the Milky Way galaxy. The story of the Hero Twins (see Chapter 2) describes the change of Venus from the morning star position to evening star position and back again. The changing of the previous ages may be a description of the precession of the equinoxes.

What Did the Maya Actually Know?

From the Dresden Codex it's apparent the Maya knew a considerable amount about our solar system and galaxy. Here's a quick list of some of the astronomical details the ancient Maya knew. If you don't know what some of these things are, take a peek at Chapters 6 and 7 where we explain what these concepts mean and why they are important to 2012:

◆ The ecliptic path of the constellations

◆ The length, rising, and elongation of the orbit of Venus, Earth, and other planets

◆ The timing of the solstices, equinoxes, and zenith passage of the sun

◆ The solar sunspot cycle

◆ The exact length of the solar year

> **Codex Cues**
>
> The Mayan solar year was estimated to be 365.2420 days minus an error of .0002. Our calendar calculates it as 365.2425 plus an error of .0003.

◆ The length of the precession of the equinox

◆ The wobble and tilt of the earth

◆ The galaxy arrangement (they depicted the galaxy as a whirling disc, indicating they knew it is a spiral galaxy and arranged along a planar axis)

◆ Where our solar system is located in relation to the galactic plane

Crossed Sticks and Other Devices

Some of the celestial information of the Maya was obtained through careful observation with simple sighting devices and procedures. Illustrations in the Dresden Codex and in building murals show astronomers using three devices: a cross-staff device, a simple pole in the ground, and a tube sighting device.

The cross-staff device was likely used to estimate angular distances between objects in the sky. It could have determined information such as the maximum elongation of a planet's orbit. It worked by sighting along the staff through the ends of a crosspiece. This was a common device of pre-technology astronomers and was used around the world.

> **Celestial Connection**
>
> Greek astronomers at Alexandria produced the first catalog of star positions in 284 B.C.E. using a cross-staff. In Medieval Europe, an improved version used a cross that slides along the staff base, allowing for adjustments in angle and distance. This was called "Jacob's staff" and was used as a navigational instrument for sailors well into the eighteenth century.

A pole in the ground was an easy way to measure the zenith passages, the days when the sun travels directly overhead. In the Maya region, the sun stands directly overhead at noon twice each year, in May and July. A pole in the ground or a standing stone was all that was needed to establish the zenith. The Maya used standing stones, which were adjusted to true vertical with a plumb line. When the sun was directly overhead, the stone cast no shadow.

The Maya also used a vertical zenith tube in the roof of buildings or in a cave-roof or dug-out hole in the ground. A vertical tube could be used to determine the zenith passages of planets as well. In some locations, artificial caves were dug and installed with a tube feature. A good example of this is Monte Alban in Oaxaca. The ancient astronomers crouched in the dug-out cave, looking through the tube for the passage of celestial objects. When the planet, sun, or moon filled the hole, the object was at its zenith. The Maya Madrid Codex illustrates this "advanced" observational technique.

Line of Sight

The Maya used their temples and buildings as simple "line-of-sight" observatories. A long line of sight is an important feature in determining events that happen on the horizon, such as the rising and setting of the sun and planets. Building on mountains or other natural features amplified this effect. There is some evidence that Mayan observatories were built in a line across the landscape, keeping a continual line of sight across the sky.

Lines of sight have always been important in many aspects of life. The Greeks and Roman used bonfires to send messages over long distances. Keeping a line of sight from one hilltop to the next, as one fire was lit, the team at the next hilltop would see it and light their fire. Messages could be sent over very long distances much faster than runners.

Trance States

It's pretty clear that simple devices together with long periods of observation can account for a lot of the Mayan knowledge—especially since the Maya were able to build on all the data from the previous culture of the Olmec/Itzpam, which means they had about 500 years of observations! Even so, this was not enough to explain all that the Maya knew about the sky. For example, the Maya knew a considerable amount about the galaxy and the earth's position in the galaxy. Where would they gain the perspective to know this? No line of sight from the earth can reveal this information!

The Maya have their own explanation. Ceremony for the Maya was an opportunity to open portals and commune with the gods. The Maya considered the sky and the movements of the celestial bodies as the message board of the gods. During ceremony, the Maya achieved trance states that allowed them to open the portals and explore the message board.

Trance states, or altered states of consciousness, were achieved through different means. Practices that involve breathing patterns and influencing the internal flow of k'ul have been described by modern-day Mayan elders. For sure we know that the ancient Maya used hallucinogenic plants. Peyote cactus and mushrooms were both used to induce a trance, as was tobacco.

In trance states, the Mayan shamans were able to perform many extraordinary feats. They were able to perform healing rites, seeming to remove the cause of illness in a type of psychic surgery. They were able to travel among the stars, possibly with the help of their Wayeb (see Chapter 2). It was during trance states that some of the advanced knowledge is claimed to have been discovered. We'll explore more about how trance states were used in Chapters 10 and 11.

Cosmic Caution

Should you be inclined to smoke a lot of tobacco and induce a trance, be advised: Mayan tobacco was much different than ours. Using our tobacco in this way may produce a trance, but it will cause nicotine poisoning far sooner!

Sacred Sites and Astronomy

The Maya left evidence of their cosmology in their architectural structures. Pyramids, temples, and city plans were designed to align with astronomical events. Some buildings were marking passages and celebrating celestial alignments, such as the Kukulkan pyramid at Chichen Itza.

Others were working observatories, discovering new information, or confirming existing data. Alignments were made to the rising and setting of stars, constellations, the sun, moon, and planets. Of course, some alignments are bound to be simply coincidental; however, alignments were repeated in different ways at each site, so coincidence becomes hard to swallow.

Codex Cues

Encrypting pyramids and drawing glyphs in stone allowed Mayan knowledge to be preserved through centuries. In contrast, the knowledge of our modern culture, which is written on paper, CD-ROMs, and other media, will disappear with us.

Most importantly, the Mayan encrypted the pyramids they built with information from their calendars. Information is reflected in the mathematics of the design and the number of stairs, angles, segments; all had relationship to the length of the Mayan ages, the solar year, specific dates, and more. In addition to being observatories, these are teaching devices, universities in stone—books to withstand the march of time!

Why did the Maya go to the trouble? It's not like they couldn't record events in the codices or murals. The most likely explanation goes back to Maya-view. Buildings and cities were doing more than lining up for astronomical observation. They were aligning to the unique energy being released from the celestial gods. The orientations they used maximized the amplification of sacred energy gathered at the site. Coding information to teach people about the calendars not only taught the information, it provided a cosmic energy link to help understand and live the knowledge.

No wonder kings were consecrated at specific times of the year in specific buildings. It added power to their rule. No wonder shamans had better results with their ceremony when performed on the top of pyramids. No wonder people today are looking toward the wisdom of the Maya. Many are looking for information on what the Maya believed is coming in 2012. Is it possible that part of what is coming is an alignment that will discharge an energy powerful enough to assist our passage through the end times of the Mayan calendar? Many think so and are looking to the world of the Maya for an approach to this transition.

Building Codes

The Maya had several techniques to create alignments. Windows were precisely placed to allow the sun to illuminate desired objects at desired times. Objects were placed in exact locations to cast shadows in very explicit ways. Some buildings were used as sight lines for observation, such as structures at Uaxactun (see next section). Some buildings simply shared an orientation with the directions of planetary risings. Many pre-classic sites are oriented with the constellation of the Pleiades and the star Eta Draconis.

Uaxactun

Uaxactun is located in the Peten Basin lowlands of Guatemala. Its original name meant "born in heaven." It's 25 miles from Tikal, and most certainly the two ancient cities traded with each other. Uaxactun flourished during the classic period between 300 C.E. and 900 C.E.

This city ruin is a perfect example of how the Maya used building arrangements as sighting instruments. Uaxactun has one main pyramid that is aligned to a platform with three temples across a plaza. The main pyramid at Uaxactun is called the Jaguar Mask Pyramid. It's a flat-topped pyramid with stairs on all four sides. Flanking the stairways are huge jaguar masks. Across the plaza is a platform with three temples.

A line of sight crossing the cornices on the three temples marks the passages of the sun. The platform is aligned north-south. From the pyramid, the southern temple is in alignment with the sunrise on the summer solstice, the north structure is in alignment with the sunrise on the winter solstice, and the central structure is in line with sunrise on the equinoxes.

Chichen Itza

Chichen Itza is probably one of the best-known ancient Mayan cities. It has a special alignment between the equinoxes and the pyramid of Kukulkan (Quetzalcoatl). The pyramid is also called El Castillo.

The temple of Kukulkan is a four-sided, flat-topped temple with stairs on all sides. The axes running through the northwest and southwest corners are oriented toward the rising sun at the summer solstice and the setting sun at the winter solstice. The balustrades on the staircases descend in the shape of an enormous serpent. Twice a year at the equinoxes, the setting sun hits the northeast balustrade wall casting triangular shadows that undulate down the staircase like a serpent slithering down the temple wall. The pyramid has a large sculpture of a serpent's head at its base. When the shadow of the serpent reaches the bottom of the pyramid, it unites with the sculpted head of Kukulkan (Quetzalcoatl). To this day, 50,000 people gather annually to see this event.

The Kukulkan pyramid also codes information from the calendars. Each of the four faces of the pyramid has a stairway with 91 steps. When added to the shared step at the top platform, the total is 365, the number of days in a year. The terraces are divided into 18 segments, the number of Mayan months in the Haab calendar. There are many more relationships and many researchers believe important information is coded regarding 2012. You'll read about this in Chapter 8.

> ### Celestial Connection
>
> The Maya built temples on top of each other, terminating old buildings when their life span was up and building new structures on top of them to contain the energy. The pyramid of Kukulkan was excavated in the 1930s when a staircase was discovered under the north side. Digging though the top, they found another temple buried below. Inside they found a statue of a god called Chac Mool and a throne in the shape of a jaguar.

Another interesting building at Chichen Itza is called the Caracol. It's a circular building that was used as an astronomical observatory. It has three important Venus alignments. A pair of turret windows each point to a different place on the western horizon where Venus pauses and changes direction in the sky. An observational platform has diagonal inscriptions directed toward the sunrise on the summer and winter solstices.

Palenque

There are a tremendous number of alignments at Palenque with more being uncovered all the time. In comparison to other sites, Palenque seems to direct the observer toward the stars and the moon. The Temple of the Count is aligned to the bright star Sirius. The Temple of the Foliated Cross is aligned to the binary star Capella. Alignments also exist to the moon at the time of its maximum elongation, the winter solstice setting sun, and the setting sun at the zenith passage.

Palenque is a great example of window placement alignments. Sunset in the Tower at Palenque illuminates an interior room through a T-shaped window, marking passages of the sun at the solstice and zeniths.

Palenque is also a good example of how the ancient Maya used architecture to commemorate legends and actions of the gods. The Palenque enactment takes place in Pacal's tomb. Pacal, sometimes referred to as Pacal Votan, was an important Lord of Palenque. He took the throne at the age of 12 and died in 683 C.E. at the age of 80. He was responsible for the growth of power and influence of Palenque and according to Mayan elder Hunbatz Men, brought wisdom and enlightenment to his people. It's said he was an incarnation of the Mayan god Votan. When Pacal died, the Maya believed he turned back into a god after his descent into the underworld. His tomb was hidden behind a secret entrance in the Temple of Inscriptions at Palenque. It was discovered in 1948 and finally uncovered in 1952.

Outside the temple, the sun sets behind a large ridge lying in alignment with the center of the temple roof. As the sun moves across the sky, rays of sunlight enter a doorway, illuminating the back wall of the temple. As the sun moves toward the horizon, the illumination slowly descends the temple stairway until it disappears into Pacal's tomb. This symbolizes Pacal's descent into the underworlds before becoming a sky god.

Codex Cues _____

If you're interested in ancient sites, here are some more you may want to check out: Cancuen (this has the largest palace found to date, three stories, with many levels and courtyards), Calakmul, Uxmal (this has the most amazing conical pyramid!), El Mirador, Tikal (truly an incredible city), Civil, and Copan.

Time and Cosmic Events

What the Mayans achieved in regard to astronomy and mathematics is nothing short of miraculous. What they did better than anyone else, however, is synthesize information. Through their synthesis they came to relate the cycles and rhythms in the sky with cycles and rhythms in human affairs, storm patterns, climate shifts, earthquakes, and more. Relationships like this are now being substantiated by science. We know, for instance, that solar flares correspond to increases in hurricanes and contribute to global warming.

In Maya-view, alignments to celestial bodies were more than physical. They displayed the bonds the Maya believed existed between Earth and the heavens. The Mayan kings timed their accession rituals to be in sync with major celestial events and especially with the Milky Way. They believed that important events happened at the end of cycles, so with every cycle transition of the calendars, they had a ceremony. Often they erected stone stele to record the event.

Observing cycles allowed the Maya to predict aspects of life and plan for planting crops, performing rituals, and so on. It also allowed the Maya to observe psycho-spiritual correlations to time. We've already seen that every day was given a meaning, as was the month and year. Each configuration expressed a certain character so it could be used for divination. People went to diviners to have fortunes told the same way people today read their horoscopes.

The Least You Need to Know

- Using a simple counting technique, the Maya were able to accurately calculate huge sums and spans of time.
- The Maya gained astronomical information through long-term observation, simple tools, and trance states.
- Celestial information was coded in the buildings, cities, and calendars.
- Information was coded in pyramids for information and for energy transmission.

Part 2

Cosmic Treasure Hunt

Now that you can appreciate the Maya, you're probably getting curious about the 2012 predictions. Where did the predictions come from? What are they based on? Are they accurate?

This part takes you into the calendars and changing ages of the Maya. The Maya measured cycles and qualities of time. Time periods were expressions of qualities and time itself determined the events that happened. The interactions and alignments of the celestial bodies reflected themselves in the events of earth. Through their timekeeping system the Maya were able to see events unfolding into the future.

In these chapters, you'll get a chance to look at the calendars, the pyramids, the skies, and the Mayan world ages to see the evolution of consciousness in its many expressions.

DO YOU HAVE ANYTHING I COULD JUST HANG ON MY WALL?

MAYAN CALENDARS

BARR

4

Pieces of the Puzzle

In This Chapter

- ◆ How the calendars work and interlock
- ◆ The Gregorian calendar versus the Mayan calendars
- ◆ Time forms events
- ◆ Interlocking cycles form alignments

The labyrinth toward 2012 begins with the Mayan timekeeping system. The system is based on more than one calendar. The calendars measure interlocking, multidimensional cycles. Before we can explore the individual calendars in Chapter 5, you need an overview of how the system works. In this chapter, we'll show you how many calendars there are, why so many were needed, and how they interrelate. Most importantly, you can see what was so unique about the Mayan view of time.

You'll also get a glimpse into how our modern calendar works and why the two systems are so different. This will give you a good framework for the upcoming chapters where we weave through the individual calendars, explore the solar system and galaxy, and then descend into the jungles to decode the pyramids.

The 20 Puzzle Pieces

Although we talk about the Mayan calendar, the truth is there's more than one. In fact there are between 17 and 20. The calendars are unique. They're extremely accurate. Their calculations of orbits, eclipses, and other astronomical events are as accurate as our measurements today. Why did the Maya need such exactness? Other pre-technology cultures survived just fine without this precision. The answer might lie in how they view time.

The Function of Time

In our calendar, we use time to measure distance or mark events. Most significantly, we use time to mark the occurrence of events, in phrases such as "it's three days away." Time to us is a measurement; it has no quality of its own. The events have qualities; time itself is just a canvass on which we write history and separate events.

The ancient Maya would not have understood us. For the Maya, time was holy. It had its own set of qualities that reflected in events. Time formed history, not the other way round. This is the basis of what today is called *synchronicity*, or meaningful coincidence. Synchronistic events are important because of their timing, not their content.

def•i•ni•tion

Synchronicity refers to a person's experience of two or more events happening simultaneously that are unrelated by cause and effect but which occur in a significant manner.

The Maya had the ability to understand time as a formative principle. It was for this purpose that they required such precision and accuracy in their measurements. Time was not a succession of days; it was the enactment of a cosmic plan. The calendars contained the map of this plan.

The Calendars

There are between 17 and 20 authentic calendars presently known in the Mayan timekeeping system. The easiest way to think about this is to consider them as almanacs. Each almanac recorded a different type of cycle and each almanac was complete to itself. Many of these calendars are still in use by the traditional Maya.

We use almanacs today to keep track of farming cycles, the fiscal year, the academic year, and so on. In our system, we record our almanacs against a constant timekeeping calendar based on the earth's solar year. Our current-era calendar is called the *Gregorian calendar*.

The Mayan system was different. Each of the Mayan calendars relates to the cycle it measures. They created calendars for the solar year of Venus, for the zenith passage of the Pleiades constellation, for the rise and fall of insect cycles, and for the cycle of the precession of the equinox. Some of the calendars do not measure physical cycles, but spiritual cycles, the periodic release from the gods of spiritual qualities. It's not correct to say that there was no timekeeping constant, like our Gregorian calendar, but it didn't reside in any single cycle. It resided in the synchronized interaction of all the calendar cycles.

def•i•ni•tion

The **Gregorian calendar** is the solar calendar in use throughout most of the world, sponsored by Pope Gregory XIII in 1582 as a corrected version of the Julian calendar.

One Calendar per Cycle

Each calendar represents a different cycle; each cycle was important, both physically and spiritually. All the cycles are interrelated. The calendars are sacred to the Maya and information about them is not released lightly. The following information is condensed from two sources: Carlos Barrios, an anthropologist and Mayan Elder; and Aluna Joy Yaxk'in, a modern-day mystic who works with many indigenous Elders. This is an abbreviated list of what some of the calendars measure and how long their cycles are:

◆ **Agricultural cycles:** Two calendars relate directly to agriculture; one was 130 days long and measured growing cycles of corn, the other was 180 days and measured insect cycles. Some insects are needed for fertilization, others are damaging to crops. Knowing the cycles was essential information.

◆ **Human gestation of 260 days:** Also related to the Venus cycle. It describes the connections between astronomical events and the human body. This calendar is called the Tzolk'in. It is a very sacred calendar at the heart of the system and will be explained in detail in the next chapter.

◆ **The solar year of 365 days:** This is the Haab cycle, which you will see in more detail in Chapter 5.

◆ **Prophetic calendars:** These are secret calendars in use by at least ten Mayan tribes today. There are five strictly prophetic calendars plus the Long Count, which has prophetic application.

◆ **The moon cycle of 29.5 days:** Measures the length of time it takes the moon to go through a complete phase from new moon to new moon.

◆ **The galactic cycle of 26,000 years:** Measures the precession of the equinox.

◆ **The 13-baktun cycle (5,125 years) of the Long Count:** Measures the changing of the "suns" in the precession. The Long Count is where the date 2012 comes from. We'll describe it more fully in Chapter 5.

◆ **Spiritual cycles:** Measures cycles of energy released to the planet. They vary in length.

Three to five calendars are yet to be released but are believed to be prophetic.

Why So Many?

All the different cycles were important to daily living. Knowing the zenith passage of the sun, for example, helped farmers know when to plant crops. Knowing the patterns of insects helped farmers know what type of crop would have an advantage or disadvantage in a given year. Knowing the cycling and release of spiritual qualities helped people to plan weddings, put extensions on their houses, and plan trips.

Codex Cues

For a complete list of the calendars, go to www.kachina. net/~alunajoy/calendars. html. This site by Aluna Joy Yaxk'in gives the names and functions of all 20 calendars as she has learned them from the Mayan Elders.

You might be wondering why the Maya didn't keep track of all their cycles in one timekeeping system. In fact, they did, it just took more than one calendar! Being less interested in timelines and more interested in interactions, they didn't need to fix events the way we do. However, it's not really accurate to say the Mayans had separate timekeeping systems; really they had one grand timekeeping device with many different interacting cycles.

How Many Are in Use Today?

Of the 17 to 20 Mayan calendars, three to five are hidden from common use but are in use by traditional Mayan Elders. They are said to be important in guiding evolutionary consciousness. We have been told that each year there is a meeting of the 441

Elders who represent the present-day Mayan tribes. They discuss the calendars, the Mayan traditions, and how much information to share with the larger world. It has been suggested to us that there will be a release of some or all of these calendars within the next several years. Drunvalo Melchizedek will be instrumental in this release. Drunvalo is an internationally known modern visionary, author, and workshop leader. You'll learn more about him in Chapter 14.

It's unknown whether there are more than the five concealed calendars at this time. Carlos Barrios is an anthropologist and Mayan Elder. He and his brother are reported to have spent years traveling among the Mayan villages in a quest for hidden copies of the calendars. Reports of their findings are remarkable. They collected many different copies of the same calendar from all over the Maya region. They were identical. In 500 years of hiding the calendars had not been altered.

Calendar Comparisons

Comparing the Mayan timekeeping system to our current Gregorian calendar is like comparing apples to oranges. The calendar reflects the beliefs of the culture, but at the same time it directs the way people think.

Calendars keep track of units of time and organize them in meaningful patterns. Some calendars relate to astronomical events, others don't. The original Western calendar was devised in 36 B.C.E. by the Romans and related the cycles of the earth's rotation around the sun, the earth's revolutions on its axis, and the cycles of the moon. It was called the Julian calendar, named after the Roman emperor Julius Caesar.

Astronomers became concerned about discrepancies in the Julian calendar that resulted in a 10-day difference between the calendar date and the actual seasons and movements of the planets. Of course, no one wanted to hear this. Astronomers argued their case and eventually proved that an adjustment had to be made.

> **Celestial Connection**
>
> During the time period when half of Europe was using the Julian and the other half the Gregorian, both dates had to be posted on all documents. In some countries, double posting is still legal. A posting might look like this: 1 March 1923/15 February 1923.

Papal Intervention

In 1582, Pope Gregory decreed that the date would change from October 4, 1582, to October 15, 1582, a loss of 10 days from people's lives; 10 days' revenue for merchants;

and 10 days of extra rent payments for renters. The people fought bitterly to stop the change, convinced it was a conspiracy of the landlords.

The Catholic countries of France, Spain, Portugal, and Italy were the first to change to the new calendar, the Gregorian calendar named after Pope Gregory. England finally joined the majority of Europe after the British Calendar Act of 1751. The final country to lose 10 days of life was Greece. In 1923, the people of Greece went to bed on Wednesday, February 15, and woke up on Thursday, March 1.

The Maya vs. Pope Gregory

The Gregorian calendar is a solar calendar, so it's based on the revolution of the earth around the sun. (The week is an example of a calendrical measure that is not related to any planet or astronomical event.) The smallest calendar unit is the day, which is the time it takes the earth to rotate on its axis. The month is the time it takes the moon to revolve around the earth. These three astronomical cycles form the basis of the calendar.

Unfortunately, the moon, sun, and earth do not synchronize very well. There are 365.2425 days in year, which adds to slightly more than an extra day every four years. There are 29.5 days in a lunar month, which means that a 12-lunar cycle has only 354 days. Periodic adjustments are made to keep the calendar in sync with the actual planets it represents.

Leap year is an example: we use 365 days for three years in a row, then add a day on the fourth year, thus correcting for the quarter day. This would work perfectly if the difference was exactly a quarter day, or 365.25, but it's not. The difference is a little more. It's 365.2425, and that .0025 adds up. To compensate, every 400 years we drop a day from the calendar. This is called the 400-year rule. To keep the moon in sync, we force the 12.5 *lunations* to fit into a 12-month period. We do this by making the months different lengths. Instead of reflecting the 29.5 days, we make our months 30 or 31 days.

def•i•ni•tion

Lunation, or lunar cycle, is the 29.5-day cycle of the moon's orbit around the earth.

The Mayan system incorporated many more cycles than the three celestial bodies of the Gregorian. Unlike the Western calendar, they didn't compensate for the lack of synchronicity. Instead they worked to bigger cycles where the sun and earth and other planets naturally synchronize. In doing this, they stayed in harmony with nature. Remember, the Maya believed their bodies had correlating points with the planets and parts of the galaxy. To stay in balance, they needed to remain harmonized to the natural cycles of the planets.

Different Calendars and Natural Rhythms

The Gregorian calendar is unnatural. It forces the sun and earth to synchronize by artificially adding and subtracting days. In a sense we are ruling time, forcing the calendar to reflect a contrived reality.

Your body is linked to the movement of the planets by your *circadian rhythm*. This rhythm is based on the effect the sun and moon have on your endocrine system. The pineal gland releases melatonin in response to shifting patterns of sunlight. Melatonin sets the hypothalamus, the body's master gland, which coordinates all the hormonal rhythms of our body. In this regard, the Mayans weren't far off in their understanding of the need to stay in harmony with natural cycles. Just look at all the sleep disorders people suffer today!

def•i•ni•tion

The **circadian rhythm** is a 24-hour biological cycle that is affected by light and dark. It's an internal cycle that controls sleep patterns, eating patterns, and hormonal balance.

As we said, the Maya did not try to synchronize the day and year. They allowed time to unfold as the planets moved. They took a long view and allowed the sun and earth to complete a 400-year cycle necessary to synchronize. Does this explain the pressure we feel in our culture around time? Everyone is always rushing to beat the clock, to fit extra hours in the day. Do you let yourself be ruled by time? Does your calendar control your life? Our view of time and calendars makes it hard to understand the balance in which the Maya lived.

Putting the Puzzle Together

The calendars fit together to create a bigger picture of the universe as a whole. The one constant is time itself. Physicists call time the fourth dimension. We live in the three-dimensional world of space where everything has length, width, and depth. We can navigate through space as long as we pay attention to these three dimensions. Because we measure time as a constant based on the earth's movement around the sun, we also tend to measure the movement of the universe against the same earth cycle. Albert Einstein taught that time is relative. It relates to the speed of movement. So how can we say that time is the same in all parts of the universe?

The Maya knew that time was the connection between objects in space. The scope of the Mayan system is much more universal than ours. Timekeeping is not based on a single orbit, or zenith passage, or constellation. It's based on synchronized alignments that allow interaction between the parts of the whole. The interactions occur because of relationships rather than closeness in space.

Celestial Connection

Albert Einstein opened our eyes to the relationship between space and time, making time a fourth dimension. His theory of special relativity shows that time is relative. It behaves differently under different conditions. The Lorentz equation demonstrates that as speed increases, length contracts and time expands.

Cycles of the Universe

To see how it all fits together, imagine each of the Mayan calendars as a disc, or sphere, with the size of the circumference representing the length of the cycle. Each disc will be a different size. The disc for the solar year of Venus will be smaller than the disc representing the solar year of Earth. Imagine that each disc has notches, or cogs, along the circumference representing time spans. All of the discs interact with each other, like the gears of a clock, only three dimensionally. All the cycles move in relation to the whole. The precision of the Maya's astronomy and mathematics was essential to enact this extraordinary dance.

Wheels Within Wheels

The dance of interlocking spheres unveils ever-more complex combinations and extensive cycles. The laws of time and nature reveal themselves as we open our minds to subtle patterns. The greatness of the Mayan system is the ability it has to expand our perception.

The problem with the cogwheel analogy is that it's easy to start to think of the universe as a machine. This is not what the Maya saw! They saw that each celestial body interacted with the whole and influenced the overall patterns. The universe is not a machine set on a course of action; it lives, responds, and changes.

Grid Work

Let's look at another aspect of the cogwheel analogy. As you know, the Maya tracked planetary alignments and eclipses. In this analogy, planetary alignments are the points of contact between the interlocking cogwheels. They allow the planets to exchange with each other disregarding distance. What are they exchanging? They're exchanging the k'ul from Chapter 2—the "vital life force."

The ancient Maya believed that just as k'ul flowed in the earth, it flowed along pathways through all planets and celestial bodies. You might think of them as intergalactic arteries, allowing the earth and other celestial bodies to exchange essential energy "nutrients." The Maya interacted with this exchange through the earth's energy grid.

As you remember from Chapter 2, k'ul lines crisscrossed the earth forming the earth grid. Places where lines of force intersect had more k'ul; like streams crossing and forming a pool. Humans were able to interact with the grid by building temples on these high-energy, or sacred, sites. Celestial bodies interacted with the nodal points on the grid during alignments, increasing the flow of k'ul through the grid lines. At the same time, energy could also flow from the earth to the celestial body, creating an intergalactic exchange.

> **Celestial Connection**
>
> All ancient cultures have a word for vital life force. It's *prana* in Sanskrit, *ki* in Japanese, *qi* or *chi* in Chinese, *mana* in Huna, *Odic force* in Germanic mysticism, etc. Many cultures believe this vital force runs in channels called meridians in people and ley lines in the earth.

The Mayan system was based on the pulsing of energy through the earth as celestial bodies come into and out of alignment. Because people are connected to the planets through the 13 major joints in their body, the effects of alignments were both planetary and personal. Modern astrologers still believe the movement of the planets affects people's moods, health, and decisions. The Maya, however, didn't limit this interaction to just planets in our solar system; all celestial objects played a role.

In Sync

A major reason for tracking so much astronomical information was to gain control and advantage over life events. All aspects of community were connected to the calendars; when wars were fought, when ball games were played, when rituals were performed. Events were planned to take advantage of celestial alignments and the energy released into the earth. Diviners were consulted for weddings, business ventures, and all personal matters. As much as the Maya used this information for material gain, it was even more meaningful spiritually.

Being in sync with the cycles, being able to "sky-walk" celestial connections, was the ultimate goal. For the Maya, the calendars were a map to spiritual evolution. The mythology of humans overcoming death and becoming gods related to the evolution of consciousness and transcending material reality. This was the great motivating force for the Maya. It's also the underlying prophecy for 2012.

The Least You Need to Know

- There are approximately 20 Mayan calendars that work together in an interactive system.

- The Gregorian calendar is based on a solar year, while the Mayan "calendar" is a group of calendars that are all based on different celestial and spiritual events.

- In Maya-view, time is formative: the quality of a time period forms the events that occur. This is the basis of synchronicity.

- Celestial alignments allow interactions, increasing the exchange of k'ul and activating the energy grid.

Chapter 5

The Calendar Clues

In This Chapter

- ◆ The main calendar systems of the Mayan calendar
- ◆ The interlocking mechanisms
- ◆ Writing and reading Mayan dates
- ◆ Determining the calendar start and end dates

We started our journey toward 2012 exploring the vastness and complexity of the Mayan timekeeping system. We discovered their comprehensive understanding of celestial patterns. Our next step is to look at the calendars themselves. What do they measure? How do they fit together?

The Maya kept meticulous records of the movements of the sky deities. Their data was recorded in the codices; every repetition of the cycle provided more information. Over centuries they refined their knowledge and began to predict future events based on the patterns of the past.

In this chapter, you'll learn about the main calendars and how they interact. You'll learn how archeologists correlated Mayan time to our own, and you'll discover how the date 2012 was determined.

Tzolk'in or Cholqij Calendar

This is the most sacred of the Mayan almanacs. It measures the intention of the gods as they express themselves through creation. The original Quiche Mayan name was Cholqij. This calendar was lost during the Spanish invasion, but the 260-day cycle was maintained by elders in the highlands of Guatemala.

Codex Cues _____

The Aztec had an equivalent calendar that clearly originated from the Cholqij. In the Nahuatl language of the Aztec it was called the Tonalpohualli.

This calendar was the center of the Mesoamerican timekeeping system. It was in use in the pre-Mayan era of the Olmec at a city called Izapa. It's believed it was initiated in 1200 B.C.E. and has been in continuous use for the last 3,000 years. Maya today use it in the same way it was used in the past—to determine the timing of religious and ceremonial events and for divination.

Using our cogwheel analogy from Chapter 4, the Tzolk'in is located in the center of the calendar gears; it's the wheel all others relate back to. It tracks something we can't really comprehend, the "divinatory year." It represents the center of the galaxy, and is linked to the center of each person. It brings the universe into alignment.

The Tzolk'in's 260-day span does not have direct correlation to planetary orbits or repeating astronomical patterns. However, it is the common denominator in the cycles of the sun, the planets of our solar system, and our moon. In essence, it links planetary and terrestrial cycles and anchors them to the human body through the 13 major joints and 20 fingers and toes. (As you'll recall from Chapter 2, there are 13 major joints in the body that connect us to the galaxy, as well as 20 galactic threads that connect to our fingers and toes.)

Days, Months, Years

Tzolk'in has been translated to mean "the Count of Days" by Yale professor Michael Coe. Each day in the 260-day cycle is known by both a number and a name. The name is designated by a glyph called a day-sign that we talked about in Chapter 3. There are 20 day-signs and 13 numbers. Tzolk'in dates were written with the number first and the glyph second, such as 1 AHAU.

Here's a list of the day-sign names of the Tzolk'in:

Imix	Akbal
Ik	Kan

Chicchan	Ben
Cimi	Ix
Manik	Men
Lamat	Cib
Muluc	Caban
Oc	Etznab
Chuen	Cauac
Eb	Ahau

Day-signs and numbers are counted alongside each other like we count weekdays. Both the day-sign and the number change each day. In our week, Monday the 1st is followed by Tuesday the 2nd is followed by Wednesday the 3rd, and so on. In the Mayan calendar, it would look like this: 1 Ahau, 2 Imix, 3 Ik, and so on. In the Tzolk'in calendar, one cycle is complete when all 13 numbers have been combined with all 20 days. You can get a sense of how this works by looking at the two rings inside of each other in the following illustration. The inner ring is the cycle of the 13 numbers, the outer ring is the cycle of day-signs.

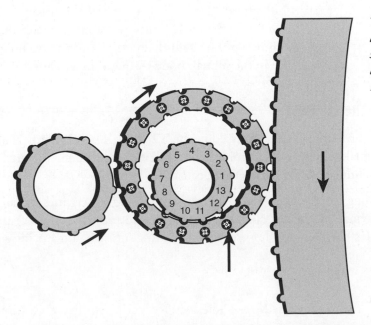

The numbers of the Tzolk'in are the inside ring, the day-signs are the outside ring, and the large ring is the Haab.

As the 13 numbers revolve within the 20 days, it takes 260 days for the same number-glyph combination to repeat. That means a complete cycle of the Tzolk'in takes 260 days. The number of times a cycle completes, or the number of Tzolk'in years, are not counted. It's a system that exists in the eternal present, one more reason it's considered the centering calendar.

What Is a Divinatory Cycle?

If a divinatory year is not tracking a specific astronomical body, what is it based on? Some say the calendar is based on the length of human gestation, or the growing cycle of corn, the sacred plant of the Maya. Others say it's related to celestial events such as eclipses, the time Venus is seen as the morning star, or the zenith passages of the sun. Some link it to the Pleiades constellation. Robert D. Penden, former lecturer at Deakin University in Australia, asserts that 260 days is the common denominator between the planets of the inner solar system, thus making it a unifying cycle.

Codex Cues

Thirteen-day periods of time are called trecenas. They were used in pre-Columbian Mesoamerican calendars. The calendars divide the 260-day cycle into 20 trecenas of 13 days each. Trecena is a Spanish word meaning "group of thirteen," and trecena is used similarly to the way we use "dozen."

In the larger picture, all these theories are valid. Together they form the basis for the belief that the Tzolk'in calendar linked celestial and terrestrial events, like the movements of the planets with the corn harvest. It's said that celestial events are linked into in the human body through the gestation cycle.

Spiritual Qualities of the 20 Suns

Let's not forget the spiritual qualities expressed in the Tzolk'in. The 13 numbers and 20 day-signs were actual deities, so the combination of deities determined the attributes of the day and influenced the events that occurred.

The glyphs representing the day-signs show pictures of meaningful activities in daily life. When used in divination, the day-signs were combined with the meanings of the 13 numbers as well. It's like reading a horoscope with both a sun sign and a rising sign.

Divination

Ah K'in is the title of the Mayan *Day Keeper*. The Day Keeper performed divination by "reading" the Tzolk'in. You might decide to go to the Day Keeper to resolve a crisis, to ask health questions when you're sick, or to find out the status of a pregnancy. If you wanted to expand your business, you might consult the Day Keeper for a wealth reading. The sacred cycle was also used to determine auspicious dates for marriages, rituals, etc. In divination, expanded meanings of the day-signs were used in multiple combinations. The Day Keeper/shaman could also answer yes and no questions.

def•i•ni•tion

A **Day Keeper** was a Mayan shaman whose job was to keep the count of the calendars. He also used the calendars to interpret auspicious dates and give "Life Tree" readings, similar to present-day astrology charts.

Birthdates

The Day Keepers were particularly interested in the combination of day-signs and day numbers at the time of a person's birth. This told the Day Keeper what spiritual qualities were present. As we saw earlier, this means that multiplying 20 times 13 gives 260 different energies or character combinations. According to your birthday, you possess one of those 260 combinations.

The Day Keeper created a birth chart for each child known as an individual Life Tree. The tree showed the energies prevailing on the date of the child's birth, but also what energies were complementary or contradictory. In some ways, this is very similar to today's astrological readings. The purpose of a Life Tree reading was to give insight into the individual path of each child.

Codex Cues

If you want to know your Mayan birth day-sign, here are some websites that will help you convert your birth date to a Mayan day-sign:

- ◆ www.pauahtun.org/Calendar/tools.html
- ◆ www.fourmilab.ch/documents/calendar
- ◆ www.diagnosis2012.co.uk/conv.htm

Modern Life Tree readings are also available. You can search the web with keywords "Mayan astrology," or check out one of these sites:

- ◆ mayandaysigns.blogspot.com
- ◆ www.mayanastrology.com

Haab Calendar

The Haab calendar is the companion to the Tzolk'in. It's a civil calendar that works with the Tzolk'in to serve the needs of daily life. The Haab originated around 550 B.C.E. The word Haab translates as "the cycle of rains."

In one sense, the Tzolk'in and the Haab together represent the secular and sacred interests of the culture. The Haab is the yearly cycle, while the Tzolk'in relates to hidden dimensions of the spiritual.

Days and Months

The Haab is a little easier to understand than the Tzolk'in. It's an astronomical calendar of the solar year and is divided into 18 months of 20 kin each (the Mayan word for "day" is *kin*). The 18 months make a 360-day year followed by five extra days that existed at the end of the Haab year, making it a 365-day cycle. The five-day extra period was called the Wayeb period. It was the transition between the end of the old and beginning of the new; a time when the spirit Wayebs could play tricks on humans.

Here are the names of the Haab months. The names in parentheses are Quiche Mayan, which are sometimes different from the more common Yucatec:

Pop	Yax
Wo (Uo)	Sak (Zac)
Sip (Zip)	She (Ceh)
Sotz' (Zotz)	Mac
Sek (Tzec)	K'ank'in
Xul	Muan
Yaxk'in	Pax
Mol	K'ayeb
Ch'en	Kumk'u (Cumku)

The Haab calendar is more like our own month and day system. Each of the 18 months is named and has 20 days. The days are numbered from 0 to 19. The zero day was called the "seating of the month" and established the new monthly cycle. Using a zero day is unique to the Mayan calendar; no other ancient or current calendar does this.

Unlike the Tzolk'in, which changed names and day number together, the Haab maintains the same month through a complete cycle of 20 days. So 0 Pop would be followed by 1 Pop, 2 Pop, and so forth, until 19 Pop. Then it would change to a new seating of 0 Wo, followed by 1 Wo and continue through the new month. Like the Tzolk'in, the years of the Haab calendar were not counted.

Famous and Exact?

Archeologists are quick to say the Maya did not know the true length of the year. You will see this isn't true in Chapter 6. Many archeologists thought the Haab was crude and inaccurate since it treated the year as having 365 days, ignoring the extra quarter day (actual solar year is 365.2425). This means the seasons were off the actual dates by a quarter day each year. Eventually, over centuries, the calendar dates no longer corresponded to the seasons at all.

You probably agree that it's important to keep dates in line with the seasons. In a solar calendar, you want the equinoxes and solstices to happen on the same calendar day every year, otherwise you won't know when to plan seasonal events. This is why we adjust our system with leap years and the 400-year rule we talked about in Chapter 4.

> **Celestial Connection**
>
> The Haab is compared to the "wandering 365-day year" of Ancient Egypt. The Ancient Egyptian solar calendar was nearly identical to the Maya. It had 12 months of 30 days each, equaling 360 days. At the end of the 360 days was a short month of 5 days, called the *epagomenes*.

The Maya were perfectly aware of the true length of the year. However, they were more concerned with synchronizing their calendar with larger cycles. They kept track of seasons by watching the changing lengths of the days; they didn't need to correlate this to a specific date. Keeping the Haab in sync with the Tzolk'in and staying linked to the 400-year earth/sun cycle was more important. We will probably never know the true reason why the Maya didn't adjust the Haab to the seasons, but we can be sure they knew about the issue!

Five Days of the Wayeb Celebration

The five Wayeb days at the end of the 18-month Haab calendar are called the nameless days, the extra-days, or the soulless days. The Wayeb was a time for both year-end rituals and New Year celebrations. On the last day of the year, all the hearth fires were extinguished to release the energy of the old year. People refrained from eating hot food, ate small amounts, abstained from sex, and tried to stay home (not like our New Year celebration!). Rituals were used to assist the completion of the past cycles.

Fires were relit during the second half of the Wayeb period to welcome the New Year. Celebrations continued until the start of the next Haab. Much speculation occurred at this time as to what the new year bearer would bring (more about year bearers in the next section).

Year Bearers

Since the Haab was primarily a civil calendar, it was used to mark civil occasions. Each Haab year was given a name that related to the Tzolk'in calendar. The Tzolk'in day-sign of the first day of the New Year became the year bearer for the next Haab cycle. The calendars mesh in such a way that the New Year can only land on four possible Tzolk'in day-signs. These are called the four year bearers and relate to the four directions and the Bacab gods who hold up the four corners of the world.

Calendar Round

As we move out from the center of the clockworks, the Calendar round is the first large cycle of the Mayan timekeeping system. It synchronizes the Tzolk'in and the Haab calendars.

Mayan dates always reflect both calendars. The Tzolk'in day was written first and the Haab day second. For example, a date would be written as 1 Kan 2 Zotz. This tells us the date is the first day of the Tzolk'in "week" of Kan and the third day of the Haab month of Zotz (remember the first day of the month is a zero day).

The Tzolk'in and the Haab calendars synchronize every 52 Haab, which is about 52 years. This means that any given Tzolk'in/Haab date happens once every 52 years. For example, if a day is "1 Kan 2 Zotz," the next time the calendar day will fall on 1 Kan 2 Zotz will be 52 years later.

> **Celestial Connection**
>
> The Calendar round was the longest period of time recorded by the Aztecs and other Meso-american peoples except the Maya. Only the Maya and their pre-Classical predecessors, the Olmec, kept longer counts.

Perfect Marriage

The Haab and the Tzolk'in calendars cycle around each other like gears of different sizes. Look at the previous illustration again to get a sense of how this works. Even as the numbers rotate within the Tzolk'in day-signs, the Tzolk'in travels around the Haab.

As we've said, the Calendar round is based on the length of both the Tzolk'in year (260 days) and the Haab year (365 days). The smallest number that can be divided evenly by both 260 and 365 is 18,980, or approximately 52 years. Among other things, the Calendar round offers an individual 18,980 separate perspectives for divination.

Year Calculations

You may have noticed that neither the Tzolk'in nor the Haab system numbers the years. So how did the Maya keep track of how old a person was or how many cycles had passed since a given date? For the average person, the answer was in the combination of the Tzolk'in/Haab date. Since a particular combination only occurs once every 52 years, the combination itself was enough to identify a time period. The average life span at the time was somewhat less than 52 years; not too many people would see a Calendar round date repeat. For more important events, like the succession of a king or the end of a successful war, the date was locked into the Long Count calendar (which we'll be discussing in a moment).

A 52-Year Celebration

The end of the Calendar round cycle was observed with massive celebration. Fires were put out for four days across the region while people waited to see the Pleiades cross the horizon. This would ensure another 52 years. The occasion was honored with the construction of a 52-year stele. The steles were inscribed with important dates of the period, events, and the passages of kings. To stay in alignment with the new energy coming in, many buildings were terminated, some were rebuilt, and new construction was begun at this time. The Calendar round stele have been important markers for decoding the dates of the Maya.

 Cosmic Caution

Among the Aztec, the end of a Calendar round was a time of public panic as it was thought the world might be coming to an end. Sound familiar?

Venus Cycle

Venus was an important icon for the Maya. The story of the Hero Twins (see Chapter 2) acts out the Venus cycle. Venus as the evening star descends into the underworlds during the time it disappears behind the sun. It re-merges as the morning star after defeating death. (The significance of Venus and the Hero Twins played itself out in the planning of wars and coronations of kings, both designed to coincide with the rising of Venus so that death would be defeated.

The Venus cycle was calculated and recorded in the Dresden Codex where six pages were devoted to its accuracy. The cycle is 584 days long, the time it takes between risings from the underworld as the morning star.

Connections

The Venus cycle is wrapped into the Calendar round where Venus and the Sun perform their continual dance through the 260 days of the Tzolk'in. Five Venus cycles equals eight Haab cycles.

The merging of the Venus cycle and the Tzolk'in happens in such a way that Venus can only emerge as the morning star on one of five possible day-signs of the Tzolk'in. Shaman/astronomers calculated the day-sign for each upcoming Venus rising. The first Venus day-sign, 1 Ahau, had special significance. It was named the Sacred Day of Venus because it marked the beginning of the next large cycle, the Venus Round.

Venus Round

The Venus Round is the time it takes for all three cycles, the Tzolk'in, the Haab, and the Venus cycle, to synchronize. It happens every 104 Haab or 2 Calendar rounds, approximately 104 years. Are you beginning to see what a remarkable accomplishment of synchronization the Maya created? No wonder they were not worried about the wandering 365 days of the solar year. They were marching to a much bigger drum.

Codex Cues _____

For a quick recap, here are some of the associations so far:

◆ The Tzolkin is 260 days composed of 20 day-signs combined with 13 numbers.

◆ The Haab is 360 days and is composed of 18 months of 20 days each, with a 5-day extra "month" at the end.

◆ The Calendar round is 18,980 days or 52 Haab years and is the synchronization of Tzolk'in and Haab.

◆ The Venus cycle is 584 days between each new morning star appearance.

◆ The Venus Round is 37,960 days or 104 Haab years and equals 2 Calendar rounds. It is the synchronization between the Tzolk'in, Haab, and Venus cycle.

The Long Count Calendar

All the calendars we've been deciphering so far come together in the Long Count calendar. The Long Count was created around 200 B.C.E. It counted backward in time about 3,000 years to a beginning date and counted forward in time about 2,000 years to the end of this era. It's a straight line of days from the beginning to the end of the current era, a span of 5,126 years. Like our own calendar, the Long Count can be used to identify when one event happens in relation to another. It can also be used to predict future events.

The calendar is not organized into astronomical cycles like the solar year or the orbit of Venus. As a result, for a long time it was believed to be independent of astronomical relationship. However, this isn't true. It's measuring a cycle so much larger than other cycles it simply dwarfs them. We'll be exploring this larger cycle in the next chapter, but first let's consider the Long Count measurements.

Measurements

The basic unit is the kin, or day, which allows it to be correlated with the Tzolk'in, Haab, and Venus cycles. The kin are counted in units based on the "20 vestigial" system we talked about in Chapter 3. Here's a quick reference:

◆ Kin = 1 day

◆ Uinal = 20 kins = 20 days

- Tun = 18 uinals = 360 days

- Katun = 20 tuns = 7,200 days = approximately 20 years

- Baktun = 20 katuns = 144,000 days = approximately 394 years

- One Great Cycle = 13 baktuns = approximately 5,126 years

- One Grand Cycle = 5 Great Cycles = approximately 25,630 years and the length of the precession of the equinox

The Maya also counted larger time spans:

- 1 pictun = 20 baktuns = 2,880,000 days = approximately 7,885 years

- 1 calabtun = 20 pictuns = 57,600,000 days = approximately 158,000 years

- 1 kinchiltun = 20 calabtuns = 1,152,000,000 days = approximately 3 million years

- 1 alautun = 20 kinchiltuns = 23,040,000,000 days = approximately 63 million years

The Long Count calendar is one Great Cycle, a period of 13 baktuns or 5,126 years. Another way you might see this written in other books is for the Long Count Great Cycle to be 5,200 years and the Grand Cycle to be 26,000 years. These numbers are using the 360-day Haab year as opposed to the astronomical year of 365.2425 days. To fit with astronomical information in the rest of the book, we are using the actual solar years.

Creation Myths

Many researchers believe the creation myths are tied in to the Long Count calendar and the Long Count calendar is a cycle within the precession of the equinox. Stories drawn in murals, on temple walls, and inscriptions on steles support this view. We'll explore this further in Chapters 6 and 8. What we need to know now is when the 13-baktun cycle started, when it will end, and where we are on the timeline.

Monuments of the Maya

Monuments found throughout the jungles proved to be the *Rosetta stones* to determine the starting point of the Long Count calendar. Steles were marked with Long Count dates for important events, like coronations, Calendar round cycles, etc. Long Count dates have five designations, or decimal places. The first position on the right is for kin, the second is for uinals, the third for tuns, then katuns, and then baktuns. The

Maya placed the positions in columns, as we saw in Chapter 3. However, researchers have made an easier notation by placing the positions in rows to match our system, separating each position with a dot. Each position increases by the power of 20.

An empty date notation would look like this: 0.0.0.0.0. If you saw this date, you might think it was the starting date of the Long Count cycle, but you would be tricked! The actual starting date of this baktun is 13.0.0.0.0, meaning it's the start of a 13-baktun era.

Hundreds if not thousands of archeological monuments bear the markings of the Long Count dating system. On a monument you would see the Long Count date for an event next to the Calendar round date. This proved to be the Rosetta stone in correlating the starting date of this era, which is 13.0.0.0.0 4 Ahau 3 Cumku.

Connecting the Calendars

Correlating the Mayan system to our own has been a daunting feat! We know the Long Count calendar beginning date was 13.0.0.0.0. We know the Tzolk'in date was 4 Ahau and the Haab date was 8 Cumku. Knowing this, can we find the Gregorian correlation?

We can't rely on information from the Spanish, because the Long Count calendar was no longer in use when they arrived. Any records that may have helped were destroyed. On top of that, the European calendar system was in its own state of disarray. The Julian calendar was inaccurate, and remember, the Gregorian calendar only came into use in 1582. The dates we're correlating are about a thousand years older than that.

Finding a Link

There was no easy way to find relationships between Mayan dates and European dates. Researchers looked for clues in steles and monuments. In the sixteenth century, the Maya were using a shortened version of the Long Count calendar called the "U Kahlay katunob," or the count of the katuns.

Researchers eventually discovered a stele inscribing a Mayan event that was also written about in Spanish records. The event on the stele was dated in the katun count as 13 Ahau 8 Xul and related to the Long Count date of 11.16.0.0.0. The event was known to have happened in the year 1539. Finding the day and month in 1539 was just a matter of counting the days on the Long Count and matching day-signs to the Katun. The Gregorian date for 11.16.0.0.0 13 Ahau 8 Xul was determined to be the 12 or 14 of November, 1539.

The accepted relationship between the Gregorian and Mayan calendars is called the GMT (Goodman-Martinez-Thompson) correlation, based on the work of three men, Joseph T. Goodman, Juan Martinez-Hernandez, and J. Eric S. Thompson. The problem is that each person came up with a slightly different day. You can see how easily this could happen, and it was still a major breakthrough. It allowed the beginning and end dates of the Long Count to be determined within a fairly tight range.

Back-Tracking Dates

What does the beginning date of 13.0.0.0.0 4 Ahau 8 Cumku in the Long Count calendar equal in the Gregorian calendar? Scholars determined that the Long Count started on August 11, 3114 B.C.E. (or August 12, or August 13).

The Long Count end date is written the same as the beginning date: 13.0.0.0.0 4 Ahau 8 Cumku, only it's 5,126 years later. Assuming the start day of August 11, 3114 B.C.E., the end date is December 21, 2012 C.E. On this date, the Long Count calendar and the 5,126 year age it records will end.

Celestial Connection

The present Kali Yuga cycle of the Hindus began just 11 years later in 3102 B.C.E. This is supposedly when Lord Krishna disincarnated and then the Kali Yuga began. Kali Yuga is the final and darkest age. For the Maya, this age began at 3114 B.C.E. The first dynasty of Egypt was established circa 3100 B.C.E. The first city in history, Uruk, was founded circa 3100 B.C.E. Uruk was founded by seven wise men at the beginning of history in Mesopotamia. If you look at the history books, you will see that virtually everything we think of as the history of civilization began at that point.

Date Debate

Many researchers agree with the GMT correlation and the end date of December 21, 2012. It has been promoted extensively with new age luminaries such as José Argüelles in his book *The Mayan Factor: Path Beyond Technology* (see Resources appendix). It's also promoted by notable alternative archeoastronomers such as John Major Jenkins in his book *Maya Cosmogenesis 2012* (see Resources appendix). This version seems to be supported by inscriptions at Palenque and other ancient sites.

However, not everyone agrees. The most notable dissenter is Swedish microbiologist and Mayan researcher Carl Johan Calleman. He believes the end date of the Long Count is actually October 28, 2011. He bases this in part on an adjustment made to the Long Count by Mayan priests in Palenque in 600 C.E. The adjustment was made to correct a 420-day error in the continuity of the calendar. Dr. Calleman bases his Mayan theories on the archeoastronomy of the Kukulkan pyramid.

Alternative Theories

There are many who believe the entire dating of the Long Count calendar is faulty. Chief among these is Vincent Malmström at Dartmouth University. He believes that the start and end dates are contrived to fit our modern understandings of the universe.

Where Do We Go from Here?

On December 22, 2012, the next age of the Maya begins. Exactly what does this mean? What are the astronomical and spiritual correlations? The Maya were spiritual timekeepers. The meanings of the ages and the changing of the ages exist in a multi-dimensional matrix. It's coded in the calendars, in the sky, and in the temples. What to expect, what to prepare for, is the focus of the rest of the book. The next step is to move our focus out of the Mayan calendars to the stars themselves.

The Least You Need to Know

- ◆ The Tzolk'in, the Haab, and the Long Count calendars are the main time-tracking calendars.
- ◆ The calendars expressed spiritual qualities of days and numbers and could be used to determine auspicious days for events.

- The Tzolk'in was especially useful in personal divination and birth charts.

- All of the calendars interact with each other within the context of larger cycles.

- The Long Count calendar is related to the creation story and is a cycle within the precession of the equinox.

- Many researchers believe that the Long Count calendar started on August 11, 3114 B.C.E., and ends on December 21, 2012 C.E.

Chapter 6

Players on the Cosmic Ball Court

In This Chapter

- ◆ The celestial players of 2012
- ◆ The orbit variations of the earth
- ◆ How solar sunspots affect Earth
- ◆ How galaxies behave and Mayan mythology

We've tracked the 2012 story out of the jungle and into the calendars. We've seen the Maya's mathematical and astronomical genius. But before the puzzle pieces come together, we must journey to the stars. You've seen how the Maya coded astronomical information into their mythology, calendar systems, and pyramids. Clearly the information they tracked and coded held great significance for them. What were the events they watched so carefully, and why were they so important?

As it happens, 2012 will be a year of amazing celestial alignments. As we turn our gaze to the sky, keep in mind that the sky game of 2012 was being watched 2,000 years ago by Mayan shamans as they plotted the calendar end date.

Let's look at some of the players in the celestial games underway. The key players are the earth, the sun, the solar system, Venus, the Milky Way galaxy, and the Pleiades constellation. Even if you don't have a mind for astronomy, you'll find this pretty interesting!

Earth's Anomalies

Our window to the universe looks out from planet Earth. Naturally, the cycles and anomalies of Earth affect our view. Even the alignments we measure are only alignments from our particular vantage point: in another galaxy far, far, away, the alignments we emphasize aren't alignments at all. On Earth, however, they affect the tides, the weather, the climate, our mental/emotional states, and by some calculations our spiritual development. It's not an urban legend that more crimes are committed during a full moon.

Let's look at the specific attributes of the earth that affect the impact of upcoming alignments, starting with the length of the year. This cycle is important in the larger synchronization of cycles.

Length of the Year

It's time to end the argument of whether the Maya knew the true length of the year. As we discussed in Chapter 5, every calendar system has the same set of problems: correlating years and days. The issue is that the time it takes the earth to rotate on its axis (a day) does not divide evenly into the time it takes the earth to revolve around the sun (a year). The solar year is actually made up of 365.2425 days. As mentioned in Chapter 4, to keep the calendar in sync with the sun we add a day at leap year and subtract a day every 400 years. Four hundred years is a unique time span: it's the only number of years whose days equal a whole number with no fraction. In 400 years there are 146,097 days. The fact that the Maya knew this and worked to the 400-year cycle confirms that they knew the true length of the year.

Codex Cues _____

Another way to calculate the Mayan year length is to take into account three items: the length of the Haab, the dates of the Long Count calendar, and the amount of time the Maya believed it took for the Earth to move through all the seasons. The result is that the Maya worked with a year length that is 365.242036. A bit more precise than the one the Gregorian calendar works with!

Eccentricity Cycle

The eccentricity cycle describes the changes in the earth's orbit. The earth's orbit around the sun is not a perfect circle; it's an ellipse, or oval. This means that at one part of the orbit the earth is closer to the sun (called the perihelion); and at the opposite time in the cycle the earth is farther away from the sun (called the aphelion). When the earth is closer to the sun, temperatures will be warmer than when the earth is farthest away.

Here's the catch: the elliptic orbit doesn't always stay the same shape. It changes from being more circular to being more oval. When the orbit is more circular, the difference in temperature between the closest and farthest positions will be minimal, say 6 percent. When the orbit is more oval, the difference in temperature between the two positions is more extreme, jumping to 20 to 30 percent.

The length of the cycle, from most oval to most circular, is approximately 100,000 years. The variation in shape is caused by the speed the earth is traveling, and the pull of the sun, moon, and other planets on the earth's gravitational field. So really, it displays the effects of celestial movement and interaction on the earth's movements. As the Maya have said, the whole system is interactive!

Obliquity Cycle

Here's another anomaly about the earth's axis. It's not straight up and down in relation to the path of the earth's orbit around the sun. The earth's axis is tilted. The tilt is what creates the seasons, and like everything else, it's not always the same. The planet doesn't always tilt to the same degree. During a 41,000-year cycle, the tilt of the earth's axis changes from 22.1 to 24.5 degrees. The current tilt is 23.5 degrees. This means there is a greater difference between seasons now than when there was only a 22.1-degree tilt.

So what happens when the cycles coincide and the most extreme perihelion falls at the same time as the most extreme tilt of the planet? You got it: extremes of hot and cold. And yes, that may be a factor in the extremes of the end-time predictions of Chapters 11 and 12.

Precession of the Equinox

The precession of the equinox is one of the more dramatic cycles the Maya understood. It's another result of the tilt of the earth's axis. You already know that the earth turning on its axis creates night and day. It's night for the side of the earth that's not facing the sun and day for the side that is facing the sun.

If the earth's spin were completely stable, every day would be the same length. But the earth does not spin on a stable axis. It wobbles. Consequently we have long days in the summer and short days in the winter.

Wobble

Spinning like a wobbling top, the axis of the earth scribes a small circle in the sky, called the precession. You can see what this looks like in the following illustration. As the earth spins, it travels along the edge of the circle it makes, changing the celestial landscape. In the time it takes to completely move around the circle, the earth moves through all the constellations in the sky. This not only changes what constellations we see at night, but also the stars and other celestial "background" features. In other words, the wobble is responsible for the movement of the constellations across the night sky.

So how long does it take the earth to turn a complete circle through all the constellations? The earth moves along the precession at an astonishing rate of 1 degree every 72 years! Consequently it takes approximately 25,600 to 25,800 years to complete the journey, called the *precession of the equinox*. Does that number sound at all familiar? A Grand Cycle in the Mayan timekeeping system is approximately 25,630 years and is believed to measure the precession of the equinox. Each baktun of 5,126 years is a cycle within the precession.

North Star

The wobble also means that the star with the most northern position, the North Star, is not always the same star. It changes over the course of the precession. Right now the North Star is Polaris. Around the time Homer wrote *Iliad* and *Odyssey*, the North Star was Kochab. The North Star of the ancient Egyptians in 2700 B.C.E. was Thuban in the constellation Draco. Around 3000 C.E., Polaris will change to Gamma Cephei. Vega will become the North Star by 14000 C.E.

The God of the North Star was an important god to the Maya. He guided merchants and was the center pole in the creation myth of raising the sky. The Maya also have a myth about the time the North Star god fell from the sky. Were they describing the changing of the North Star?

The Ecliptic Path

The tilt of the axis not only scribes a circle around the celestial North Pole, it also draws the path the sun and planets travel when they cross the sky. The ecliptic path passes through the equator twice a year. When the sun crosses the equator, it marks the equinoxes.

The ecliptic was represented in Mayan cosmology as part of the Sacred Tree of Life. If you remember the symbolism of the Sacred Tree from Chapter 2, the Tree creates a connection between the three worlds: the underworld, the earth, and the heavens. The Sacred Tree was seen in the sky as the crossing point of the ecliptic with the Milky Way. The trunk of the tree, the Axis Mundi, is the Milky Way, and the main branch intersecting the tree is the plane of the ecliptic. The intersection was considered the sacred doorway or portal between the worlds. The crossing of the ecliptic with the Milky Way was known to the Maya as the Crossroads.

Mayan Creation and the Precession of the Equinox

Many researchers believe the Mayan creation stories are linked to the precession of the equinox. The precession is a Grand Cycle of 25,630 years. It's made up of 5 Great Cycles of 5,126 years each. There are two versions of how the creation story is linked. In the first version, each world in the creation story equals a Great Cycle (baktun) of 5,126 years. The five worlds, or ages, together equal one precession cycle. In this view, we are in the fifth age of creation and are completing the end of one Grand Cycle. This is the most commonly held view.

In the second version, a Mayan creation age is equal to one entire precession cycle. Each of the five subdivisions of the Great Cycles is called a "Sun," which is different from an age or world. In this version, we are in the fifth sun of the fourth world.

Celestial Connection

You've probably seen images of the famous Aztec sunstone calendar. The sunstone is actually older than the Aztec civilization; the Aztec borrowed it from the earlier Izapa/ Olmec culture. It was brought to fame when the huge Aztec rendition was found in the pre-Columbian ruins of what is now Mexico City. The sunstone depicts the five ages of creation. The four previous ages are located in the four square boxes around the center circle. The figure in the center represents the fifth and final age. Some think we are in the fifth age; others feel that we are in the fourth age preparing to enter the center spot of the fifth age.

The Milky Way

The Milky Way was central to the mythology of the Maya. It was the main component to the Sacred Tree of Life. But before we look at the significance of the Milky Way, let's take a closer look at galaxies in general. How much do you know about galaxies and how they act? It's pretty neat!

Galaxies

Galaxies are large systems of stars along with their orbiting solar systems, space debris, comets, dust, etc. Everything in a galaxy is held together by gravity. In the center of most galaxies is something called dark matter. Dark matter has an extra amount of gravitational pull and usually indicates the presence of a *black hole*.

def•i•ni•tion

Black holes are regions in space where the gravitational field is so powerful that nothing can escape once it's fallen past the event horizon. The name comes from the fact that even electromagnetic radiation, or light, is unable to escape. This makes the interior invisible to us.

The Milky Way galaxy is called a spiral galaxy. A spiral galaxy is one that spirals out from the center with streams that look like arms. It's spread out along an axis called the galactic plane. The Milky Way bulges in the middle where the largest concentration of suns and solar systems live. In the very center is an area called the Dark Rift, where the dark matter accumulates.

Thanks to NASA and the Hubble telescope, we have remarkable pictures taken in space of other spiral galaxies like our own. This helps us to know what our galaxy looks like, a benefit the Maya didn't have. From the side, it looks sort of like a disc with a bulge in the middle.

How Galaxies Interact

An interesting feature of galaxies relates to how they interact with each other. When they pass in space, each is affected by the other's gravitational field. Sometimes they just spin by each other, slightly changing each other's direction, rotation, etc. If they are the same size, they might merge and form one larger galaxy. If one galaxy is very large and the other is very small, "galactic cannibalism" may occur as the large galaxy swallows the small one. What more proof do we need that the universe is not a mathematical machine but an interacting system?

After cannibalism has occurred, the large galaxy emits powerful radio emission from the black hole at its center indicating it has just received fresh matter. The Sagittarius dwarf galaxy is currently being devoured by our own Milky Way.

The Galactic Equator

Our solar system is located in the galaxy at the outer reaches of one of the spiral arms, the Orion arm, about 26,000 light-years from the center. Our solar system orbits around the center of the Milky Way along with 200 to 400 billion other stars and possible solar systems. Our solar system doesn't orbit in just a circle around the center; as it orbits it follows a path that travels above and below the equator of the galactic plane.

Looking at the galaxy from space gives an interesting perspective of this movement. As the galaxy rotates, our solar system looks like a spiraling sine wave crossing back and forth over the *galactic equator*. We cross the galactic equator every 30 million years. According to some astronomers, we're passing into the outer edge of the galactic equator now.

def•i•ni•tion

The **galactic equator** (or **equator of the Milky Way**) is the line running down the precise middle of the plane of the Milky Way, dividing it into two hemispheres. If you think of the galaxy as a pancake, the plane of the galaxy is the edge of the pancake and the equator is the line that runs down the middle of the plane, dividing the pancake into top and bottom halves.

When our solar system passes through the galactic equator, we pass through an area with more asteroids, comets, and space debris. We've already entered the edge of the galactic equator, thus increasing the number of asteroids on a potential collision course with Earth.

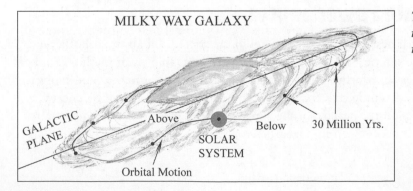

This represents the motion of the solar system as it rotates through the galaxy.

It's estimated that it takes the solar system between 225 and 250 million years to rotate one time around the galaxy. Since the approximate age of our sun and solar system is 4.5 billion years, we can estimate that the solar system has orbited around the galaxy a total of 18 times. Keep this in mind as you read Chapter 8. You might decide the Maya knew this piece of information, too.

The Dark Rift

The Dark Rift is a feature flowing through the Milky Way galaxy. Clearly visible on a dark night, the rift divides the light-filled part of the galaxy in two. Physically, it's a cloud of gas and particles that don't reflect light from the surrounding stars. It looks like a dark streak streaming into the galactic center. The Maya saw it as a two-way road; the road moving into the center was known as the "dark road," and led to a portal into the underworlds. The roadway out of the center was the "birth canal," streaming out from the "womb of the world" (the Mayan name for the center of the galaxy).

The Milky Way in Mayan Mythology

The Milky Way was a central player in Mayan mythology. The center of the Milky Way, the "womb of the world," was the place where the Maya believed all stars were born. Modern science seems to agree that the stars of the Milky Way were born in the black hole at its center. One Mayan glyph depicts the center of the Milky Way as a whirling disc, much as we might draw a black hole. If the Maya did not inherit this information from Atlantis, then their trances were pretty powerfully accurate!

Did the Maya know about galaxy cannibalism? One depiction of the Milky Way is as a great reptile extending across the entire sky. It's a two-headed beast, one head creating life and the other consuming it. Again, science theorizes that the material consumed in galactic cannibalism is the raw material used to create new stars and planets.

The Sun: Ultimate Power Source

Our sun, like our solar system, is around 4.5 billion years old. Of all the celestial bodies, the impact of the sun on the earth is by far the greatest. In Mayan mythology, the Sun god ruled the heavens during the day and the underworlds at night. The sun was the source of life. It's certainly true that all life on our planet is powered by energy from the sun. Activity on the surface of the sun also causes electrical storms on the earth and impacts our climate, an important factor leading toward 2012 that we'll discuss in Chapter 15.

Sunspots

A sunspot is a dark area seen on the sun's surface. It's essentially a planet-size magnet created by concentrations of magnetic flux on the sun's surface. Sunspots have north and south magnetic poles and arise in pairs of opposite polarity. One member of the pair lives in the northern hemisphere while its partner lives in the southern hemisphere. They're linked together by loops of magnetic energy that arc across the sun between the two partners. They move in unison across the face of the sun. The life span of a pair of sunspots can be an hour, a day, or several months. Sunspot activity rises and falls in phases every 11 years. Sunspot activity creates enough electromagnetic energy to affect the electromagnetism of earth.

Sunspot Cycles

There's always some type of sunspot activity happening on the sun's surface. However, every 11 years there's a surge of activity, called the solar maximum. Five to six years after the surge, or maximum activity time, there is a minimum activity period, called the solar minimum. During the surge, all the sunspots in the northern hemisphere of the sun have the same polarity and all the sunspots in the southern hemisphere have the opposite polarity of those in the northern hemisphere. During the next sunspot cycle, the polarities reverse.

Solar Flare

A solar flare is a sudden and dramatic release of energy near or in a sunspot. A flare can last for a few minutes to a few hours. During a solar flare, the ionization of the earth's atmosphere increases. This causes an increase in aurora borealis activity and magnetic storms across the earth, which can cause radio interference and other technical problems.

Aurora Borealis

The aurora borealis, also known as the Northern Lights, is caused by the interaction between the earth's magnetic field and the charged particles that come from the sun called solar wind. It's usually seen in the northern parts of the North Hemisphere such as Alaska and Siberia. The same thing happens at the South Pole, where it's called the aurora australis, but as this is the tail of the *magnetosphere*, it's less dramatic.

def•i•ni•tion

The **magnetosphere** is the ionized magnetic field around the planet. It's generated by movement of the molten core center of the earth. It absorbs energy from the sun in pathways called the Van Allen Belts, protecting us from space radiation.

The aurora borealis looks like beautiful ribbons of multicolored lights streaking across the sky. They undulate and scintillate, emitting bursts of electrified light. People watching say the stream of light looks alive and seems to interact with their thoughts and feelings.

Big changes happen in the auroras as the result of substorms in the magnetosphere. Substorms cause increases in brightness, size, shape, and movement of the Aurora. The northern lights can be seen quite far south during such a magnetic storm and can disrupt compass needles, cell phones, and other forms of technology.

Magnetic Impact on Weather

The magnetic storms that cause changes in the aurora borealis also affect weather. When the earth's magnetic field shifts, it shifts the jet stream, causing changes in weather patterns. Magnetic storms pour tremendous amounts of energy into the magnetosphere creating violent weather patterns.

Science shows that the La Niña and El Niño weather shifts are related to sunspot activity. The cycle of the El Niño pattern directly matches the escalation of sunspot cycles. Sunspot escalation takes 4 to 5 years to maximum activity and de-escalation takes 4 to 5 years to minimum activity. El Niño's cycles vary every 4 to 6 years, increasing with increasing solar activity. The next solar maximum will be in 2012 and is expected to produce severe storms and electromagnetic disruption.

The Pleiades Constellation

The Pleiades constellation is a cluster of 500 stars, most of which we cannot see, even with a pretty good telescope. It's commonly called the seven sisters after the seven brightest stars that we can see with the naked eye: Alcyone, Atla, Electra, Maia, Nerope, Taygeta, and Pleione. These stars reflect blue light because they are "hot" young stars emitting energy in a high frequency range.

Nebula

The Pleiades is currently moving through a great dusty cloud of interstellar matter and gas called a nebula. The dust particles reflect the light of blue stars, creating an illusion of a blue halo around the seven sisters. It's especially bright around the star Nerope.

Does a Photon Belt Orbit the Pleiades?

A photon is the smallest unit of light or electromagnetic radiation that we can measure. A popular theory suggests that the nebula around the Pleiades is actually a photon belt. There's much controversy as to the actual existence of the photon belt, but here's the theory in a nutshell.

An immense belt of photons is traveling through space and is currently orbiting the Pleiades. The belt is moving toward Earth and we will encounter it in 2012. Believers say it will affect our technology, weather, and spiritual growth.

At present there is no evidence that the photon belt exists, but it's a common 2012 theme. Proponents suggest that the photon belt is a spiritual energy that won't be detected by devices until our science advances.

The Reverse Rotation of Venus

Venus is frequently called the earth's twin. It's the second closest planet to the sun and the closest planet to the earth. Interestingly, the rotational spin of Venus is reverse to all the rest of the planets in our solar system. This can't be observed with the naked eye or even with a telescope because the featureless, thick atmosphere of Venus prevents observing any surface landmarks.

One scientific theory suggests the reverse rotation is due to a massive ancient collision between Venus and another celestial body. It's thought Uranus was also impacted, resulting in the exaggerated tilt of the Uranus axis.

Although the collision theory is not accepted by all astronomers, it's interesting to consider in the light of the *Popol Vuh* creation story. In the first few pages of the *Popol Vuh*, it describes how Venus tried to take the place of father Sun. This happens at the end of the age of the wood people (see Chapter 2) and results in a series of cataclysms that ends the third/fourth age. Mayan Elder Carlos Barrios relates that the oral tradition of the Maya describe a collision between Venus and another body that knocked

Venus out of its orbit, putting it very close to Earth. Venus then tried to "take over the position of the sun" and outshine the sun and moon. In the story, Hunab K'u intervened and put Venus back in its orbit. Is it possible the story relates to actual fact, as so much of the rest of Mayan mythology seems to?

Venus Transits

A Venus transit occurs when Venus passes in front of the sun. Venus transits happen in pairs and are rare events. A Venus transit lasts for six to seven hours. Once a Venus transit occurs, its partner transit occurs eight years later. The most recent pairs of transits occurred in 1518 and 1526, 1631 and 1639, 1761 and 1769, and 1874 and 1882. The first transit of the current pair occurred in 2004. Its upcoming partner will occur on June 6, 2012. It will be visible from Northwestern North America. There won't be another pair of Venus transits until December 11, 2117, and December 8, 2125.

The Least You Need to Know

- The variations of the earth's orbit create changes in our celestial landscape, creating the ecliptic pathway of the constellations, the changing of the North Star, and the precession of the equinox.

- The precession of the equinox represents the 25,630-year Grand Cycle of the Maya.

- The Long Count calendar age of 5,126 years is one fifth of the precession cycle. The Mayan ages of creation are linked to the precession of the equinox.

- The Milky Way galaxy was known to the Maya as the creator of stars in our galaxy.

- Increases in solar sunspots cause increases in weather severity on Earth.

Chapter 7

Alignments of 2012

In This Chapter

◆ What happens on December 21, 2012

◆ Eclipsing the center of the galaxy

◆ Strange events in the black hole of the Milky Way

◆ The importance of the Pleiades

◆ New energy for a new age

Now you've met all the players, just what is it they're supposed to be doing? The astronomical events of 2012 are actually a series of pretty unique and unusual alignments. Each alignment in itself is rare; for all to happen in the same year is exceptional. As anticipated, everything culminates in an alignment on December 21, 2012.

John Major Jenkins, Mayan researcher and author, believes the Mayan specifically created their calendar to end on December 21, 2012, to match this alignment. You can see what the sky will look like in 2012 in the following illustrations. If the Maya geared their calendars to this alignment, then they had an understanding of cycles and time that far exceeds our own. It also means the GMT correlation, which we discussed in Chapter 5, was extremely accurate. What was so important about this alignment that it was coded into calendars, temples, stele's codices, and myths?

Cosmic Crossroads

Let's start with the Grand Finale for 2012 and look at what happens on December 21. Our solar system has been passing through the galactic equator. John Major Jenkins claims that the rising of the solstice sun on December 21, 2012, will be in alignment with the center of the Milky Way galaxy, and will in fact eclipse it. An alignment with the center of the Milky Way happens once every precession cycle and can be considered the starting/ending point of the precession. If the Maya knew this, as it seems they did, what significance did it have?

Here are the stars you'll see from Guatemala at noon local time on December 21, 2012.

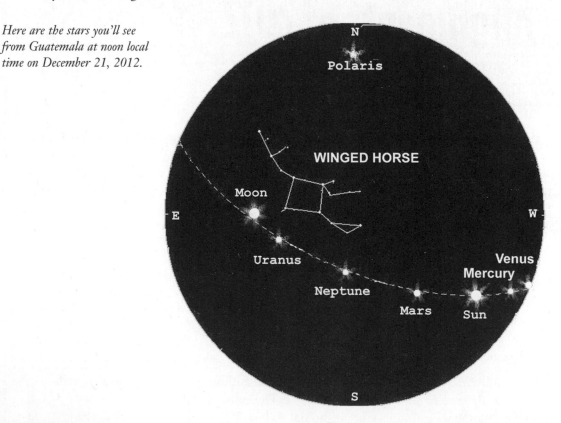

Galactic Crossing

The ecliptic is the path traveled by the sun, moon, and planets across the sky (see Chapter 6). The path of the ecliptic crosses the Milky Way, forming the cross of the Sacred Tree. As our solar system passes through the galactic equator during 2012, the cross of the Sacred Tree will be formed across the galactic equator in alignment with the center of the galaxy. What does this mean? The ancient Maya believed the center of the galaxy, birthplace to the stars, was the home of the creator god, Hunab K'u. Hunab K'u sends emissions from the center of the galaxy that pulse through all the celestial alignments, bringing enlightenment. It's believed that the alignment of the sacred cross with the center of the galaxy will create a portal; a direct connection to Hunab K'u, accelerating the transmissions from the center of the galaxy.

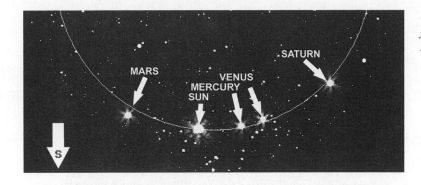

Here are the stars you'll see from the northern hemisphere at noon local time on December 21, 2012.

However, there is another component. This alignment is eclipsed by the solstice sun. An eclipse is the movement of one object in front of another, "eclipsing" the view. Usually we think in terms of the moon eclipsing the sun, or Venus eclipsing the moon. In this case it's the sun eclipsing the center of the Sacred Tree and the center of the galaxy. During the time of the eclipse, the emissions from the center of the galaxy will be interrupted. As the eclipse passes, the emissions will be resumed, but they will not be resumed in the present age. They will be resumed in the next age when the transformative power of the alignment with the Sacred Tree and the center of the galaxy will be felt. It's the eclipse itself that marks the end of the Long Count calendar and the beginning of the next age.

Codex Cues

To learn more about the 2012 alignment, read *Maya Cosmogenesis 2012* by John Major Jenkins (see Resources appendix).

Reality Check

All of this sounds impressive, but how certain is the timing of the alignment with the galactic equator? In his book *Mathematical Astronomy Morsels* (Willmann-Bell Publishing, 1997), astronomer Jean Meeus calculated when the precise center-point of the body of the sun would align with the galactic equator. His calculation was that the alignment would occur in 1998.

John Major Jenkins explains that since the sun occupies half a degree of space, it takes approximately 36 years for the sun to cross the galactic equator. Therefore, the "galactic alignment zone" is between 1980 through 2016 (1998 +/– 18 years). Theoretically, the alignment can take place any time during this period.

The exact date of December 21, 2012, comes from the Mayan calendar. Many feel the exact timing has too many variables for certainty. In the grand scheme of things, if the Maya were gearing their Long Count to this event, a 36-year range is pretty close! Many people think the precise date is not as significant as the time period itself. They point to a process of change over time as opposed to cataclysmic change. The exact nature of the change is twofold: the destruction of the old age and the transformation into a new, better age.

Mythological Crossing Point

The importance of the crossing of the Sacred Tree is shown throughout the Mayan culture. We saw it in the creation story and in the way the Maya centered their towns, cities, temples, and homes. Now we may see a new significance. Remember Pacal's tomb from Chapter 3? As the sun sets, rays of light move through a doorway such that light descends the stairway disappearing into Pacal's tomb. While the lighting effects depict the descent of Lord Pacal into the underworlds, the lid of the tomb has even more significance. The lid is thought by some to symbolize the events of December 21, 2012.

Lord Pacal Votan is the central figure on the lid of the tomb. You may remember that Pacal Votan brought wisdom and enlightenment to his people. He was believed to be a reincarnation of the god Votan and after his death and descent into the underworlds he was resurrected to the sky. The picture of him on the lid shows a picture of the Sacred Tree of Life extending from his umbilicus. Many Mayan stories represent the Sacred Tree as an umbilical cord because of the way it nourishes the realms. The Mayan word for Lord also means sun. Some researchers believe this image shows the alignment of the sun with the Sacred Tree at the end of the Long Count calendar.

The myth of Pacal Votan tells us he started as human and was elevated in the course of his life to sky-god. Some believe this represents the double nature of the end times: a destruction of the old and transformation into the new. They believe the lid of Pacal's tomb shows that the alignment of 2012 will open a portal through the Sacred Tree, through the solstice sun, to the heart of the heavens. This will release an energy that will flow through the earth and raise humanity to a higher spiritual level. The 2012 solstice sun will birth a new year and a new age.

The Mysterious Black Hole

Scientists say that most galaxies have black holes at their center, producing the energy the galaxy lives on. Black holes are super-dense gravity fields that draw energy and matter inside. Like a devouring monster, they consume everything in sight, but black holes have another side. They're creators as well as destroyers. When a black hole feeds, powerful emissions fly into surrounding space. These emissions jump-start the formation of stars. It's pretty clear to most scientists that we have a black hole in the center of the Milky Way and right now, in the center of our galaxy, strange things are happening. Is the Mayan prophecy unfolding? Is there really a stream of energy coming from the center of the galaxy? Astronomers have discovered three unique events in the center of the Milky Way: a loop-like structure 20 light-years across, unusual gravity waves, and radio emissions. Are these signs of changes happening in the heart of the galaxy?

Going Loopy

A loop-like structure was found in 2005 by a team of astronomers, including scientists from the University of Leicester and the Max Planck Institute for Extraterrestrial Physics. The structure was viewed from a European x-ray satellite, XMM Newton, as part of the XMM Newton Galactic Center Survey project. It's the first time anything like this has been detected in our galaxy. The scientists believe it's producing sub-atomic particles with massive amounts of energy, acting like a cosmic particle accelerator. This does sound like the center of the galaxy is emitting energy, as the Maya say!

An interesting thing about the loop is that it's nonthermal (meaning its not hot). So whatever the structure is, scientists say it's not stationary and is part of an ongoing process. It may, in fact, relate to high-energy cosmic "rays."

Gravity Waves

You've heard of electromagnetic energy waves, and you've heard of light waves, but how many people have heard of gravity waves? Einstein theorized the existence of gravity waves, but until now there was no way to detect them. New research facilities are being built to measure gravity waves hitting Earth. The research is being conducted by the California Institute of Technology and the Massachusetts Institute of Technology.

Gravity waves are "ripples in the fabric of time-space" and are caused by violent events in the universe, such as the collision of two black holes or by supernova explosions. They're emitted by accelerating mass. When gravity waves pass through matter, they create vibration. There may be a correlation between gravity waves and earth events such as earthquakes, tsunamis, and volcanoes due to the geological vibration they cause.

Codex Cues _____

The Laser Interferometer Gravitational-Wave Observatory (LIGO) is a facility dedicated to the detection of cosmic gravitational waves and the harnessing of these waves for scientific research. You can find out more at www.ligo.caltech. edu/LIGO_web/about/factsheet.html. For more information about the correlation of gravity waves with past earthquakes, such as the December 26, 2004, Indonesian earthquake and tsunami, go to www.etheric.com/GalacticCenter/GRB.html.

Radio Waves

What else might lie at the center of the galaxy? A press release from the Naval Research Laboratory published on March 2, 2005, tells of a new discovery. Low-frequency coherent radio waves have been detected coming from the heart of the galaxy. Astronomer and professor Dr. Scott Hyman and his research team discovered the signal. It was made up of five highly energetic radio emissions of equal brightness. They lasted 10 minutes each and appeared every 77 minutes over a 7-hour period from September 30 to October 1, 2002.

It's not unusual to have radio emissions from space. They've just never been detected coming from the center of our Milky Way. Usually a galactic center emits radio waves after its black hole has consumed a large meal of matter. What's causing the emissions from the Milky Way is presently unknown.

Maybe the heart of the galaxy, Hunab K'u, is preparing for a life-creating emission. Maybe this is the event the Maya were portending.

Involvement of the Pleiades

There will be two solar eclipses in 2012 that involve the Pleiades. The first eclipse will occur on May 20 when the sun and moon *conjunct* Pleiades. Interestingly, the second solar eclipse on November 13 will conjunct the sun, the moon, and the constellation

Serpens, or the serpent. The placement of these two alignments is referred to as the "serpent that ate its own tail," or the infinity sign.

Pleiades and Chichen Itza

Remember the Pyramid of Kukulkan at Chichen Itza from Chapter 3? On the spring equinox, the shadows cascade down the north balustrade like a serpent descending

the pyramid. At the base of the stairs, the shadow meets its head in the huge plumed serpent sculpture. This represents the return of Kukulkan or Quetzalcoatl. It also heralds the return of the zenith sun on May 20, the date of the zenith passage over Chichen Itza. In 2012, the zenith passage of the sun coincides with a solar eclipse that conjuncts the Pleiades. For the Maya, this alignment opens the door for the return of Quetzalcoatl energy.

def•i•ni•tion

Conjunction is a term used in positional astronomy and astrology for when two celestial bodies appear near one another in the sky. It's another term for alignment.

Photon Belt Hypothesis

Following right along with the Pleiades is the photon belt (see Chapter 6). As we align with the galactic equator, we're moving into a densely populated part of the galaxy. There are more suns, more solar systems, and more space debris. If you subscribe to the photon belt theory, there are also more photons.

If you remember, the photon belt is traveling through space and will engage earth in 2012. Followers of this theory believe that this engagement will be apocalyptic, resulting in the interruption of electricity and causing social upheaval. Or it will initiate a spiritual transformation. Which occurs will depend on the state of mankind's spiritual receptivity.

This theory was popularized in an article republished in 1991 by *Nexus* magazine, an Australian publication. It was originally published in 1987 by the Australian *UFO Magazine*. In the *Nexus* article, "The Photon Belt Story," it was claimed the earth would go through this belt in July 1992. When this clearly did not happen, the date was changed and now we're to go through the photon belt in 2012. Although the photon belt has not been detected with instruments, proponents claim that its effects can be observed through its interactions with our sun. Plasma particles in the sun's heliosphere become excited in the presence of highly charged particles. Russian scientists have reported seeing "excited plasma energy" in the *heliosphere*, indicating to believers of the photon belt that we're starting our movement through the belt, or some other energy source.

def•i•ni•tion

The **heliosphere** is an immense magnetic bubble emanating from the sun's magnetic field surrounding our solar system. It extends well beyond the orbit of Pluto.

In keeping with Mayan belief about energy, as energy particles interact with the sun they charge the sun's energy pathways. This in turn is transmitted to the planets, increasing the energy throughout the solar system.

The Venus Appearance in 2012

Venus, too, will make a grand appearance during 2012. The second half of this infrequent transit will occur on June 5–6, 2012. These transits happen in pairs eight years apart. The 2012 transit is the second transit; the first appeared on June 8, 2004. The 2012 transit will occur directly through the center of the sun over a period of eight hours.

2012 will also see a conjunction between Venus and the Pleiades. This was an important alignment to the Maya. Venus represents overcoming death and some say the Pleiades are part of the Mayan origin mythology. Specifically, Venus will conjunct with Alcyone, which is the central star of the Pleiades system. This conjunction will not be the closest that Venus and the Pleiades will come to each other. They will have a stronger conjunction in 2036; however, this is the closest they have been in the last 1,000 years and it brings its own unique energy to the 2012 alignments.

Transits of Venus are thought to be correlated with advances in social technology and communication.

The Next Solar Maximum

Sunspot activity will also increase as the next solar maximum is 2012. Adrian Gilbert and Maurice Cotterell discuss the 2012 sunspot cycles in their book *The Mayan Prophecies* (Element Books, 1995). They state that the end of the Great Cycle will coincide with the culmination of a series of powerful sunspot cycles. They claim the intensity of the magnetic influx will flip the sun's magnetic field, causing earthquakes and flooding on earth.

On the positive side, they claim the change in the magnetic field will alter the pineal gland and affect hormone production. Because the pineal gland is associated with the third-eye energy center, they say this could be a fine-tuning that will help people adjust to the shifting magnetic fields on the planet and in the solar system.

The Bottom Line

You've heard the planetary events underway, the mythology and the theories from Mayan researchers. What does it all mean? Here is the viewpoint that emerges.

The Maya were pointing to 2012 for a reason. The "alignment zone" may not narrow down to exactly 2012; however, the events being marked are real events. The Maya felt they were important enough to place big neon markers saying, "Look Here." What is the message? Let's pull it all together.

The Maya were concerned with spiritual evolution and the alignments of planets bringing in k'ul. They believed the Milky Way galaxy was the birthplace of stars and planets and also the double-headed monster that ate matter. Hunab K'u lives in the center of the galaxy and it's his energy that streams forth feeding the galaxy with vital life force.

The 2012 alignment will interrupt the flow of energy reaching the earth from the galaxy. The birth of the solstice New Year will also be the birth of a whole new age filled with new energy. As the eclipse passes, the energy from the galaxy will once again reach Earth bringing new frequency. The loops and strange events happening in the galaxy center may be the beginning of the new energy of Hunab K'u.

The many additional alignments throughout the year serve to prepare the way for the increased energy from the galactic center, preparing the planet for the new age being born. How difficult or easy the birth is remains to be seen.

The Least You Need to Know

- December 21, 2012, is the date of an eclipse of the galactic center by the solstice sun. This will interrupt the energy flow from the galactic center to the earth.

- Scientists are discovering many unusual energy phenomena happening in the center of the galaxy that may relate to the Mayan predictions.

- The Pleiades will conjunct with a solar eclipse of the moon twice in 2012. This may represent an opening for the return of Quetzalcoatl.

- After the December 21 eclipse of the galactic center, new energy will stream into the galaxy in sync with the starting of the next age of the Mayan creation story.

Chapter 8

Changing of the Ages

In This Chapter

◆ What age are we in?

◆ The five ages of creation and what they represent

◆ Cosmic day: Mayan evolution of consciousness

◆ The coming of a new age

As Mayan mythology plays across the sky, stargazers are being treated to extraordinary celestial theater. To fully appreciate the unfolding drama, expand your view still further.

There is evidence that the Maya tracked time for much longer periods than the precession. In fact, they may have visioned time to the birth of the galaxy and beyond to the birth of the universe. The Kukulkan pyramid at Chichen Itza and a timekeeping stele from Coba tell the story of creation and evolution complete with a timeline. This amazing discovery was made by Mayan researcher Carl Johan Calleman.

With all this talk about ages and changing ages, let's take a look at just what the ages are and what to expect in the new one. We're helped in this by using the creation mural from the ruins of San Bartolo, which we discussed in Chapter 1. The ruins were excavated in 2003, revealing a creation mural from 100 B.C.E. It perfectly matches the *Popol Vuh* creation story, written 600 years later, and helps us to understand parts of the story.

End of an Epoch

As you know, a Mayan creation age corresponds to the precession of the equinox. We discussed in Chapter 6 that there are two versions of how this happens. In one version, a creation age equals 5,126 years, the length of the Long Count calendar which is a Mayan Great Cycle. There are five ages in the creation and five Great Cycles in the 25,630 Grand Cycle of the precession. In this version, we are in the fifth age of the Maya.

In the second version, each creation age equals one Grand Cycle, one trip around the precession, and each creation age is subdivided into five "Suns" equal to 5,126 years each. In this version, we are in the fifth Sun of the fourth World. In both versions, we are at the end of a precession cycle. This is known because of the upcoming alignment of the Sacred Cross of the Maya to the center of the galaxy, something claimed to happen once per precession and marks the end/beginning of the cycle.

What does it mean that the Long Count calendar ends as we are coming to the end of a Grand Cycle? Does it matter what world, age, or Sun we are in?

What Sun Is Rising?

Deciding what age we're in has generated a lot of controversy. Is this the fourth age going into the fifth? Or are we in the fifth age and at the end of the creation story? What does it mean that none of the creation stories talk about a sixth age? The picture is further confused by the Aztec creation story, clearly based on the same events as the Mayan creation story. According to the Aztec legend, we are firmly in the fifth age.

Some researchers contend that the problem is one of interpretation. They say it depends on when you start counting. If you start counting at zero, we are in the fourth age moving into the fifth. But if you start counting at one, we are in the fifth age now; for example, starting at zero: 0 1 2 3 (4) 5, or starting at one: 1 2 3 4 (5) 6. This doesn't really answer the question, as it still means we are living in the fifth age, whatever number you give it.

Popular Mayan researchers put us squarely in the fifth age, leaving a Grand Cycle on 2012. Mayan Elders say we are in the fourth age, moving into the fifth age which lies at the center of the sun disc calendar. The sun disc is a beautiful Mesoamerican sun calendar that incorporates the changing of the ages. The sun disc predates the Mayan calendar originating in the Izapa/Olmec culture.

You're going to have to decide this one for yourself. Let's look at what each of the five ages represents and you can figure out what makes sense to you. As for us, we agree that the story belongs to the Maya. Taking their word for it, this must be the fourth age.

Overview of Creation

Each world of the creation has its own Tree of Life holding up the sky and connecting the realms. Each world also has to deal with a particular challenge. At the end of each world is death and destruction followed by resurrection and rebirth.

The creation story is similar to the myth of the Hero Twins from Chapter 2. The Hero Twins go into the underworld and face five challenges in order to defeat death. In the creation story, at the end of each world, the gods use natural disasters to destroy humans. Symbolically, the life the gods created was sacrificed. As the Hero Twins are reborn from death, each age is reborn from the one that came before.

First Age

In the first age of creation, the gods created the earth, mountains, trees, and animals. The gods were lonely, however, and decided to create humans for company and worship. There is no actual destruction of this world and it becomes the foundation for future creations. Each world builds on the one before. This world is about manifesting form and substance. It's said to represent the body.

In the first world, the Sacred Tree of Life is depicted in the San Bartolo murals as a staff with three fish. This is interesting in relation to the Aztec creation story. In the Aztec story, the first world is inhabited with animals and people. The first world is destroyed by floods that are sent by the gods. Some people whom the gods favor are saved by being changed into fish. In many cultures, fish represent the element water and the development of emotions as a type of awareness.

> **Celestial Connection**
>
> The five ages of the Aztec vary from the Mayan ages but the cycle is essentially the same. A series of destructions and rebirths occur at each level of creation. In the Aztec version, the new world cannot be created until a god sacrifices himself to become the new sun and life of the next world.

Second Age

In the second age, the gods created humans out of clay or mud. Because the people were unable to move or speak, they were pretty poor company and didn't worship at all. The gods weren't happy about this, and the second world was destroyed. The second world is about manifesting consciousness, and is said to represent the mind.

In the Aztec myths, the second age was destroyed when the sun fell from the sky and burned the creation in a fiery blaze. Some people survived but were eaten by jaguars.

The murals on the walls at San Bartolo provide a date for the end of the second age. As of yet, the analysis of the date is either incomplete or has not been published. When it is, it will provide insight into the creation timeline.

Third Age

In the third age, man was made of wood. Humans could walk and talk, but once again they were defective. This time the gods forgot to add a soul. Without a soul, humans forgot to worship and again the world was destroyed. This age was about the need to add heart and soul, or individual essence.

In the *Popol Vuh*, the world was destroyed when the gods "rained blackness on their heads and tore them apart." In the Aztec legend, the gods "rained gravel and fire" until the world again caught fire. The gods took pity on some people who were saved by being turned into birds. The San Bartolo murals show the third age with birds in the sky and on the Tree of Life.

Fourth Age

In the fourth age, the "true people" were formed out of maize, or corn dough. Corn was considered sacred by the Maya. Maybe the reason the true people were not destroyed (so far!) is because of the sacredness of the maize that formed them. Some say this age defines the union of spirit and soul with matter—the unity of mind, body, and spirit.

In the Aztec story, this age came to an end with a great hurricane that "raged across the land and blew the people off the face of the world." Some people survived by being changed into monkeys.

The San Bartolo murals have a glyph that may provide a date for the end of the fourth age. When it's revealed, we might end the debate on what age we're in!

Fifth Age

According to today's Mayan Elders, the fifth age is still to come. The first four ages existed in three-dimensional reality; each one relating to one of the cardinal directions, a color, and an element. The sun disc represents all four of them, showing them on the same level, circling the fifth age at the center.

The fifth age will take a leap forward, into higher-dimensional reality. The fifth age jumps to the center of the sun disc and is the fifth direction, the direction of the Axis Mundi. The center of the sun disc encompasses all that came before, all the information of the four directions and four worlds. It's an age of synthesis, an age of harmony. If the other ages were represented by directions, colors, and elements, this age is represented by expanded consciousness.

The San Bartolo creation mural shows all the people of the four worlds working together in the fifth world. This world is the age that brings the other four together into something new, a higher level of consciousness.

The fifth age of the Maya is the return of Kukulkan. This time Kukulkan will not be an external god but the god in each of us coming to fruition. We will each become Kukulkan.

In the Aztec legends, the fifth age is currently underway. It's a time for sacrificing blood to the gods. This age is destroyed when people stop sacrificing and the gods run out of blood. Then the world will be shattered by earthquakes. There is no sixth world.

Maybe this is a good time to fully join the Maya in the fourth world!

End of a Cosmic Day

Okay, let's take a longer view—in fact, a much longer view. A cosmic day is the amount of time it takes the solar system to travel around the galaxy once. It's between 225 and 250 million years. So about every 10,000 precession cycles the solar system travels around the galaxy once. Given the age of the solar system, it has traveled 18 times around the galaxy; it has lived 18 cosmic days. Our species has only experienced about 10 minutes of these 18 days. But hey, who's counting? Other than the Maya, of course.

According to Carl Johan Calleman, the Maya have recorded dates and named cycles that span 16.4 billion years. Before your mind boggles, take a look at the evidence.

Coba Stele

Coba is a Mayan site in the Yucatán. It unearthed the most important stele time-keeping "document" yet. Amazingly preserved, this stele provides a timeline beyond imagination. Inscribed 1,300 years ago, the dates are written in powers of the largest numbers in the Mayan system. They represent time spans along a continuum of 16.4 billion years. According to Calleman, the time cycles recorded on the stele represent evolutionary ages of our planet. Shockingly, the timeline of Mayan evolutionary ages matches almost exactly the evolutionary epochs of modern science. We may indeed need to rethink the origins of the Maya!

Codex Cues _____

More information can be found in Carl Johan Calleman's books: *Solving the Greatest Mystery of Our Time: The Mayan Calendar,* and *The Mayan Calendar and the Transformation of Consciousness.* (See Resources appendix for details on both books.)

Pyramid Power

Combining the geometry of the pyramid with the insights of the Coba stele is illuminating. Calleman saw the progressively smaller steps up the pyramid as the progressively smaller evolutionary periods of modern times. The calendars culminate with the end date on the top platform; each step up represents an evolutionary age. Remember from Chapter 5 that Calleman has calculated a different end date than the accepted 2012. His calculations take into account an adjustment to the calendar made by Mayan priests in 600 C.E. Calleman establishes an end date of October 28, 2011.

Time Progression

You may notice as you look at the time pyramid that the evolutionary cycles are based on progressions of 13, one of the magic Mayan numbers. Look at the following table for a quick review of the numbering system. You can see that each pyramid level increases by powers of 20, the second magic Mayan number. Finally, notice that the top step on the pyramid, the step before we reach the platform, is 260 days, the final magic Mayan number. 260 brings the entire pyramid structure into resonance with the Tzolk'in calendar, the calendar of spiritual cycles. The combination of 13, 20, and 260 resonate with the human structure, connecting us to the larger universe, dimensions of time, and spiritual cycles. (Don't recall this? Go back and check out Chapters 3 and 5.)

kin	1 day	
uinal	20 kins	20 days
tun	18 uinals	360 days
katun	20 tuns	7,200 days (20 years)
baktun	20 katuns	144,000 days (394.26 years)
Great Cycle	13 baktuns	5,126 years
Grand Cycle	5 Great Cycles	25,630 years
pictun	20 baktuns	2,880,000 days (7,885 years)
calabtun	20 pictuns	57,600,000 days (158,000 years)
kinchiltun	20 calabtuns	1,152,000,000 days (3 million years)
alautun	20 kinchiltuns	63.1 million years
hablatun	20 alutuns	1.26 billion years

Calleman has another theory about time and the pyramids. It's called time acceleration. At the bottom of the pyramid, there's a lot of time but not much growth. With each step up the pyramid, growth and development happen faster. In essence, time appears to be accelerating. This has certainly been noticed before; we all feel time disappearing, but this is the first time it has been quantified. We can measure the speed of time acceleration. Each time a new cycle starts, time is 20 times faster.

Celestial Connection

Do you have difficulty thinking about time as elastic? Time acceleration or deceleration is a foreign concept, and yet it happens all the time. In Calleman's pyramid, each cycle is 20 times faster than the one before. The amount that has to be thought about and acted on in a short space doesn't seem to relate to actual clock time. It's a strange but real experience. Time is anything but static. Have you ever been in an accident? Did you experience time slowing down as you had nanoseconds to respond? Everything becomes extra slow, allowing thoughts and action "time" to prevail. Or when you're totally engrossed in something, time seems to disappear. We could say that "time" is a variable experience.

Resonance

Resonance, or "sympathetic vibration," is a central Mayan concept. In the Mayan time-keeping system, humans are connected to the celestial universe and the dimension of time through resonance with cycles of 13, 20, and 260. This is accomplished through vibration. In this case, the magic Mayan numbers establish a vibration that resonates with the human body and we become connected to the spiritual cycles of the Tzolk'in.

You have probably experienced resonance with a musical instrument. For instance, if you have a piano or harp and strike the middle C note, all the strings for other C notes in different octaves will vibrate. If you hit the note hard enough, you will be able to hear this. Only the C strings vibrate, not all the other strings, because the other strings are tuned to different notes. This is resonance, things that are sympathetic to each other vibrating together.

The entire Mayan calendar system is based on the resonance of cycles and time dimensions. By tuning in to the calendars, you are tuning in to the soul transformation underway.

Evolution of the Soul

You might remember from Chapter 2 that there are three different realms of creation: the heavens, the earth, and the underworld. The realm of the underworld is divided into nine levels. Calleman believes the nine levels of the underworld and the nine evolutionary cycles on the stele are the same. The evolution of the underworlds marks the evolution of soul and consciousness.

What if the realms of creation are metaphors for states of consciousness? Then they take on a whole new meaning. In fact, Calleman suggests the trip up the pyramid steps is a trip through the development of consciousness. When the platform is reached, transformation occurs. Tuning in to the calendar's resonance assists individual transformation.

We're on the eighth step of the pyramid on the countdown (or up) to Calleman's date of 2011. When we reach the ninth step, we will be in complete resonance with the Tzolk'in calendar and in resonance with spiritual cycles. For the next 260 days, we will accelerate to meet the new age.

> **Celestial Connection**
>
> Imagine if every metaphor you used was taken literally. For example, astronomers talk about the movement of the solar system across the galactic plane as a carousel. When an astronomer talks about the "carousel in the sky," it's understood the metaphor is describing the pattern of movement. No one really thinks the solar system is attached to a carousel that pumps them up, down, and around in circles in the sky. Yet we take literally every metaphor ancient cultures used. We assume the Maya believed the earth was flat because of the metaphor they used.

End Date

Whether you use the end date of 2011 or 2012, whether you believe this is the fourth age or the fifth age, the message is the same. We are coming to the end of an epoch. The cycle that is ending was focused on a split between the spiritual and material worlds. The result has been technical and material growth with a loss of connection to the sacred essence residing within matter. Divine spirit has been lost as the planet struggles, bearing the brunt of our folly. Inspiration comes from the calendars who proclaim that there is a divine spirit in life and a cosmic plan for its realization.

End of the Present Age

Every previous age ended because humans either could not or would not worship the gods. You may have laughed inside at the thought of gods so hungry for human worship. But what if this, too, is a metaphor? What if worshiping the gods means acknowledging the god force within and putting that impulse first in your choices and actions? What if, as author Michelle Small Wright asserts, we need to "behave as if the god in all life matters"?

If this age is destroyed by angry gods, is it the god within each of us who rises in anger at what we have created and what we have forgotten? And why is the world destroyed? To create another; to build on what we have learned in the evolution of consciousness. To the ancient Maya, we are on the path and the cosmic plan is unfolding as designed.

> **Cosmic Caution**
>
> There have been five historical mass extinctions on the planet, the dinosaurs being the most recent. They may have happened due to super volcanoes, asteroids, and major climate shifts.

Transitions are never easy. In Mayan belief, the ending of cycles is always accompanied by difficulty. At the 52-year Calendar round celebrations, people hid in their houses with all the fires out to avoid the difficulties of ending the old. Endings were traumatic; despite the record of history, the gods might not grant renewal.

Coming of the New Age

The interesting thing about the new age is that we are writing it now. If we are in the sixth age, the creation story ends with the fifth. There are no guides from the past to lead us forward.

Some say there is no creation story for the sixth world because 2012 is the end of the world. Others say it's because we are entering a time when we become the Kukulkan and create the next stage of the story ourselves. The *Chilam Balam* stated that the masters of old will reincarnate at the end of the 13 baktuns to return wisdom to the land. If they are here now, are we listening? Is it possible, as some think, that the next age is outside of the four dimensions we currently live in? In that case, there is no calendar because we don't know what time means in the fifth dimension.

The Least You Need to Know

- The ages of the creation story may be metaphors for the development of consciousness.

- The Maya knew the age of the universe and the evolutionary leaps of life on earth. This information was written on a stele at Coba.

- According to Carl Johan Calleman, time is accelerating as we move up the pyramid of consciousness evolution.

- The end times may not be the end of the world but the beginning of an age when humans evolve into higher spiritual beings.

- We are creating the next age with the thoughts and actions we bring into the end of this epoch.

Part 3

Predications of 2012

2012 is not about the world ending, it's about the world changing. You won't necessarily wake up and everything will be different, but everything *is* changing. 2012 will be the flash point; the point where enough energy has been put into the system to ensure ignition.

What will this be like? To know the answer to that, we need to look at the actual written prophecies of the Maya, the katuns, as well as other 2012 and end-time predictions. We also need to consider what other prophets in other times have to say, what religious systems can add to the picture, and what science and metaphysics include.

Most important, let's remember that the future is not written in stone. We create it in each moment with every thought and every action and every word.

Chapter **9**

Mayan Prophecy

In This Chapter

- ◆ The two sides of the Mayan prophecy
- ◆ What the katuns tell us
- ◆ What to expect in the end times
- ◆ Hope for the future

Whatever age you believe we're in, whatever end date you believe to be accurate, we are clearly completing an important cycle. In both versions of how the creation story links to the precession cycle, the end of this Long Count completes a creation age. What will the end of the cycle bring?

The ancient Maya say surprisingly little about what will actually occur at the end of the calendar. They don't talk at all about the celestial events we have been describing. References to the end times come from the katun prophecies in the book of the *Chilam Balam*. We know there will be a time of purification and we know there will be a time of transformation, the return of Kukulkan. This chapter will tell you about the katun prophecies and what they reveal. It will also tell you what to expect in the end times, what purification entails, and what the return of Kukulkan might bring.

The Mayan Prophecy in a Nutshell

There are two sides to this coin. On the one hand, we're going through a difficult time leading into 2012. These difficulties are the result of our own disharmony of spirit. Governments and religions will let us down and lead us astray. Resources will be scarce and people will be afraid. Natural disasters will increase through the period and the age will end with destruction by fire.

On the other hand, Kukulkan returns representing a rising of consciousness. People are reunited with the wisdom of the past as a new age unfolds. Not only does Kukulkan return but Mayan masters and initiates also return to help spread the wisdom of the Maya. People are drawn to the temples and ruins to remember the past age of knowledge. It's a time for recording and writing things down.

As we return to lost wisdom, we also return to living with the natural cycles represented by the calendars. People begin to elevate their own consciousness through the evolution of the energy centers in the body. We write the next phase of earth, the next age, together as people from all places unite. What happens in this phase depends on us. The "Golden Age" of the Maya begins. This is a synthesis of the katuns. Curious as to the details? Read on!

The Katuns

The prophecies are part of the katun cycles and were written in the *Chilam Balam*. The book, however, holds much more than the simple katuns. It holds the visionary predictions of the author of the *Chilam Balam*, nicknamed "the singing Chilan." The katuns were read for divination and prediction in tandem with the Tzolk'in.

The last day of the Tzolk'in "week" was named Ahau. The Maya named things on the last day of a cycle rather than the first, so all the prophecies occur on Ahau days. There are 13 katun prophecies, 1-13 Ahau. They do not occur in numerical order, but in the order that synchronizes with the Tzolk'in calendar.

Prediction Methods

The Maya watched life unfold and wrote the events they saw into the daily record. They believed cycles repeat and used the past records of cycles for prediction. It's not as simplistic as it sounds. Every number had a quality. Studying the events that happened and how the number's quality was expressed provided insight into how it might express again in the future. However, katun prophecies did not predict events; they only determined the quality of the cycle. Like a mathematical fractal, the same information was repeated over and over in a symmetrical wave. Understanding this allowed the Maya to organize their lives.

Codex Cues

Here's a one-line synopsis created by J. Eric Thompson from the books of *Chilam Balam* of Chumayel and Tizimin. The katuns always end on an Ahau day in the following order. This order synchronizes the "katun short count" with the Tzolk'in calendar.

11 Ahau.	Miserly is the katun; scanty are its rains, misery.
9 Ahau.	Drought, famine.
7 Ahau.	Carnal sin, roguish rulers.
5 Ahau.	Harsh his face, harsh his tidings.
3 Ahau.	Rains of little profit, locusts, fighting.
1 Ahau.	The evil katun.
12 Ahau.	The katun is good.
10 Ahau.	Drought is the charge of the katun.
8 Ahau.	There is an end of greed; there is an end to causing vexation, much fighting
6 Ahau.	Shameless is his speech.
4 Ahau.	The Quetzal shall come, Kukulkan shall come.
2 Ahau.	For half the katun there will be bread; for half the katun there will be water.
13 Ahau.	There is no lucky day for us.

The Shaman's Role

How the katuns worked and what rules were followed in naming and numbering them is complex, not a simple matter of just reading the past. The actual predictions required that the shaman enter a trance state and read the "flavor" of the future. Each katun was only a few paragraphs long; the predictions were developed by the shaman. The *Chilam Balam* reveals many predictions gained in trance. Here's what the katuns have to say about the times we're in, 2012, and beyond.

The katun translations we summarize in this book are from *The Book of the Jaguar Priest: A Translation of the Book of the Chilam Balam of Tizimin* by Maud Worcester Makemson, 1951.

The Present Katun

The present katun is 4 Ahau. It's believed by those who follow the 2012 end date that this katun began on April 6, 1993, and ends with the Long Count/creation age on December 21, 2012. This katun warns of scarcity of resource, food shortages, and many people dying. It also talks of "remembering (old) knowledge and writing it down."

The Mayans predicted the coming of the Spanish to Maya lands, stating that their knowledge would have to retreat before the advent of the "wooden cross," but would resurrect again at the end of the calendar. The *Chilam Balam* states that Kukulkan (Quetzalcoatl) returns during this period to establish the new world and guide the way. The Maya believed in reincarnation and talk of the return of the Mayan masters prior to 2012. The *Chilam Balam* writer says: "My part is to interpret to you, your part, later, as well as my own, is to be born again." The purpose of coming back during the end times is to spread the wisdom and knowledge of the Maya, to ease the time of the purification, and to open the door to the transformation.

End of the World, 2012–2032

The katun 8 Ahau is the katun of the end date. The *Chilam Balam* states: "This is a time of total collapse where everything is lost. It is the time of the judgment of God. There will be epidemics and plagues and then famine. Governments will be lost to foreigners; wise men, and prophets will be lost."

The katuns have a number of prophecies relating to the "end of the world," which comes at the completion of the Great Cycles that started on 13.0.0.0.0 4 Ahau 8 Cumku. Remember, the start and end date are the same. Also, a katun lasts for 20 years, so a katun prediction covers the entire 20-year period.

The katuns refer to this time as the final days of misfortune at the end of the Long Count calendar. They predict earth changes in the form of storms, earthquakes, famine, and pestilence. In this time people lose confidence in religion, priests, government, and officials. In fact even the omens that connect the Maya to the gods are questioned. The omens themselves are said to be broken by the dishonor prevalent in the times.

In *The Book of the Jaguar Priest*, Maud Worcester Makemson translates from the *Chilam Balam* the actual events of the end times. From the sound of it, the Sacred Tree of Life itself falls. The days turn upside down, stones fall from the sky, and fire consumes everything. Many think this description sounds a lot like a massive super volcano and a magnetic pole shift where the earth actually turns onto a new axis. The description of the Sacred Tree of Life falling might describe the Milky Way changing position in the sky. Both of these possibilities are discussed in Chapter 10.

After speaking of great destruction and disillusionment, the *Chilam Balam* ends by saying, "These are the words which must be spoken: the prophecies are a solemn trust from ancient times. They are the first news of events and a valuable warning of things to come."

Codex Cues

The *Chilam Balam* refers to a time when the calendars themselves will "pass away," and the separation of time into periods will be no longer. It's believed the reference is to the end of the Long Count calendar.

After 2012

What happens to the calendars if we have moved into the sixth age? Does the katun cycle just roll over and reset like your car's odometer? This is how it worked in the past, but the sixth age is unknown. If the katuns do just roll over, here is the next in the cycle.

Katun 11 is the first katun and therefore always opens the new cycles. This was the katun that brought Spanish rule to the Yucatan. It predicts the end of traditional rule and the arrival of foreigners that invade and disperse the population. It also predicts scarcity of resources and food.

But again, there are two sides to the coin. Even as the katun talks of difficulty and death, it also predicts great opportunity. It's a time when gifts are given by the gods. In fact, the gods actually come to visit, bringing enlightenment. They talk of life after death. The destruction is spoken of as purification: cleansing the old before creation of the new. The *Chilam Balam* claims that after the time of trial and tears the "divisions in the earth will be one; one Ahau in the heavens, one Ahau in the earth as the ancient prophecies say." This seems to be the Mayan version of "As above, so below." After this time of travail the Golden Age of the Maya begins.

It's clear that the road to better times will not be easy and we may be in for a rough ride. Looking at the traditions and history of the Maya may give some insights into what's to come. The general Maya tradition believes that cycles of any length end with purification, followed by renewal.

A Period of Purification

You might think of change happening with the start of something new. So naturally you think more about what will happen when 2012 arrives than what is happening now.

In Maya-view, change happens at the end of the old cycle. All cycles end with a period of purification as the old is taken down so the new can be constructed. You'll remember from Chapter 2 that the end of cycles was marked with termination rituals for the buildings that had been part of the old cycle. Past structures were removed and new ones rebuilt in alignment with the energy of the new cycle. The five-day period at the end of the Haab calendar was for the same purpose: to cleanse the old before welcoming the new.

According to the *Chilam Balam*, the purification period for the Long Count calendar starts "on the first day of the last Uinal before the end of the 13th Baktun." In English that means the last 20-year period before the end date, which means we're already purifying. As you may have noticed, challenges of extreme weather, distrust of our leadership, and economic distress are already here!

Fruits of the Past Age

In Maya-view, matter and spirit are both important aspects of creation. One is not necessarily better than the other; they both work together for the purposes of consciousness. However, it's easy to get lost in the material world and forget the spiritual. In this past age, we've forgotten the sacred essence and have acted as if the material is all there is. The progressive loss of connection to the sacred created a duality. In the duality, we forgot how to work with spirit creatively and have tried to get what we want through the force of our will. In a sense, we have forced our will on nature. Force of any kind is bound for disaster because it suppresses one thing for another. Resonance brings things together; force drives them apart. Once spirit was removed from matter people were justified in treating the creation any way they wanted. The result has been devastating. In the words of author Michelle Small Wright, "The only thing worse than man's inhumanity to nature has been man's inhumanity to man."

Loss of Harmony

The Mayan calendar system kept the Mayans in sync with creation. When the calendar system was destroyed, harmony was, too. Did the Maya help keep the whole world in balance by living with the calendars? Or are they an example for what we need to do in this time of purification?

Purification is the necessary first step in renewal and returning to balance. The process, however, seems destructive. Before the new temple is built, the old is destroyed. During the purification cycle, all imbalances get bigger. They get so big they tear themselves apart; they collapse under their own weight. It's a time to look in the mirror and face our own shadow, face the consequences of living out of balance. As Mahatma Gandhi said, "You must be the change you wish to see in the world."

Social Tension and Suppression

As the energy of purification builds, social divisions increase. Strife between people and groups of people increases. Resources diminish and the competition for necessities increases. Since we have forgotten how to work with spirit to manifest what we need, people and nations try to get it through force.

A big issue in this time is that differences are not tolerated. Suppression of dissenting voices in all areas of life occurs. Political, religious, and cultural differences are suppressed, creating more and more civil unrest. Nations suppress other nations, groups suppress other groups, and the use of violent force increases.

Earth Changes

The changing of the ages was often the result of natural disasters sent by the gods. Past ages were destroyed by forces such as earthquakes, hurricanes, tsunamis, and volcanoes. The destruction of the current age is said to be by fire. It's described as stones and fire falling on our heads.

Descriptions could fit massive volcanoes, nuclear bombs, or even asteroids from space. Many people predict Earth changes for this time, as we will see in the next few chapters. But could it equally be the fire of the spirit destroying the strongholds of our ego and materialistic viewpoint?

Cosmic Caution

Many believe the Maya deserted their cities at the end of the classic era because of ecological stress. As populations grew, the environment was overstressed, causing an ecological crash. We are very much facing the same today. The destruction of the rain forest, the melting of the ice caps, weather changes, pollution, and so forth are indicators of global ecological stress. Grave ecological consequences may have to be faced. The katuns forecast drought, famine, and pestilence during this time.

The Return of Kukulkan

As we discussed in Chapter 8, Carl Johan Calleman is pretty convincing that the calendars of the Maya are actually tracking the advance of consciousness. The end of the Long Count raises us to the top platform of the pyramid, coming out of the nine levels of the underworld. Many think the return of Kukulkan is also a metaphor for the raising of consciousness.

Hunbatz Men, a Mayan Elder, says that during this time before 2012 people will come together and the initiates will "return to the sacred land of the Maya to continue the work of the Great Spirit." As expressed in the *Chilam Balam*, those who were part of the Maya were told they would return to pass on the prophecy they were receiving. Remember: "My part is to interpret to you, your part, later, as well as my own, is to be born again."

Spirit Rising

Many people today are noticing changes within themselves. They may feel more synchronicity in their lives, feel attuned to nature and natural cycles, even experience more energy awareness. We will discuss these processes more in Part 6 of this book, but what does it mean?

As the planets are moving toward the alignments of 2012, they are increasing in frequency. The vibration affects everything that resonates with it. People who respond to the frequency feel the effects in their body, mind, and spirit. Their consciousness responds and awareness increases. The result is a greater connection to the spirit behind and within matter.

According to Hunbatz Men, the *solar priests* of the past are returning. He says they are walking in many ceremonial centers, awakening those who visit. This awakening is part of the impact of the alignments. Hunbatz says, "The Mayan masters will begin to manifest in the trees, in the sun, in the moon and in the stars. They will appear also in homes to inform families that the new time to begin the initiation of cosmic work has commenced. Many will not understand because this will happen when people are asleep." Pay attention to your dreams, and the time in between wake and sleep; not only your Wayeb but the Mayan masters may be visiting!

Codex Cues

Solar priests are the keepers of the spiritual wisdom of the Mayan people. Depicted in different murals as carrying the "Cycles of Time," it is thought that they awaken people to their energy centers and oversee the transitions of the ages.

A Return to Natural Time

The katuns talk about "tying up," or ending, the Long Count calendar. They warned of the ending of a significant time cycle and the end of the present age. They also talk about a time when there will be no divisions or periods to time. Some people think this refers to the end of the calendars, possibly indicating a new dimension. Others think it refers to a return to natural timekeeping. The Gregorian calendar aligns people to periods of time that are artificial. Our biorhythms are not in sync with the time cycles of an artificial clock, disconnecting us from our inner balance and deeper spiritual awareness. The return to a nature-based cycle is thought to bring us back to our essence and reconnect us to the spiritual world we inhabit.

Balance with Nature

Returning to the awareness of the unity of matter and spirit brings us back in harmony with nature. The k'ul that the planet receives from the universe is sent out along pathways to sacred centers. All of nature feeds from this energy. When humans are in touch with nature, they receive the flow of k'ul. Spending time in nature or spending time at sacred sites reconnects us to our source of true power.

Charging Your Power Cords

Getting through the challenges ahead will require that you become like the Hero Twins and develop your awareness. We all have energy structures in our bodies that the Maya were aware of. The Maya performed energy breathing and exercise techniques to keep their energy centers clear. You may know of the energy centers as *chakras*. To learn more about chakras, check out David Pond's book *Chakras for Beginners* (see Resources appendix). It's one of the best we've seen.

You may already use many techniques for keeping your energy structures clear and connected. Have you noticed that when things get tough, it's easy to forget to use your energy routines? It's important to remember them! Meditation, Qi Gong, Tai Chi, yoga, sound healing, and energy breathing are all ways you can clear and charge your field. In addition to breathing and exercises, the Mayans used sun meditations,

def•i•ni•tion

Chakras are energy centers in the body that look like wheels of light. There are seven traditional centers starting at the base of the spine and moving up to the crown of your head. Each center has a specific color, sound, and lesson.

drawing on the energy and consciousness of the sun to charge their system. You'll learn some techniques to help in Chapter 21. You will feel the benefit immediately when you start to take care of your energy field.

The Least You Need to Know

◆ The katun prophecies tell of the need to purify and return to balance with nature. Masters of the past will return to help the process.

◆ The purification will be marked by increasing social, political, environmental, and spiritual unrest and tension.

◆ After 2012 there will be a difficult adjustment period followed by the rising of spiritual consciousness. A period of peace follows.

◆ You can help yourself get though difficult times by caring for your own energy centers, the chakras.

Chapter 10

2012 Global Predictions

In This Chapter

- ◆ Extreme solar maximum
- ◆ Can the magnetic poles reverse?
- ◆ Cracks in the earth's magnetic field
- ◆ Super volcano at Yellowstone
- ◆ Traveling through the photon belt
- ◆ Shifting consciousness

The mystique of the Mayans has initiated a 2012 awareness phenomenon. Coincidentally, or synchronistically, 2012 has become the benchmark for a number of cataclysmic, end-of-the world theories. It's also become a dominating presence in theories of human spiritual evolution. Perhaps if these events did not coincide with the end of the Mayan Long Count calendar we wouldn't pay much attention to them. But they do and so we wonder why.

All of the geophysical conditions we describe in this chapter are real and can be stimulated by the celestial events of 2012. Whether they will result in catastrophe is speculation. No one really knows. In this chapter, we'll look at changes in the earth's magnetic field, changes in the solar sunspot activity, and the effects of galactic energy waves.

2012 Solar Sunspot Cycle

On July 31, 2006, a sunspot appeared on the sun. Not surprising in any way, but this sunspot heralds the start of the next sunspot surge. How do we know? Because its magnetic polarity was reversed from the polarity of the previous cycle. You know what that means from Chapter 6: the new sunspot cycle has begun.

Solar Maximum

Solar sunspots occur in cycles of minimum sunspot activity followed six years later by maximum sunspot activity (see Chapter 6). In 2006, the shift away from solar minimum toward solar maximum occurred. NASA reports that 2012 will be the most intense solar maximum since 1958, when sunspot activity bombarded the earth with enormous amounts of electromagnetic energy, boosting the aurora borealis so far south it was seen in Mexico! Scientists are predicting that the next sunspot cycle will be 30 to 50 percent stronger than the last. A sunspot cycle of this intensity has major consequences in today's technological society.

Sunspots and Weather

What do hurricanes, tornadoes, and blizzards have to do with sunspots? Well, quite a bit, actually. Large influxes of energy from the sun drive extreme weather patterns. This influx of energy not only makes an incredible display of the Northern Lights, it also creates the La Niña and El Niño jet stream patterns. The result? Super hurricanes like 2005's Katrina.

> ### Celestial Connection
>
> Sunspots and solar flares dump a lot of energy into the earth's magnetic atmosphere. The energy is channeled along the lines of the earth's magnetic field, causing the aurora borealis. The large influx of energy shifts the earth's magnetic field, which shifts the jet streams, which shifts the ocean currents. The cumulative effects are El Niño and La Niña, which equal big bad storms.

What does this mean in the larger picture? A 50 percent stronger solar cycle could be catastrophic—huge, Katrina-size storms battering the coastline; not just one, but one after another. Imagine it: bridges gone, power supply interrupted, oil refineries destroyed, communities devastated, infrastructures ruined, lives lost. Weather alone could result in the collapse of economies, energy shortages, and massive loss of life. But it would take a lot of different factors coming together all at once for this to happen.

Sunspots and Technology

In 1958, there was very little satellite technology. Compasses, not GPS, were used for direction. Telephones used land lines and no one had a cell phone. Computers were almost exclusive to research or government facilities.

Today the influx of magnetic radiation would have enormous impact on our technology. Electromagnetic interruption of satellites could knock them out of commission for days. This can affect a lot more than GPS systems, cell phones, and the Internet. Magnetic radiation could potentially jeopardize nuclear warhead devices, national warning systems, airplanes, jets, and really all aspects of life. The technological age we live in has its Achilles heel in the electromagnetic flux.

Magnetic Pole Reversal

You probably thought that the magnetic north pole always pointed north. Not so. In fact, it's always moving a little bit. In addition, the earth is subject to something called "geomagnetic reversal." This is a change in the orientation of the earth's magnetic field. North pole becomes south and south pole becomes north.

Magnetic Field Strength

A pole reversal usually follows a decline in the earth's magnetic field strength. The field strength recovers rapidly after the new orientation has been established. Of course, we don't really know how rapid the recovery is since the last pole reversal happened 780,000 years ago. But we do know reversals happen; they leave their magnetic imprint in the magnetized volcanic minerals on the ocean floor.

Reading the ocean floor tells us that reversals happen on average every 250,000 years.

Cosmic Caution

Don't confuse the magnetic pole reversal with a pole shift. A pole reversal is the reversal of the magnetic field. A pole shift represents movement in the molten lava core of the planet that actually shifts the earth's axis of rotation. This could happen, for example, after an impact with a large object.

Many people think we are in for one now. The earth's magnetic field has undergone a gradual decrease in strength that may indicate a coming reversal. Over the past 150 years the field has decreased by 10 percent.

Cause of Pole Reversal

It's not known for sure what causes a pole reversal. Many scientists think it's a natural part of a dynamic system; after all, the sun reverses polarity every 11 years. Another theory is that the earth's magnetic field becomes unstable. In the earth, a decline in magnetic field strength creates instability, which may spontaneously flip the poles into the opposite direction. In the case of the sun, magnetic field instability occurs with an increase in magnetic strength from increased sunspot activity.

Another theory is that a pole reversal can be caused by an intense influx of energy from the sun. Enough energy entering the ionosphere of the earth can destabilize the magnetic field, especially if the field is already weak. Archaeoastronomist and astrophysicist Paul LaViolette describes experimentally creating pole reversals in magnets by bombarding the magnets with a lot of strong particles. The increased amount of energy along the magnetic lines has the effect of reversing the fields. The extra-strong sunspot cycle coming up together with the current weakening of the earth's magnetic field could have some serious effects on earth. LaViolette has written four books and many articles. You can learn more at his website, www.etheric.com.

Codex Cues

The Geomagnetic Polarity Time Scale (GPTS) measures the rate at which reversals occur. It demonstrates that the rate of reversals varies considerably. It can maintain a single orientation for tens of millions of years, and then start shifting every 50,000 years.

What's the Result?

We don't really know what happens in a pole reversal. Will there be major cataclysms? Storms? Tidal waves? Speculation is that the reversal could agitate the molten core of the planet, increasing internal pressures. This might cause movements in the tectonic plates, causing earthquakes and floods. Increased pressure may also set off volcanic activity.

Less dramatic problems can be equally difficult. Interference with animals' sense of direction can disrupt migration routes of birds and whales as well as activity cycles of bees and other insects. Not only will animals show up in places they've never been before, but crop pollination and ecosystem balance will be impacted as well. Our own navigational system will almost certainly be disrupted. Once again satellites, radar, and navigational systems may be knocked out. Obstruction of the electric grid, radio waves, airplanes, cell phones, cars, and national security systems might occur. Daily life as we know it has the potential to be inalterably changed.

The good thing? Evidence supports a slow reversal over a thousand years or more as opposed to the fast reversal suggested for 2012.

Celestial Connection

Recent discoveries by Canadian geologists have confirmed that the position of magnetic north is moving. Magnetic north is always moving a little; however, for the last 400 years, it has stayed within northern Canada. Now the North Pole has moved out of Canada and is heading toward Siberia. According to geologists, the movement of the poles could be related to massive earthquakes. For example, the quake that caused the massive tsunami of December 26, 2004, in Indonesia was powerful enough to alter the shape of Earth and jar the planet into a slightly different axis of rotation. It could be partly responsible for propelling the magnetic North Pole toward Siberia.

Cracks in the Earth's Magnetic Field

The earth's magnetic field (magnetosphere) forms a shield around the earth that protects it against harmful solar radiation. Cracks in the field were discovered in 2003 by both NASA and the European Space Agency. The immense cracks can remain open for hours, allowing solar winds to flow into the atmosphere. The largest crack is over the Atlantic Ocean between South Africa and Brazil. It's known as the South Atlantic Anomaly and is a 100,000-mile crack. Crewmembers in spacecrafts that pass through the crack require higher shielding, and satellites have been damaged during transit.

NASA explains that the cracks are due to changes at the earth's core. As the molten center of the earth moves, it generates the magnetic field that creates the magnetosphere and determines the north and south poles. Fluxes in the core cause the magnetic poles to shift. NASA thinks this might be causing the cracks. If this is the case, then cracks in the magnetosphere are actually signs and symptoms of a magnetic flux, which can lead to a pole reversal.

Check out the following illustration to get an idea of the magnetic poles.

The earth's magnetic field.

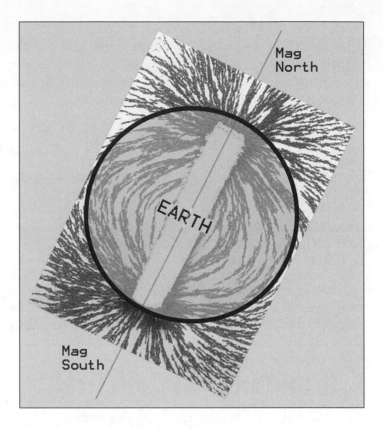

Here's the scene: it's 2012, the solar maximum is stronger than ever, a huge solar flare sends a massive wind of electrified particles into the earth's magnetosphere. The Southern Atlantic Anomaly crack is open, allowing the solar wind to blow through the atmosphere. The Northern Lights can be seen in South America, the jet stream goes haywire, and extreme weather pounds the planet. Impossible? Not really.

Super Volcanoes

You may have thought that a super volcano is the same as a regular volcano only stronger. Yes and no. A super volcano is stronger, as powerful as 1,000 Hiroshima-type nuclear bombs. But they look much different and can easily hide for centuries with no one knowing they are there.

A regular volcano looks like a mountain with a large cone-shaped funnel. A super volcano is a depression, called a caldera, forming a basin. It's like an upside-down volcano with the cone going into the earth. Super volcanoes are called "hot spots." The basin usually fills with water, hiding the signs of the lurking volcano underneath the calm surface of a lake.

Yellowstone

The largest super volcano hot spot ever discovered is at Yellowstone National Park in Wyoming. Identified in 1993, it lies right under the beautiful glacial lake. Underneath the calm surface, within the depression, flowing along underground tributaries and

rivulets is a searing caldron of magma, solid and liquefied rock, and highly combustible volcanic gas. It's estimated to be an 8 on the Volcano Explosivity Index, the highest possible level.

Covering 136 acres, the area under the lake has been rising since 2004, forming a bulge. This indicates activity in the caldera. Areas of the lake have been closed to the public and water temperatures have been rising.

Codex Cues

To keep track of seismic changes at Yellowstone, tune in to the Yellowstone Volcano Observatory, a U.S. geological survey project that provides regular updates on monitoring findings. Go to http://volcanoes.usgs.gov/yvo.

The Making of a Super V

Super volcanoes form at the boundary between the molten core of the planet and the mantle. Columns of smoldering rock move slowly upward through the boundaries of the tectonic plates. Most of them exist on the ocean floors because this is where the plates come together. Iceland, Hawaii, and the Galapagos Islands were all formed from explosions of past super volcanoes. But don't think super volcano explosions are all in the far distant past; the most recent explosion of a super volcano happened in 3500 B.C.E. in Greece. That's not so long ago in the scheme of things. More importantly, super volcano activity is being monitored at several locations around the world.

Yellowstone is different than the ordinary super volcano. It's fueled by underground accumulations of uranium, formed over millions of years. When this volcano blows, it will spew radioactive lava across the states of Wyoming, Nebraska, Montana, and parts of Canada.

Will Yellowstone Blow?

Evidence suggests yes; the Yellowstone super volcano shows signs of activity. Temperatures in the glacial lake have been rising. The bulge in the lake floor has gotten larger. Steam vents along the Norris Geyser basin have raised soil temperatures significantly. Seismic activity and other signs are being monitored. The question is when, not if. Of course no one knows when and there is no way to predict it. But people are thinking 2012. Why? Because the earth is part of an interactive system. As solar maximum approaches and more energy input occurs along our magnetosphere, changes are felt at the molten core of the planet as well. These changes can precipitate an explosion.

If the Yellowstone super volcano blows, huge rocks, molten lava, and magma will be ejected through the air at supersonic speeds. The states in the immediate area will be devastated. The next circle out will be poisoned with radioactive fallout. An ash cloud will spread over the continent, stopping air travel for an estimated three to five years and blocking rays from the sun. The result? Temperatures dropping with the potential of a "nuclear winter." No air travel, no satellites, interference of radio waves, and radioactive fallout. The interference with technology leaves some people thinking an eruption of Yellowstone will end civilization as we know it.

2012: The Tipping Point

Volcanoes provide an important balancing function for the earth. In the past, it was thought the main function was to release internal pressure. While true, it's now thought that the main function is to balance temperatures on the planet. The ash spewed into the air provides protection from the sun, bringing temperatures down. With global warming, holes in the ozone layer, and cracks in the magnetic field, we may be due for a planetary cooling off. The truth is, we really don't know the cycles of the planet. Holes in the ozone, cracks in the magnetic field, and super volcanoes may all be part of balancing mechanisms that play off each other through the eons of time. We haven't had the ability to monitor for long enough periods to truly know what's going on. However, 2012 researchers believe another factor may play a hand. If the sun and earth undergo a magnetic pole reversal at the same time, it's thought an eruption may be triggered.

Codex Cues

Weather can always cause problems, and even temporary disruptions can create havoc in your life. It's always a good idea to be prepared. Don't know what to do to be prepared? Look ahead to Chapter 20 for ideas.

What About the Photon Belt?

As you'll recall from Chapter 6, although there's no physical evidence of the existence of the photon belt, it's a recurring theme in 2012 predictions. Believers say it represents a frequency of energy that scientists are currently unable to measure. They suggest it comes from other dimensions and is assisting a spiritual awakening on the planet. We're scheduled to enter the belt in December 22, 2012. This date has been chosen because of the Pleiades alignment we discussed in Chapter 6 and because of the Mayan calendar end date.

The Passage

According to advocates, the belt is divided into three sections. The near side and far side perimeters are called the null zones; the middle is called the main belt. First the solar system enters the null zone, which takes five to six days to traverse. During this passage, there is a three-day period of total darkness. Passage through the main belt will take 2,000 years. During this time, there will be 24 hours of daylight. Moving out through the far side null zone will again take the solar system five to six days, and the earth will experience three days of darkness. How do we know? Hmm. Good question.

Cosmic Caution

Although many people believe in the photon belt, there is no real evidence. Before believing in any new theory, be sure to check out the source. A lot of times when something is repeated enough by many different people, it gets accepted as real. A little digging is always important before leaping aboard.

Spiritual Light

The theory is that photon radiation will excite molecules and atoms, increasing their vibration. Matter will essentially be raised in spiritual energy. It's believed this will allow the solar system to elevate to a higher dimension, leading to a golden age of spiritual realization. Of course, not everyone will want to have their vibration increased. These people will find themselves in a lower-dimensional universe appropriate to their level of development.

Physical Manifestation

The photon field is said to have the effect of reducing solar radiation. It's unclear whether the sun is actually dampened or whether its strength is the same, but the solar radiation is interfered with by the photon energy. In either case, it is claimed the rotation of the planet will be affected, temperatures will drop, and we will have another ice age. The rotational axis will shift, followed by melting of the ice caps and flooding across the planet. After the cataclysm is the beginning of a new age of peace and attunement with higher spiritual planes.

Additional Causes of Disasters

There are more theories of end-of-the-world scenarios and 2012. Most of them don't have enough information to substantiate them, and some are pure speculation. Many simply need more time for scientists to uncover the physics involved. Here are a couple to contemplate.

Gamma and Gravity Waves

Some scientists, such as Paul LaViolette, are studying "super gamma waves" being emitted from the center of the galaxy. Dr. LaViolette calculates the gamma emissions occur in waves every 26,000 years. 2012 is the estimated time of arrival of the next major shot. There are claims that the effects are already being felt as the front wave of the emission is hitting us now. Gamma waves are said to travel with, or on, gravity waves, so the effect is said to be twofold: an increase in earthquakes and a boost in spiritual energy.

Asteroids

Many people believe that as the solar system moves through this more densely occupied area of the galaxy it becomes inevitable that the earth will be hit by an asteroid. NASA has a program that constantly monitors space for this eventuality. Right now, nothing is on the horizon until 2029, when an asteroid is expected to come within 18,600 miles of Earth!

Consciousness Shifting

We've mentioned that a prevalent theme to 2012 is the double-sided coin of physical catastrophe and spiritual enlightenment. We're moving into celestial alignments, sunspot cycles, etc., which contain significant energy. The release of this energy has the power to cause earthquakes, super volcanoes, and super storms. If solar winds and gamma waves have this effect on physical bodies, what effect do they have on spirit?

Luminosity

We talked in Chapter 7 of the sun's heliosphere lighting up as we go through a part of the galaxy with more highly charged energy particles. These highly charged particles interact with the plasma field in the heliosphere, increasing the sun's luminosity. What might these highly charged particles be doing to us?

As the sun's energy increases, the earth is charged as well. People also experience the increased charge physically, emotionally, and spiritually. Clairvoyants who see energy fields say that the energy field, or aura, around our body is becoming more luminous. This happens as the electromagnetic energy from the sun impacts the grid lines of the planet, charging sacred sites. Ceremony and meditation at these sites at this time is said to increase spiritual consciousness.

Physical Evolution

Many people believe that not only is consciousness being changed, but the physical bodies we inhabit are being changed as well. The thought is that our nervous systems and body structures have to be upgraded to manage larger amounts of energy. Your DNA, your cellular vibration, your nervous system, your endocrine system, and your entire physical body have to change to manage larger amounts of energy. We'll take you further on this part of the journey in Parts 5 and 6 of this book.

Attitudes

At a very basic and real level, we evolve or devolve into better or worse people through our day-to-day experiences. How we respond either develops our resources and spirit or reduces us to our greatest fears. Most of this happens in our mind. How we think determines whether something is a threat or an opportunity. What we think determines how we respond. As society gets more stressed, we have a choice: cooperation or competition? Anyone who has lived through war knows that it brings out both. Sometimes in order to appreciate the magic that life is, we have to be challenged. The end times might be a self-created mandate for growth. We are living evolution with every thought.

The Least You Need to Know

- The solar maximum of 2012 will cause extreme weather and technological interruptions.

- The earth's magnetic field is weakening, which may indicate an upcoming reversal of the magnetic poles.

- Scientists are measuring cracks in the earth's magnetic field that allow high levels of solar radiation into the earth's atmosphere.

- The largest super volcano ever discovered is at Yellowstone National Park in Wyoming. It's showing signs of eminent eruption.

- The photon belt is a recurring and much-written-about event with no basis in reality.

- The changes of 2012 are thought to bring about a rising of consciousness and spiritual evolution.

11

Past Parallel Prophecies

In This Chapter

- ◆ Hopi words of wisdom

- ◆ The quatrains of Nostradamus

- ◆ Biblical end times

- ◆ End times according to Edgar Cayce

- ◆ The Kali Yuga forecast

While you're watching the news, you may be starting to wonder if ancient prophecies are being fulfilled in our time. You're not alone. A 2002 TIME/CNN poll reveals that 35 percent of the population agrees. And 59 percent of the population believes the end times will happen in this time ("Apocalypse Now," *Time Magazine*, June 23, 2002). Let's not forget, however, that in every era during uncertainty and upheaval, belief in the end times rises. The fall of Rome, the Black Plague, and World War II are good examples.

Are you curious if there are other ancient prophecies pointing to 2012? In fact, there are a lot of predictions that fit the general scheme of the Mayan prophecy. However, none of them comes with an actual date.

Many researchers lump them together, building the case that 2012 was universally foretold as the end times. It's not really true, but it is true that the end times have been foretold. Let's take a look at some of the more prevalent past prophecies of the Hopi, Nostradamus, the Bible, and more. One thing they all have in common: they are double-sided, being cataclysmic and uplifting.

The Hopi: Red Road or Black Road?

The Hopi, whose name means "peaceful people," are a Native American tribe of the Four Corners area of the Southwestern United States. Their reservation is in Arizona. They live on a large mesa in two key communities, Oraibi and Hotevilla. Like the Maya, they have an extensive prophecy with extreme accuracy. The prophecy dates back several thousand years as an oral tradition. There is also a sacred rock with a pictogram that reveals part of the Hopi prophecy. Called the prophecy stone, it is still preserved, revered, and protected from public viewing by Hopi Elders. A pictogram is a picture or series of pictures that tells a story, describes an event, or relays a concept. The Hopi prophecy stone tells the story of the Hopi prophecy.

The Hopi prophecy rings with a breathtaking spiritual authority. It doesn't give dates when events will happen, but gives signs. In the Hopi prophecy, we have a choice: we can travel the red road of spirituality and attain harmony with the earth, or the black road of the material world and cause the ruin of the earth. The road of the material is doomed to destruction at the hands of greed and avarice. The red road leads to higher spiritual reality.

Individuals may be traveling one road while society follows the other road. It's the individual's responsibility to walk the red road for the Great Spirit. The prophecies are meant for society, the road that is being taken by the masses. The prophecy gives many signs to alert society to the road being traveled; there are crossroads or junctions where society can choose to rejoin the red road if we are lost on the black road. The farther along the track of the black road society goes, the harder it is to rejoin the red road. Eventually we will reach the point of no return.

What road are we on and where are we now? The Hopi prophecy given here is a synopsis taken from lectures and writings of Hopi Elders Thomas Banacyca and Dan Evehema; *The Book of the Hopi* by Frank Waters; and the words of a man named White Feather as told to Reverend David Young in 1958.

The Worlds of Creation

Like the Maya, the Hopi believe there have been four or five previous worlds that have been destroyed as part of a purification process. Purification was necessary to cleanse the world from corruption and greed. The majority agree that this is the fourth world, but some believe it is the fifth.

Humans were created in four colors as part of the fourfold creation process: four directions, four elements, etc. Each color or race has ruled one world. The last world was ruled by the red race, the present world by the white race, and the next world will be ruled by the yellow race. This is a tradition shared by the Toltec/Aztec wisdom schools as well.

Celestial Connection
The belief in four guardians, colors, directions, and elements is not exclusive to indigenous cultures of the Americas. Similar beliefs are found in Celtic lore, Egyptian legend, and the Aborigine in Australia. The concept is found in Sanskrit as the Four Kings or Guardians of the world, in Chinese as the Four Heavenly Kings, and in Korea, Japan, and Tibet as well.

At the creation of the fourth (or fifth) world, humans were told to travel to all four corners of the world and keep the ways of the Great Spirit. The Hopi stayed on the Oraibi Mesa to keep the sacred ceremonies for the return of the Great Spirit. The white race went to the east. The Hopi were told in their prophecy that the white man would return bringing either peace and harmony or destruction. Eventually the true white brother would return to help the Hopi transform the continent into a spiritual paradise: the fifth world.

The Hopi and the Maya both have a legend of coming to this land from either tunnels under the water or by boats after the destruction of their homeland by floods and fire. Both seem to refer to Atlantis as the home base. Both also have a legend that the white brothers, Kukulkan or Pahana, leave to the east promising to return and bring peace and harmony.

Prophecy Stone

The Hopi have a prophecy stone that has been preserved for thousands of years. It contains a pictogram of the prophecy. The Hopi were told they would recognize the true "white brother" (called Pahana) because he would come with a fragment of stone that would fit into and complete the prophecy stone.

The return of the true white brother is eagerly awaited. It's abundantly clear that the white man who did return brought destruction. The Hopi are charged with keeping the traditional ways and traditional lands and to assist the passage into the fifth world. It's their duty to their family, the animals, and all of nature to keep this land protected and in harmony.

The prophecy stone holds the signs we are to watch for to know which road we follow and where we are on the journey.

Signs

There are nine main signs that are referred to in the Hopi prophecy related to the road society is taking. The prophecy states that when the nine signs have all been fulfilled, the fourth world will end and the fifth will begin. As you read the signs and their inter-pretations, you may agree with many Hopis who say that there are few signs left to fulfill. The signs are said to have been relayed by White Feather of the Bear Clan of the Hopi tribe and were written in Frank Waters's 1963 book, *The Book of the Hopi* (Penguin Books, 1977). Waters lived with the Hopi for three years while writing his book. Here's a condensed version of the signs, which can be read directly in Waters' book.

> *The first sign* refers to the coming of Europeans to America. The people who arrive on Native lands are described as "white-skinned" people who steal the land of the Native tribes. They carry "thunder sticks" with which they strike the tribes. Thunder sticks are thought to be guns.

> *The second sign* foretells of the coming of covered wagons across the plains. They're described as "spinning wheels filled with voices."

> *The third sign* is the arrival of longhorn cattle. They're described as "strange beasts" similar to the buffalo but with larger horns. They overrun the land that was once the home of buffalo and Native tribes.

> *The fourth sign* is the coming of the railroad tracks, described by White Feather as "snakes of iron."

> *The fifth sign* is the erection of power lines and cables, which are as a "giant spider's web" crisscrossing the land.

> *The sixth sign* is the construction of concrete roads across the landscape. The description of the roads includes the fact that over long stretches they have mirage-producing effects.

The seventh sign relates to pollution. It tells of "the sea turning black, and many living things dying." This is believed to refer to oil spills in the ocean.

The eighth sign is this: "You will see many youths who wear their hair long like our people, come and join the tribal nations to learn our ways and wisdom." This is thought to refer to the hippie movement of the 1960s.

The ninth and final sign talks of a "dwelling place in the heavens" that falls from the sky. It's described as looking like a "blue star" and will herald the end of the ceremonies of the Hopi people. Some people think this sign was fulfilled with the bringing down of Russian space station Mir in 2001. Others think it refers to a comet that will arrive in the sky sometime during the end times.

The Blue Star

The prophecy states that if society continues down the black road there will be a time when the Hopi ceremonies that keep the world in balance will be suspended. According to Frank Waters, this will occur "after the Blue Kachina removes his mask while performing a ceremonial dance in the plaza before non-Hopi's."

Performing sacred ceremony in front of the white man is considered taboo among traditional Hopi Elders, so this represents a breach in tradition. The Blue Kachina may be the same as the Blue Star in the ninth sign and is often called the "Blue Star Kachina." Many think this sign was fulfilled with the falling of the Russian space station Mir in 2001. Others think it relates to a comet.

> **Celestial Connection**
>
> Comet Hyakutaki in January 1996, Comet Neat in December 2002, and Comet Holmes in November 2007 have all been considered the Blue Star. The Blue Star is to be followed by a red comet seven years later. People are searching the skies.

The Last Sign: End Times

At least eight of the nine prophecies have been met, putting us pretty near the end times. Five years is a number that echoes along the hallways when this subject is discussed. The last part of White Feather's warning is the description of the end times themselves. It sounds strangely familiar but with added detail.

The prophecy describes atomic bombs, calling them "columns of smoke and fire," which cause people to die in great numbers and leave behind a strange disease. The bomb had "great heat, equal to the heat of a sun." It's often referred to as a "gourd of ashes" that when dropped upon the earth "will boil everything within a large space and nothing will grow for a very long time." The development of the atomic bomb is a prelude to the destruction of the fourth world.

Waters reports that the destruction of the fourth world coincides with the earth "rocking to and fro." Also there will be war with the people who "possessed the first light of wisdom." This is an interesting description of the Middle East, where many aspects of civilization first developed.

The people who will be safe through all this will be those who continued to follow the ways of the Great Spirit, who understood the prophecy, and who lived in the protected lands of the Hopi. After the destruction of the fourth world, these will be the people left to rebuild. They won't have to do it alone, however, as Pahana (the true white brother) returns to help. With his arrival comes the beginning of the fifth age. White Feather says, "He [Pahana] shall plant the seeds of his wisdom in their hearts. Even now the seeds are being planted. These shall smooth the way to the Emergence into the Fifth World." Are you struck by how similar this is to the Mayan prophecy of the return of Kukulkan and the solar priests?

Codex Cues

According to a Hopi Elder, "Those who return to the ways given to us in the original teachings, and live a natural way of life will not be touched by the coming of the Purifier. They will survive and build the new world."

There are additional prophecies about man going to the moon, meetings of the Hopis at the United Nations, and many other significant events. The Hopis warned that bringing "rocks from the moon" would create an imbalance in nature and would mark the beginning of weather changes. They believe the mission to the moon was the fulfillment of this prophecy.

The Hopi prophecy also seems to describe a pole reversal where the earth turns over several times, thus "rocking to and fro." If there is a pole reversal in 2012, it would provide another link between the Hopi prophecy and the time frame of the Mayan prophecy.

Hope from the Hopi

The Hopi and Mayan prophecies have much in common. They warn of the end of this world due to "greed and corruption." They also promise a period of peace after the purification when humankind returns to balance. Not only will the "Great Spirit" or "Kukulkan" return in the end times, but in both cases masters, Pahana and the solar priests, return before the end and help plant the seeds for the transitions. In both traditions, people are taught to hold to a spiritual practice and to help maintain the traditional lands. Sounds like good advice!

The Predictions of Nostradamus

Nostradamus (1503–1566) is the most famous end-time prophet. Although his prophecies are often used to support the 2012 end date, they're not specifically linked to 2012. His predictions are written in quatrains (verses or poems of four lines that can rhyme or not rhyme) and are vague and difficult to interpret, at least before the event. Hindsight seems to be 20/20, and Nostradamus has been credited with predicting Napoleon, Hitler, World Wars I and II, and the 9/11 attacks. Still to come is a comet; natural disasters such as earthquakes, plagues, pestilence, and giant storms; another antichrist; and World War III. But take heart, this period of mass destruction is followed by a period of peace and enlightenment!

Born in France, Nostradamus was an apothecary (pharmacist) who was also a well-known astrologer and seer. His most famous book is *Les Propheties*, published in 1555. Since his death this book has rarely been out of print. He wrote in prose that's ambiguous and vague yet he has drawn a large following who believe he is extremely accurate.

Vision Power

Nostradamus studied mystery school techniques for prophesying. The technique he used is called *scrying*, which means "to reveal." The technique requires concentration on a shiny object, crystal ball, bowl of water, mirror, etc. until normal vision recedes and other visions are seen. Nostradamus used bowls of water. He surrounded his writing table with candles and waited with quill and ink while he gazed into the bowl.

The Maya also used this technique of scrying using smoky obsidian mirrors. In modern times, this technique has been scientifically studied by near-death and after-death researcher Dr. Raymond Moody at his research institute, the John Dee Memorial Theater of the Mind. At his institute, he has created a room of mirrors that induce an altered state conducive to perceiving paranormally.

Nostradamus had visions, which he translated into words. The problem is that many of the things he saw in the future had no words or even comprehension in his time. He wrote what he saw as best he could describe. This may explain some of the vagueness of his quatrains.

Past Prophecies

These quatrains make a lot of sense when we know the event they refer to. But if you were reading them in advance, they wouldn't give enough information to provide warning or guidance, or be particularly useful.

Here is an example of a quatrain describing an event of World War II. Keep in mind that Nostradamus had no modern words to describe what he was seeing. It's thought to describe land-sea vehicles:

QUATRAIN #1-29

When a fish (traversing) land and water
By force of waves and sand shall be thrust,
Its strange form, both wild and horrific,
Through the sea to the walls, very quickly toward the enemy.

This one is said to describe the twin nuclear bombs of Hiroshima:

QUATRAIN #2-6

Near the harbors, within two cities,
There will be two catastrophes, such as never before seen.
Intense in torment, an unparalleled proportion of human lives ended.
Cries for help from the great God immortal.

And here is one that is thought to describe events after the end of World War II:

QUATRAIN #1-63

The Luster passes, the world shrinks
For a long time peace inhabits the land
They will travel by air, land, sea and water
This is when new wars arise

Many think Nostradamus saw the attack on the World Trade Center on September 11, 2001. Here are the quatrains that support it:

QUATRAIN #1-87

Earthshaking fire from the center of the Earth
Will cause the towers around the New City to shake:
Two great rocks will war for a long time,
And then Arethusa shall color a new river red.

The sky will burn at forty-five degrees latitude
Fire approaches the great new city
Immediately a huge, scattered flame leaps up
When they want to have verification from the Normans [French].

It all makes sense after the fact and you can see how easy it is to read what you want into the prose. Here's one about the antichrist that has been translated to be Saddam Hussein (supporters believe that Mabus spells Sadam (actually, it's Sudam) when held up to a mirror):

Codex Cues

Check out the prophecies of Nostradamus at the following websites: www.sacred-texts. com/nos/index.htm, www. crystalinks.com, and www. godswatcher.com/quatrains2.htm.

> QUATRAIN #2-62

Mabus then quickly at this time will commit mass murder
There will come upon men and beasts, one horrible fate.
Then will all see the coup of vengeance.
There is great taking (of lives), thirst, anger, when the comet will pass.

Here's another translation:

Mabus will soon die, then will come
A horrible undoing of people and animals,
At once one will see vengeance,
One hundred powers, thirst, famine, when the comet will pass.

Nostradamus's End-Time Predictions

It's difficult to follow the quatrains because Nostradamus didn't have his visions in historical order. They're random and difficult to put into context. Essentially, the quatrains state that there will be a third world war. It will involve the Middle East and a nuclear weapon and come after destructive earth changes.

Nostradamus predicts that a comet will come, coinciding with earthquakes and volcanoes. Also mentioned is a conjunction of planets. Some interpret the words to describe a pole shift. In any case, the earth changes bring famines, droughts, and social upheaval. Civilization will be changed; continents will be split apart with waterways. Powerful nations will be weakened. The social upheaval will allow an antichrist to come into power precipitating World War III.

Nostradamus admonishes that people should be prepared spiritually and intellectually, and be more aware of survival abilities. This indicates that people do survive despite the odds. But what does he mean by survival skills? Would you be prepared to survive after a disaster without modern technology and power tools? Maybe we should all be thinking of how we can prepare ourselves to survive in times of crisis. We have more on this in Chapter 20.

You'll be happy to know that after destruction, as with the Maya and Hopi prophecy, a period of great peace, union, and concord occurs.

Biblical End Times

There are many references in the Christian New Testament to the end times. Consider these in the gospels of Matthew, Mark, and Luke:

> You will hear of wars and rumors of wars, but see to it that you are not alarmed. Such things must happen, but the end is still to come. Nation will rise against nation, and kingdom against kingdom. There will be famines and earthquakes in various places. All these are the beginning of birth pains. (Matthew 24:6-8; Mark 13:7-8 NIV)

> Then he said to them: "Nation will rise against nation, and kingdom against kingdom. There will be great earthquakes, famines and pestilences in various places, and fearful events and great signs from heaven." (Luke 21:10-11 NIV)

Book of Revelation

Luke and Matthew set the stage for the Book of Revelation, the last book of the Bible. Revelation is one of the best-known texts on the end times. The book was written by John, thought to be John the Apostle, while in exile as an old man on the island of Patmos. The book is written in symbolic language that is often hard to understand. It lends itself to different interpretations. There's no doubt, however, that Revelation gives an excellent description of the end times.

The Seven Seals

The first chapters in the Book of Revelation are a message from Christ to the seven Churches of Asia Minor. Following the message, John saw seven seals, or scrolls, on which were written the events to take place:

◆ *Seal one:* There appears a white horse whose rider goes forth to conquer with a bow and a crown.

◆ *Seal two:* A red horse is released with a rider who is given permission to take peace from the world so that people will butcher people. He is given a huge sword.

◆ *Seal three:* A black horse is called forth and the rider holds a balance scale. A voice says: "A quart of wheat will cost a day's pay and three quarts of barley will cost a day's pay, but do not damage the olive oil and the wine."

◆ *Seal four:* A pale green horse emerges with death as the rider and Hades is following right behind. They are given authority over a fourth of the earth to kill the populations with famine, disease, and by the wild animals of the earth.

◆ *Seal five:* John sees the souls of those who have died in the name of Christ, waiting for their deaths to be avenged. They call out: "How long Master before the Judgment of Earth?" They are given long white robes and are told that the forces of destruction are about to be turned loose in the world. They may have to endure even greater torment, but if they are faithful they will be redeemed whose names are written in the book of life.

◆ *Seal six:* With the opening of the sixth seal a huge earthquake occurs, the sun becomes black, the full moon becomes red, and the stars in the sky fall to earth. The sky splits apart and every mountain and island is moved from its place. Kings, governors, generals, free people, and slaves all hide from the wrath and judgment of God.

◆ *Seal seven:* The opening of the seventh seal was followed by silence. It's said to be the period of silent preparation for the awful judgments that were to descend on earth with the sounding of the seven trumpets and release of the four winds.

Four Angels

After the scrolls have been opened, John sees four angels with the four winds of heavens that will blow through the world and initiate the events described. The angels are told to hold back the winds until Christ has placed seals on the foreheads of the servants of God. There are 144,000 worthy servants who will not be touched by the destruction to be unleashed on the world. When the seven angels blow the trumpet of judgment, the physical ruin described in the scrolls begins.

The prophecy also says there will be an antichrist who assumes world domination. He has a companion, a false prophet, and together they oversee a one-world government and religion. The antichrist rules the world until the battle of Armageddon. At this point, Jesus returns to earth; the 144,000 worthy servants ascend to heaven; and Christ destroys the armies of the antichrist. The false prophet and the antichrist are thrown into the lake of fire. As these events unfold on earth, war is happening in heaven, too. The angels fight the "dragon" Satan and he, too, is thrown into the lake of fire.

> **Celestial Connection**
>
> Nearly every ancient people has a prophecy relating to the return of the masters in the end times. The Hopi, the Maya, the Egyptians, the keys of Enoch. It's a pervasive cross-culture belief.

Return of Christ

After evil is slain, 1,000 years of peace will follow. The 144,000 are kept safe in the city of god. The streets are made of gold and the walls are made of jasper and apparently sorrow and crying are over. "Death is no more."

What Does It All Mean?

As you can imagine, there have been many times in the past when political unrest, disease epidemics, or war convinced people the end times had arrived. Today people are again wondering if the end times are here. The war in the Middle East is being called the beginning of Armageddon, and everyone has their own favorite applicant for antichrist.

> **Cosmic Caution**
>
> By focusing so much attention on which signs of a prophecy have been fulfilled and looking for confirmation of what is coming, we're in danger of creating the outcome we're looking at. We need to be careful how we think, because our thoughts can create the reality!

The third seal that speaks to the cost of wheat and barley is thought to indicate economic distress. (Maybe we can substitute the word "oil" for "wheat and barley.")

The only link to 2012, however, is the description of the sun turning black, the moon turning red, the stars falling from the sky, and the mountains and islands changing position. You probably recognize this as what can happen with a pole reversal. Actually it sounds extreme enough to describe a pole shift, where the crust of the planet actually moves. (See

Chapter 10 for a refresher on this.) As with Nostradamus and Edgar Cayce, discussed next, it's not the date of 2012 that the predictions relate to, but the earth changes people expect might happen in 2012.

Edgar Cayce: The Sleeping Prophet

Edgar Cayce (1877–1945) has been heralded as one of the greatest prophets of all time. He gave over 14,000 readings in his career, focusing on health, spirituality, and the origin and destiny of man. He also had a considerable amount to say about the end times.

Born in a small Kentucky town, Cayce came into his talent when he was 21. Threatened with throat paralysis, he went into a spontaneous trance, giving himself a health reading. His prescription and treatment restored his voice. In addition to the 14,000 personal consults, 300 books have been written on the content of the readings.

Cayce used a hypnotic trance to perform his readings. He simply lay down, went through a hypnotic exercise, and went to sleep. His super-conscious mind provided the answers. Cayce himself never remembered the content, earning himself the title of Sleeping Prophet. In fact, as a solid Methodist he had serious conflict with some of the content of the readings he gave. However, because the readings provided people with such help, he continued to provide them.

Past Prophecy

Cayce correctly predicted the start and end of both the first and second world wars. He predicted the deaths of two presidents in office, the civil rights movement, and the Depression. He dated the sphinx at 10,500 years old, a date that has since been confirmed. In 1935, he spoke of the coming holocaust in Germany. His track record is significantly better than most psychics, which is why he has such a long-standing following. His readings are specific and leave little ambiguity as to their meaning.

Cayce's End-Time Predictions

Edgar Cayce's prophecies of the end times are often used to support 2012 scenarios. However, he never gave 2012 as an end-time date. He predicted the end times would happen within a generation of his prediction, which places it between 1958 and 1998. So far, the end-time scenario has not happened in the time-frame given. Although the basic prophecy fits, the only relationship to the timing and 2012 is the possibility of a pole shift. And the pole shift is not a definite for 2012 (or anytime in the next few hundred years).

Here are some highlights of Cayce's end-time prophecies:

◆ The Atlantic and Pacific coasts of America will be altered; New York City, San Francisco, and Los Angeles will disappear.

◆ Russia will become the spiritual hope of the world.

◆ Intense earthquakes will destroy California and the Baja Peninsula will disappear.

◆ The Pacific Ocean will meet Arizona and Nebraska.

◆ Mount Etna in Sicily will erupt, signaling the start of real changes.

◆ The Great Lakes will drain into the Gulf of Mexico through the Mississippi River. The Niagara River may run dry.

◆ Japan will go under the sea.

◆ There will be a pole shift and the artic caps will melt, starting severe flooding.

◆ New lands will rise out of the oceans, off the Bimini Islands and Bahamas. The lost lands of Atlantis and others will rise.

You can read about the predictions in more detail at www.crystalinks.com/caycearthchanges.html, or read one of the many books from Edgar Cayce's Association for Research and Enlightenment.

Codex Cues _____

Many prophecies do not have dates associated with them because it is believed that free will can change the future. A prophecy is only a glimpse of a probability. Situations can change. We may want to remember this and work now to avoid predictions of earth changes to come. How? By changing our thoughts, beliefs, and behaviors.

The Hindu Kali Yuga

The Hindu tradition has a close similarity to the Maya and the Mayan timeline. Like the Maya and the Hopi, Hindus believe in four world ages that correspond to stages in human development. The Hindu names of the ages are the Satya Yuga, the Treta Yuga, the Dvapara Yuga, and the Kali Yuga. The present cycle is the Kali Yuga, which began at midnight on January 23, 3102 B.C.E. (Gregorian calendar), only 12 years difference from the Maya's Long Count calendar. Lord Krishna predicted that approximately 5,000 years into the Kali Yuga a golden age will start and will last for 10,000 years.

Prior to the coming of the 10,000 years of light would be a time called the dark ages when spirituality declines. During this time, there would be corrupt rulers, famine, and disease with earth calamities and destruction. Much like we have been hearing.

So 5,000 plus 3102 B.C.E. equals 1898 C.E. Well, just 120 years off. Not so much in the scheme of things. Certainly there are enough similarities to take note, but not enough to claim a specific 2012 connection. However, with the similarities of starting dates, let's not rule it out completely, either!

Celestial Connection

Another ancient system that may point to 2012 is the Chinese book of the I Ching (Book of Changes). It's one of the oldest Chinese texts and is an oracle used through the ages. It's based on a formula that is unknown in present times. Before his death in 2000, New Age theorist Terrence McKenna believed he found the formula. His work in the 1970s involved the use of fractal mathematics, which led to a formula he called "time wave zero." Using this approach with the I Ching, he independently came to the date 2012 as the end of the world. You can read about his theories at www.alternativeculture.com.

The Least You Need to Know

- The Hopi prophecy has nine signs of its completion. We are well through eight of them.

- The Nostradamus quatrains predict earthquakes, famine, war, and other signs of destruction during the end times.

- Biblical end times also share the same descriptions of destructive events as did the Mayan and other prophecies.

- Edgar Cayce predicted earth changes, melting ice caps, war, famine, and disease in the end times. His prediction time frame was the end of the twentieth century.

- In Hindu tradition, there are four ages; the present age is the fourth age of the Kali Yuga. It began in 3102 B.C.E. The end-time predictions and end-time dates are similar to the Mayan prophecy.

Chapter 12

New Age Viewpoints

In This Chapter

◆ New Age methods for divination

◆ General messages about 2012

◆ Specific predictions from channels and intuitives

◆ New technology prophets

If the last few chapters have left you feeling hopeless and overwhelmed, this chapter is for you. The prophets of the past were pretty well geared toward the doom-and-gloom aspect of the end times. Yes, they acknowledge that after destruction comes a golden era of peace and harmony, but their main focus was on the difficulties along the way.

Present-day prophets, however, focus on the spiritual opportunity of the end times. Rather than being helpless victims of the mistakes of the past, we are encouraged to be empowered creators of the future. The end times are viewed as a push toward evolutionary development. According to biologist and shaman Alberto Villoldo, there is a "great slumber across the land," which he refers to as a "cultural trance."

In Chapter 13, we'll take a more skeptical look at the New Age prophets, but first, let's see how present-day prediction works and what the general message is. In this chapter, you'll hear views from some of the main New Age speakers.

Modern Methods of Prediction

Prediction today is seen as an extension of normal abilities. Just as we all have musical abilities or mathematical abilities, so do we all have the ability to see into different time realms. As with math and music, some people are better at it than others.

Prediction today is also influenced by quantum physics. Science doesn't see time the same way it used to. Time in science is no longer linear but can fold back on itself, creating the possibility of time travel. Using modern technology to predict the future is more common than we know. Weather models not withstanding, technology prediction can be pretty accurate, as you'll soon see.

Psychics

Psychics are people who receive information that cannot be obtained through everyday intellectual pursuit. They may have visions (clairvoyance), hear voices (clairaudience), or simply "know" something (gnosis). Many of them need to shift into a state of heightened awareness, often called a trance, to receive information. Biblical prophets were often said to "be struck down" or "fall into trance" before hearing the voice of God. This is also true today, although many psychics remain in normal everyday awareness when they interact with other realms.

Channelers

Channelers "channel" communications from other sources of intelligence and are separate from the information they pass on. They're like radios: they tune in and let the program speak through them. Sometimes they are aware of what they are saying; this is a conscious channel. Sometimes they remember nothing. Edgar Cayce (see Chapter 11) is an example of a trance channel who had no conscious involvement in the information given.

In most cases, channels do not have any personal input into the information they give. The downfall of channeling is the desire the channel may have to interpret the information coming through. Interpretation lends to the bias of the person and so may decrease the spiritual accuracy.

In channeling, the source of the information is unclear. Sometimes people claim it's the voice of god, angels, or spiritual guides. Others claim it's the higher self, people who are dead or ascended masters, alien intelligence, or even multidimensional beings. In all cases, the source is considered to be from a realm with greater spiritual access.

Intuitives

This type of information is an example of gnosis, or simply "knowing" something. Using extensions of the ordinary senses, intuitives sense and follow energetic information the way a bloodhound follows a scent. When they connect with a piece of information, they may realize it through a combination of images, words, and an internal sense of knowing. It forces them to extend themselves and expand their consciousness. This technique is very organic and lends itself well to people who are feelers rather than thinkers. The downside of this technique is that it also lends itself to the force of imagination and being manipulated by the bias of the intuitive.

Remote Viewing (RV) Technique

Another method for using visions to see into events of the past, present, or future is *remote viewing (RV)*. This technique is very similar to the way the ancient Maya described traveling through the portals and among the stars to find astronomical information. It's a technique that can be taught to anyone, although some people are better at it than others. There are two general formats, one based on the idea that we are living in a holographic universe, the other that our awareness can travel outside of our body. In the holographic model, as with your DNA, all the information in the whole exists in each part. Inside of yourself is all the information about everything in the universe. Accessing it is a technique. In the other model, it's believed people have the ability to project their awareness outside of themselves and travel to different places, times, and events.

def•i•ni•tion

Remote viewing (RV) is a form of extrasensory perception that allows a person to visualize information from a remote, distant, and hidden target. This is a valued method of obtaining secret information by some governments and can be extremely accurate.

Whatever model you use, learning remote viewing allows people to extend their senses to another place and time by going deep inside themselves. They have the experience of viewing people, actions, and places from above and watching events unfold. There is room for error with remote viewing, and yet the Pentagon had a huge remote viewing spy program overseen by Colonel John Alexander; it must have had some level of accuracy! (We discuss remote viewing in more detail later in the chapter.)

Technology Predictions

Modern methods of prediction also use computer technology. This approach looks to find patterns or codes coming from the subconscious mind, or the *collective unconscious*, and projected into society. This technology is being used on many fronts: for marketing, stock market analysis, and military information. Two projects underway right now are the Web Bot project and the Princeton Global Consciousness Project. Both rely on patterns found in randomly generated events. We'll discuss both projects in more detail later in this chapter.

The Bible Code, discussed later in this chapter, is another predictive method relying on computers. Computers search the pages of the Bible to find word and letter patterns that form identifiable relationships to events. The Bible Code was able to accurately identify both the date and event of Princess Diana's death and the World Trade Center terrorist attack. Both, of course, were looked for after the fact. The truth is we don't know what to look for until after it's happened. World War III has also been predicted; we'll have to see how accurate it turns out to be.

def•i•ni•tion

Carl Jung coined the phrase the **collective unconscious**. It is the part of the psyche that holds and transmits the common psychology everyone shares. The unconscious mind is able to access all human memory, even humanity's future. Jung believed the unconscious mind emits universal symbols and processes we all understand.

2012: The General Message

The general New Age message for the end times is empowerment. The end times are a time of accelerated learning. Time is accelerating and so are human opportunities and abilities. Humans are infinitely powerful when we use an activated intent. Our thoughts and feelings create the world we live in. In these times, we're being taught to take responsibility for what we have created in the past and to become fully realized spiritual beings as we continue to create the future.

The bottom line is that the human body/mind is evolving. Some say we are evolving into multidimensional beings, others that our DNA is being activated to increase our spiritual abilities. If this is exciting to you, you'll be happy to know that human development, not punishment, is the purpose of the end times. In the words of José Argüelles, "Everything that we know, everything that we are, is about to undergo a substantial and radical alteration."

José Argüelles

José Argüelles is arguably the person who put the Mayan end date on the map. He is a university professor who became famous in the 1980s for establishing the Harmonic Convergence. Remember the Harmonic Convergence? Argüelles claimed it would open the door to new energies of light that represented the end of the nine Mayan underworlds. It was supposed to herald a global awakening of love and unity through divine transformation.

Harmonic Convergence

Argüelles picked the date for the Harmonic Convergence based on his studies into the Mayan calendars. He claimed it ended 22 Calendar Round cycles of 52 years each. He then divided the 22 cycles into 13 heaven cycles and 9 hell cycles. He claimed the heaven cycles began in 843 C.E. and ended in 1519 C.E. Then the nine hell cycles began, ending 468 years later in 1987 at the Harmonic Convergence.

In addition to beginning a new age of peace and unity, the harmonic convergence marked the 25-year countdown to the end of the Mayan calendar in 2012. The end of the calendar to Argüelles meant the end of the evils of the modern world.

Celestial Connection
The Harmonic Convergence was a worldwide peace initiative that took place on August 16 and 17, 1987. Conceived by José Argüelles, it signified the end of the nine cycles of the underworld and heralded a 25-year period of spiritual growth leading to the end of the current age in 2012. Massive numbers of people gathered at sacred sites all over the planet awakening the energy grid.

Argüelles claimed to have based his dates and theories on Mayan cosmology, but the Maya disagree. It turns out they were right, Argüelles's work does diverge significantly from Mayan cosmology. Argüelles now claims to have channeled his information from Pacal Votan, our friend from Chapters 3 and 7. We'll talk more about this in Chapter 13.

Argüelles's Philosophy

José Argüelles believes that humans lost connection to natural cycles when we switched from the lunar-based calendars to the Gregorian solar calendar. We became immersed in an artificial perception of time that moved us away from the natural order of the universe. 2012 is meant to bring us back into alignment with natural time.

Argüelles proposes that losing connection to the cyclic nature of time closed down the creative, intuitive, powerful part of who we are. Using the Gregorian calendar locked people into mechanical rhythms and habitual thinking, making us slaves to time. To counteract the unnatural state of affairs, Argüelles designed the Dreamspell calendar. Using the calendar puts people back into a 13-moon/28-day rhythm. He claims that using his system will attune people to natural time, preparing them for 2012.

What Happens in 2012?

According to Argüelles, 2012 is a marker, a wake-up call in our DNA. The climax of this cycle will occur during "the seven last moons of the thirteen baktuns" or June through December 2012. If you want to avoid the difficulties of the time approaching 2012, Argüelles suggests you switch to his lunar-based calendar now, allowing your body to align with natural cycles.

He and his wife Lloydine founded the Planet Art Network in 1983 as a worldwide peace organization. It focuses on promoting the worldwide adoption of the Dreamspell 13-moon/28-day calendar. The calendar book *The Dreamspell Calendar of Planetary Service 1995* (Dreamspell, 1995) by José and Lloydine Argüelles can be obtained at amazon.com.

Gordon Michael Scallion

Gordon Michael Scallion became famous in the 1980s. An intuitive, Scallion calls himself a futurist. In 1979, he experienced a number of out-of-body visions that showed him what the world would look like after the turn of the century. He spent the next three years drawing a map of the new earth and writing about how to survive the earth changes that were coming. He published his map along with a book, *Earthforce* (Lotus Press, 1989). He travels internationally, giving lectures on earth changes to this day. You can obtain his map and current books at www.matrixinstitute.com/store.

Warning Signs

Scallion saw a number of warning signs leading up to the earth changes. He was very clear that nothing he saw was written in stone. Human intention could change the outcome at any time. What he saw was the outcome if we stayed on the path we were on at that moment. He did believe, however, that we would see World War III. Scallion included with his map a list of warning signs. If these signs happened, people would know the earth changes were underway and they should find a safe place to live as shown in his maps. Here is a list of his signs:

- Erratic global weather patterns
- Earthquakes that come from deep within the earth
- Increase in frequency and magnitude of earthquakes
- Melting of the poles
- Increase in wind velocity
- Increase in tornado frequency
- Humming sounds coming from beneath the earth

Many of these warning signs have come to pass, including the humming sound from beneath the earth. This hum has been heard in Britain since 1977 and in New Mexico since the early 1990s. We assess Scallion's predictions further in Chapter 13.

Scallion's Predictions for 2012

Scallion believes that energy is pulsing faster and faster until we hit the year 2012. At that time, we will have stabilized the pulse and will be living at a higher frequency. This will bring an awakening that allows people to open their minds to ideas and concepts they would have thought crazy in years before. He calls the post-2012 age the "Intuitive Age."

Barbara Marciniak

Barbara Marciniak is a channel who receives information from a group calling themselves the Pleiadians. She has been giving channeling sessions on all aspects of human consciousness since the 1980s.

According to Marciniak, the Pleiadians are focused on the time period from 1987 to 2012 as a time of enormous change for people and society. It is a unique opportunity for spiritual growth. She says the choices we make now will determine the future evolution of the planet.

Cause of Change

The Pleiadians support the end of the Mayan calendar as an end of an era. They also agree with Carl Johan Calleman that as we approach 2012, time is accelerating. Marciniak channels that the acceleration is due to the fact that the solar system is passing through high-energy particle zones in space. The high-energy particles are bombarding us and affecting us on a subatomic level.

Although this sounds a lot like the photon belt discussed in earlier chapters, to our knowledge, the Pleiadians have not called this zone the photon belt. It's possible they are referring to the same high-energy gamma waves we discussed in Chapter 10 that were researched by Russian scientists. So what happens to us when we go through this energy wave?

Cellular Frequency

As high-energy waves hit your body, they create an increase in cellular frequency. Let's explain this a little: all the cells inside your body are vibrating. The rate of vibration is your cellular frequency. Everything that exists has a frequency. You may wonder if it matters what speed you vibrate at. If everything that is getting hit with high-energy waves starts to vibrate faster, the result is acceleration. Even your thoughts and actions become accelerated. According to the Pleiadians, the rate of cause and effect is also accelerating.

What exactly does it mean to increase the rate of cause and effect? Every thought you have has an effect. This is easy to see in some cases, like you think about something scary and your heartbeat increases while your palms get sweaty. Pretty clearly cause and effect. It's harder to see in other cases. Suppose you were very critical of someone, judging them for a decision they made that you didn't approve of. Years later you might find yourself in a similar situation to learn compassion and nonjudgment. It might be harder in this example for you to see the cause and effect of your situation, but your thoughts created the experience you needed to learn. Essentially, as everything speeds up, how your thoughts create your reality becomes more and more obvious.

According to Marciniak in an interview published in *Inner Connections Network*, "In the past, what would have taken months or years for a cause, like a good or evil deed, to have its effect, will begin to happen within days, hours, and minutes. It will become blatantly obvious to all of us that we are the creators of our reality, and by changing our thinking, we can change ourselves and our circumstances. This is self-empowerment." You can read more about Marciniak's channeled information in her book, *Path to Empowerment: New Pleiadian Wisdom for a World in Chaos* (New World Library, 2004).

What the Pleiadians Say About 2012

In 2012, humans will be reconnected to the galactic center. To the Pleiadians, this means something different than to the Mayan researchers. To the Pleiadians, it means humans get to take our place outside of our solar system as part of a larger picture. We are in fact multidimensional beings and as our DNA is activated, we will be able to use the energy structures of our body as a vehicle to travel dimensionally.

> ### Celestial Connection
>
> Energy structures in the body have been written about by all cultures. They consist of an aura, the light structures with the aura, and the chakras. The aura is the electromagnetic/ spiritual energy field around your body. It has seven discernable layers. The light structures are geometries within the aura that manage the flow of energy, especially higher levels of energy. The chakras are vortexes that translate spiritual energy into physical energy and vice versa.

The Pleiadians say that we not only have the ability to create our lives, we have a duty to do so as well. Accepting responsibility for the conditions of our lives and changing our negative traits is our main task during the period before we are reconnected to the galactic center in 2012. Marciniak says in the *Inner Connections Network* interview that "At the solstice of 2012, the end of the Mayan Calendar, we will have moved into a new era, and it is critical that we properly prepare for this in order to maximize our gain in consciousness and realization of ourselves as multidimensional beings."

Remote Viewing in Action

Remote viewing (RV) has been used by the United States government as a means for gathering secret information. Remote viewers gather information on targets that are hidden from the physical perception of the RV "viewer." The term was introduced in 1974 by physicists Russell Targ and Harold Puthoff. Harold Puthoff worked in the National Security Agency on its top-secret remote viewing project. In 1972, he joined Russell Targ at the Stanford Research Institute to investigate remote viewing in a public forum.

The United States government began researching the use of extrasensory perception in intelligence work after the Second World War. The government became interested upon learning that both China and Russia had such programs. Government programs started in the 1970s have since become private-sector programs.

Celestial Connection

Dannion Brinkley was a CIA operative who had a near-death experience in 1975. After being struck by lightning, he was pronounced dead on arrival at the hospital, only to wake up 28 minutes later in the morgue. While dead, Brinkley saw future events, some related to 2012, including a "return of the energy system that existed here a long time ago," a pole reversal, and the opportunity for humanity to raise its consciousness. Says Brinkley: "You are a great, powerful, and mighty spiritual being with dignity, direction, and purpose." Finding this out may be the purpose of 2012. For more, check out his website at www.dannion.com or read his book, *Saved by the Light* (Harper Torch, 1995).

Protocol

The target is given to the viewer in a sealed envelope as a set of coordinates. The project manager does not know what's in the envelope or what the target is. The viewer, without opening the envelope, zeros in on the target. He or she then gives details as to what is physically present at the target site. Questions can be asked of the viewer as they observe. Neither distance nor time is an obstacle to the viewer's perceptions.

2012 Results

Edward Dames was in charge of a U.S. Defense Intelligence Agency team of remote viewers. He then began his own remote viewing company, Psi Tech, and is now executive director of the Matrix Intelligence Agency. He teaches his own method of remote viewing to others and is considered to be one of the best viewers.

Dames's remote viewers are unable to see past 2012. They're not suggesting the world will end, but that global change is so large and unrecognizable that seeing beyond it is too confusing. On *Art Bell's Coast to Coast* radio show on December 3, 2000, Dames claimed that the best answer his team could find is that time itself changes after 2012. "Something happened on earth, in the past, that affects the entire earth in the future, all at once, and when you look around everything is different. You appear to be somewhere else, and in fact you have leapt onto a different trajectory, a different time, a parallel time if you will."

Dames is not alone in seeing the end of the Mayan calendar as the end of a way of seeing time. If time is a dimension, we may be about to enter a new dimension.

Codex Cues _____

To assess the accuracy of remote viewing, consider this report by near-death researcher Dr. Kenneth Ring. A woman had an out-of-body experience during surgery where she found herself floating above the hospital. While there she noticed a red shoe on the hospital roof. When the surgery was over, she recounted her experience to the doctors. The shoe was later retrieved by maintenance personnel.

Tibetan Monks and Remote Viewing

The Tibetan monks also use remote viewing although they don't use that term. Tibetan monasteries have engaged in remote viewing for thousands of years, and the technique is part of their spiritual practice. According to *India Daily* (www.indiadaily. com), Tibetan monks mention that during 2012 world politics will be in turmoil and very serious conflict will begin but that "extraterrestrials" will intervene. The monks also mention that beyond 2012 our current civilization will understand that the final frontier of science and technology is in the area of spirituality and not material physics and chemistry. People will learn the essence of spirituality, the relationship between the body and the soul, reincarnation, and the fact we are connected with each other and all part of "God."

Bible Code: Encoded Messages

The Bible Code was discovered by Dr. Eli Rips, a famous Israeli mathematician. He discovered that within the five books of the Hebrew Bible, known as the Torah, are encoded messages. His work was popularized by investigative reporter Michael Drosnin, who wrote the book *The Bible Code*, published in 1997.

The process is simple. The letters of passages of the Torah are placed at equal intervals formatted to fit inside boxes like a graph paper. High-powered computers look for sequences with a program called skip sequencing. It skips one, two, and then three letters, locking onto the specific spacing that provides meaningful words. Of course, it doesn't come and say things like, On November 22, 1963, in Dallas, Texas, John F. Kennedy will be assassinated by a sniper named Oswald. What it actually does do is show individual words or phrases such as: "John F. Kennedy," "Oswald," "name of the assassin who will assassinate," "Dallas," "marksman," "sniper," "he will strike in the head, death." The words are not in sequence or along the same line. Remember the hidden word puzzles from childhood? Just like that, the names and phrases may be forward, backward, or diagonal. They are usually all three.

Predictions

The Bible Code is claimed to be very accurate, with some rather significant exceptions. Here's a list of some of the hits:

◆ Assassinations of Yitzhak Rabin, Anwar Sadat, John and Robert Kennedy, along with dates and names of killers

◆ Hiroshima

◆ Great Depression

◆ Apollo moon mission

◆ The Persian Gulf War

◆ World War II and Hitler

◆ Napoleon

◆ Marconi discovering radio waves

◆ "Twin Towers," "Terrorist Atta," "Egyptian Man"

And the list goes on and on. What did the Bible Code get wrong? "Bush," "Arafat," "Sharon," "End of Days," "World War," and "2006." However, many feel these words were indicating that in 2006 a third world war would begin in the Middle East.

Was the Code wrong or did free will change the timeline? And most importantly with all this, how does free will impact anything? The Bible Code makes these difficult questions. The Bible was written approximately 2,000 years ago and presumably was coded for the future (and perhaps past) at that time. So how can free will now change what was coded then? It seems possible only if the present has the power to change the past. Or are all possibilities present in the code and we pull out and find only the one that is most probable at the time we look for it?

Bible Code and 2012

So what does it actually say about 2012? It claims a comet will hit the earth and annihilate it. Or the comet will be intercepted and "it will be crumbled." It also says "I will tear it (the comet) to pieces." Is the "I" in the passage a mistake, not really part of the phrase, or is there a personality hidden behind the messages? Who might we be talking to?

The Web Bot Project

This project has been underway since the late 1990s. The person who originated it prefers to remain anonymous and just calls himself "Cliff." It relies on a system of "spiders" that "crawl" the Internet, much like a search engine, looking for particular kinds of words. According to Cliff, the spiders "target discussion groups, translation sites, and places where regular people post a lot of text. No, we don't do e-mail scanning: that's what we have the government for."

This technology is used by many governments in watching e-mail traffic for terrorist activity. We can assume the keywords are much different!

> **Codex Cues** _____
>
> For updates on the Web Bot project and predictions, check out www.halfpasthuman.com and www.urbansurvival.com.

How Does It Work?

Whenever the spider finds a keyword, it takes a small 2,048-byte snip of the surrounding text and sends it to a central collection point. Over a period of time the "chatter points" concentrate, revealing a spike in intensity. Like the Bible Code, the technology doesn't come out with direct messages. It gives words or phrases that reflect people's thought processes. Web Bot technology appears to tap into preconscious awareness, or the collective unconscious. It finds patterns before events occur and presumably before people are talking about them.

So what has Web Bot predicted?

◆ The crash of American Airlines flight 587

◆ Elements of the DC sniper case

◆ The space shuttle Columbia disaster

Technology Problems

The main problem with the technology at this point is the amount of "chatter" unrelated to the "preconscious" mind. For example, the crash of American Airlines flight 587 was predicted ahead of time, but as a terrorist event. Remember, eyewitnesses believed they saw a land-launched rocket. This belief was projected into the Web Bot information. Who knows, maybe they did see a rocket. In any case, what they believed was as real as what actually happened and was picked up ahead of the event—another indication that we need to watch what we focus our minds on. We could collectively be creating a 2012 disaster!

Web Bot and 2012

When the Mayan calendar end date is used as a keyword, there is only one Web Bot prediction. It predicts a pole shift in 2012. Since this is a main theme people are discussing, you may wonder what use it has. The interesting fact is that the spikes arrive before the events, not after.

Princeton Global Consciousness Project (GCP)

Another initiative watching events in the collective unconscious is the Princeton Global Consciousness Project. The project is based on a random generator. Random generators are devices like a lottery number generator. It throws balls into the air, then drops them where they randomly fall into different chutes. Although the technology used by the GCP is much more advanced, you get the idea. The project maintains 65 generating sites around the world.

The theory is that events that have significant human impact may affect the randomness of the data. In fact, what the project has demonstrated is that just seconds before a significant event that impacts large numbers of people, the generators become less random.

You might wonder why this matters, but in fact it does. The Global Consciousness Project can detect "disturbances in the force" prior to the disturbance. It has been described as the bow wave of a boat. The energy of an event precedes it, disturbing the "time" field even before the event occurs. Results of these studies indicate that mind and matter are interactive in fundamental ways.

Codex Cues

You can watch events emerge on www.boundaryinstitute. org/randomness.htm and www.boundaryinstitute.org/ articles/timereversed.pdf.

Give yourself a minute to feel this. Have you ever felt someone coming before they arrive? Or known the phone was going to ring, or who was calling? Maybe you felt the bow wave of the event.

Dean Radin, from the Institute of Noetic Sciences, writes that in laboratory situations, people react to an event six seconds *before* it takes place. Does it mean we all perceive six seconds into the future? Or that highly charged events send shock waves into the past that we perceive in the future? Get your head around that!

The Least You Need to Know

◆ New Age information accepts a time of global disruption as the old ways crumble but focuses on the spiritual renaissance it will bring.

◆ Earth changes and political and social unrest are part of the disruption to come. This is a rectification period to bring us back into natural balance.

◆ Channeled information suggests that you can expect changes at the physical, emotional, and spiritual levels as we approach 2012.

◆ Channels and intuitives see the future as a time of mass empowerment.

◆ Modern technology is providing new ways of viewing time and predictions.

Chapter 13

A Healthy Dose of Skepticism

In This Chapter

- ◆ Controversy around the findings of Argüelles, Jenkins, and Calleman
- ◆ Skeptics weigh in on the predictions
- ◆ Don't believe everything you read
- ◆ Doomsday predictions that didn't come true
- ◆ Beware the self-fulfilling prophecy!

As you can imagine, both skepticism and fanaticism abound regarding 2012. Healthy skepticism enters a debate with an open mind but maintains critical thinking: asking questions and not stopping at easy answers. Unhealthy skepticism begins the debate by already believing it knows the answer. It doesn't ask questions and doesn't listen to evidence. We can say the same thing about healthy belief and unhealthy belief, or fanaticism. Unhealthy skepticism and unhealthy belief are equally dangerous.

In this chapter, we'll look at controversy surrounding the Mayan theories and overall skepticism surrounding the 2012 predictions. We'll start with the Mayan theories. The three key researchers are José Argüelles, John Major Jenkins, and Carl Johan Calleman—all of whom you've met in earlier chapters.

You may already have noticed the first problem. There are no Mayan Elders. One of the major criticisms of the "Mayan" theories is the lack of native Mayan input. Criticism of the rest of the 2012 predictions tends to be based on the reliability of the "prophet," his or her personal credibility, and the probability of the prediction.

Critique of Argüelles

José Argüelles has been a proponent in the Mayan calendar revival since the 1980s. He started researching in the 1950s, formulating his own theories about Mayan timekeeping. He believes that "time is the frequency of synchronization." He promoted the Harmonic Convergence in 1987 as an energy shift in the 25-year countdown to the end of the Long Count calendar. He also created his own calendar, the Dreamspell calendar, meant to harmonize the users to natural cycles by using a 28-day, 13-month calendar. (See Chapter 12 for a review.)

Argüelles's work is unsupported by Mayan scholarship. Argüelles is accused of co-opting ancient traditions and reframing them in modern New Age terminology. In addition, Argüelles's Dreamspell calendar doesn't properly coordinate with the length of the year and month.

Here's the problem: the Dreamspell calendar claims to synchronize with the Calendar round. If you remember from Chapters 5 and 6, the Calendar round synchronizes the Tzolk'in and Haab calendars. You may remember that the Haab does not adjust for leap year. This means the Haab calendar deviates from the Gregorian calendar by one day every four years. Every four years, the Haab calendar's New Year happens on a different Gregorian date. However, the Dreamspell calendar is fixed to July 26 as the Mayan New Year. This means two things: Dreamspell is not synchronized to the Mayan Calendar round and it doesn't reflect the true cycles of nature. In addition, the 28-day month of his calendar doesn't reflect the cycle of the moon. The lunar cycle is 29.5 days.

Channeling Pacal Votan

Argüelles originally published his work claiming it was based on Mayan scholarship. Under criticism, he admitted that Mayan scholarship played an important role but direct inspiration was the major component. He says he channels an ancient Mayan, Pacal Votan (see Chapters 3 and 7), and claims to be the "heir of his legacy and instrument of his prophecy." He also states that the Dreamspell calendar is "correct and biologically accurate." Argüelles refers to himself as the reincarnation of Pacal Votan.

Mayan Support

Mayan Elders today don't support Argüelles or the Dreamspell calendar. Some, such as Carlos Barrios, actively speak out against him. Argüelles's predictions about the significance of and expected social changes after the Harmonic Convergence are largely thought to have been wrong. However, Argüelles does have a large following of non-Mayan supporters who point out many social changes in the years since the Harmonic Convergence. The collapse of the Berlin Wall in 1989 is one example. These supporters claim that nine Mayan Elders have recognized Argüelles as the "Closer of the Cycle" awarding him a staff in honor of his efforts to "wake up humanity to the meaning of 2012."

Critique of Jenkins

John Major Jenkins is author of the theory that the Maya were aware of the precession of the Equinox, a time span of almost 26,000 years; that the ages of the creation story are each one fifth of the precession cycle; and that the Long Count calendar is one age within the precession. In addition, he correlates the end date of the Long Count to the alignment of December 21, 2012, with the solar system crossing the galactic equator and eclipsing the center of the galaxy.

Celestial Connection
Jenkins is extremely well researched. He draws from the research of notable Mayan authorities such as Barbara Tedlock, Anthony Aveni, Michael Coe, Gordon Brotherston, and Linda and David Schele. In addition, he applies fresh insight into the steles, murals, and astroarcheology of the Izapa site where the Long Count calendar was established. Combining archeology, mythology, and astronomy, he has developed a theory whose scope is truly stunning.

Criticism of Jenkins focuses on the following topics.

Precession of the Equinox

Many people don't think the Maya were aware of the precession cycle and believe Jenkins overstates their astronomical ability. Jenkins supplies evidence from the University of Essex researcher Gordon Brotherston, who found the connection between the Mesoamerican sunstone and the precession cycle. Jenkins provides extensive evidence in his book *Maya Cosmogenesis 2012* (see Resources appendix).

Celestial Anchor

Some people doubt that the end date of the Long Count was tied to a celestial event. The Mayan Long Count was established in about 200 B.C.E. The Day Keepers counted backward to a start date of August 11, 3114 B.C.E., and forward to an end date of December 21, 2012 C.E. Two things are true: the 5,126-year time span of the calendar was chosen for a reason; and the calendar was either fixed to the start date or to the end date.

Jenkins demonstrates a celestial anchor by relating the time span of the Long Count to a "creation age" which is one fifth of the precession cycle. He also claims the Mayans fixed the cycle to the end date. He chose the end date because the Mayans typically name cycles for the end of the cycle, not the beginning of it. From that premise, Jenkins looked to the stars to see what would be happening at the end date of the Long Count. He found the alignment with the galactic center. Critics feel this was contrived and that the start of the calendar should be the fixed date, not the end.

Galactic Center

Some claim the Maya did not understand the location of the galactic center. Jenkins counters with the many accurate references of the Maya to both the function and location of the galactic center in mythology and astronomical glyphs. He points out that the features of the galactic center are visible to the naked eye.

Galactic Alignment

The most serious criticism of Jenkins's work is his claim that the 2012 solstice sun is in exact alignment with the galactic center. Jenkins counters by declaring his position: the entire period from 1994 to 2030 is the "galactic zone." Throughout this period, the solar system will be in relationship to the center of the galaxy. Every solstice sun during this 36-year time zone will have relationship to the galactic center. However, December 21, 2012, occurs in the center of this time zone and coincides with the end of the Long Count calendar. He is not claiming an exact alignment, although his followers certainly do.

Critique of Calleman

Carl Johan Calleman began to study the Mayan calendars in 1979 after a trip to Guatemala. With a biology background, he had a unique insight into what the Mayan time delineations might refer to.

Calleman's theory was developed after seeing the dates on the Coba stele. The stele marks dates going back billions of years. Looking at the progression of dates, he theorizes that the 16.4-billion-year evolutionary history of the planet was known to the Maya, directly written on the stele, and coded into the Kukulkan pyramid. A rendition of his diagram of the evolutionary pyramid can be seen in Chapter 8. His theory is intricate, detailed, and compelling. It identifies an end date of October 28, 2011; an unprecedented application of sevven days and six nights of the underworld to the Long Count calendar; and a belief in time acceleration. His main focus is on the evolution of spiritual consciousness.

There are many criticisms of Calleman's work. First, his relating the seven days and six nights of the underworld to the Long Count calendar is unsupported by mythological or archeological evidence. He is accused of rejecting established facts in favor of his own inspiration. He chooses the end date of October 2011 based on an adjustment he believes was made by Mayan Day Keepers in Palenque. The supposed Palenque change was made 1,000 years after the start of the Long Count and consisted of an adjustment of 420 days. Not everyone agrees this is correct. Calleman believes that as the date gets closer, the frequency of the time shift will draw people to his conclusion.

Objections to Calleman's work are reminiscent of those leveled at Argüelles. In short, the history of discovering the Maya has been a dedicated collaboration between painstaking research and inspiration. Every leap of inspiration is backed with evidence. The criticism aimed at Calleman and Argüelles is that their inspirations are not supported with evidence. Given the archeological correlations Calleman demonstrates, this criticism seems overstated.

Codex Cues

Major breakthroughs in all fields of study are usually precipitated with leaps of inspiration that break all the rules. Einstein's theory of relativity is an excellent example. What's important is for all parties to continue debate with an open and flexible mind.

Finding Common Ground

In the end, the differences between these three luminaries are far less than their similarities. When we're looking at spans of time as long as 26,000 years or the evolutionary ages of the planet, trying to nail a major shift to a single day may be simplistic. Change may be more gradual and time zones more realistic than single one-day changeovers. Looking at the differences instead of similarities may be likened to not seeing the forest through the trees.

Similarities

If we look at the similarities of the three, we see something more encouraging. Each has been inspired by the mathematics and astronomy of the Mayans. Each offers a unique and valuable insight into the puzzle. They are all teachers of change, promoting new ways of seeing the world. They all inspire people to find higher and better parts of themselves. In essence, they're all part of the changing paradigm.

Elder Input

The Mayan Elders do not seem to solidly support any one theory. Instead, they express unhappiness with people usurping Mayan knowledge, interpreting it from a nontraditional perspective, and speaking for the Mayan Elders. A more respectful approach might be to use the research to open the door for Mayan voices to fill the arena. We'll talk more about this in the next chapter.

At the time of the Spanish invasion of the 1500s, the use of the Long Count calendar was already interrupted. Consequently there isn't any one person or group holding complete continuity with the past, and the Mayan Day Keepers don't have an exact end or start date for the Long Count calendar. The Elders today have mostly accepted the GMT correlation and the end date of approximately December 21, 2012. They do not necessarily accept the interpretations of what will happen.

Carlos Barrios speaks out against Argüelles and also against anthropologists and others who "study the Mayan calendars and misread the signs." He seems most disturbed by the focus on the end of the calendar as being a time of destruction. He and other Elders look at this as a time of transformation into the fifth age.

Skeptics' Corner

There are several problems with 2012 predictions. First of all, many do not come with dates, or are vague and can't be interpreted until after the fact. Second, if a prediction does come with a date and/or specific correlation, if it turns out wrong, the date of the prediction is often simply changed. Finally, what is the purpose of a prediction? If it's going to be useful, it has to provide warnings before the fact. Many predictions, such as the Bible Code (see Chapter 12) and those of Nostradamus, cannot be interpreted until afterward, so are they useful?

Criticism of Nostradamus

The Nostradamus quatrains are wide open to skepticism. Although followers of the quatrains are adamant that they are accurate and important, they are so vague that they are useless for prediction. They are only recognizable after the fact, and then only with much twisting of meanings. English translations are poor quality and are often, it is said, translated to fit the event they are meant to portray.

Assessing Gordon Michael Scallion

The predictions of Gordon Michael Scallion (see Chapter 12), with some exception, have failed to come true. However, his map of earth changes is still selling; his followers say that free will has changed the timeline, causing some events to be averted and others to be delayed. Scallion is still speaking and writing, warning people of the earth changes to come.

As a partial hit, Scallion predicted that three earthquakes would strike Los Angeles, each one larger than the one before. The first happened on April 22, 1992, and measured 6+ on the Richter scale. The second happened on June 28, 1992, and was 7.5 on the Richter scale. The third was predicted to occur before December 1995 and would start the breaking up of the American landmass. It didn't happen.

Codex Cues

Scallion had a hit when he predicted in the early 1970s that a "hum" would develop coming from deep within the earth. He said the hum would make people sick with flu-like symptoms, chest pains, and nausea. In fact, since 1977 in Britain, and the 1990s in the United States, a low-frequency, persistent hum has been heard. It has been causing people insomnia, nosebleeds, anxiety, irritability, and illness. In 1993, public outcry in Taos, New Mexico, a main site of the hum, became so great that a congressional research team was formed to investigate. As of today, there is no known source.

On the other side, many of the changes Scallion predicted were based on increased volcanic activity, earthquakes, and a pole shift all to be set off by solar flares. Given the new information regarding the weakening of the earth's magnetic field and the expected solar sunspot season, maybe Scallion did see the changes to come, he just missed the exact time frame. In the same light, global warming and its effects on rising sea levels may also bring about the geographical changes Scallion predicts.

Accuracy of Edgar Cayce

Edgar Cayce's followers claim a 97 percent success rate with his predictions. Like Scallion, he provided dates or ranges of time so his predictions can be checked. In relation to the end times, his events may turn out to be right, but his timing is certainly off. He writes: "Portions of the Earth are going to be wiped away in the coming years. I feel very sure of that. The Earth changes will start in the final years before the new Millennium, and the sea will cover the western part of our nation."

This and the other Cayce prophecies mentioned in Chapter 11 related to end times have not happened in the time frame they were predicted for. As with Scallion, he bases his earth changes on a shifting of the magnetic poles. And again, it is tempting to change the goalpost and move the predictions to 2012.

Evaluating the Bible Code

The measure of a system of prediction is how well its predictions turn out. The Bible Code's big failing is that it's easier to find codes after the fact than before the fact. After the fact, the correct hits are amazing. On the other hand, two predictions made ahead of time have turned out, after the fact, to be false. The codes predicted a nuclear war in 2000. They also predicted the earth would be hit by a comet in 2006, bringing on a pole shift and major earth changes. Neither occurred.

Codex Cues

Information on using the Bible Code technique on any book can be found at http://cs.anu.edu.au/~bdm/dilugim/data.

In addition to criticizing the results, the Bible Code has been criticized for its method. As you'll recall from Chapter 12, the letters of passages of the Torah are placed at equal intervals inside graph boxes. A computer searches for sequences with a program called skip sequencing. It skips one, two, and then three letters, locking onto the specific spacing that provides meaningful words. It appears if you use this technique on any book you can get the same predictive results as in the Bible Code. Could that really be true? In response to this criticism, investigative reporter Michael Drosnin challenged his critics: "When my critics find a message about the assassination of a prime minister encrypted in *Moby Dick*, I'll believe them" (*Newsweek*, 1997).

Researchers at the Australian National University, led by Brendan McKay, took up the challenge. They applied Drosnin's technique to *Moby Dick* and found the assassination of John F. Kennedy, Abraham Lincoln, Martin Luther King, Jr., and Indira Gandhi, to name only a few. They also found the death of Princess Diana and of Michael Drosnin himself. According to the study, you can apply this technique to any book and get relevant results.

Bad Science: Don't Believe Everything You Read

A major criticism from skeptics is the use of unproved science to support metaphysical concepts. As science develops greater understandings of energy and energy interactions, these concepts are often applied to metaphysics. This is fair enough when speculating, but often it is applied as proof.

For example, it's one thing to speculate whether new advances in understanding DNA can explain the mechanisms of telepathy, or the ability to "read another person's mind." It's another thing to use the advances in understanding DNA as proof that mind reading is real. We fall into this same trap with many 2012 predictions.

Return of the Photon Belt

The photon belt and other energy particle speculation is a good example of misapplying science in 2012. We reported in Chapter 7 that increased activity in the heliosphere indicated the solar system is contacting high-energy particles. While this is true, it's not proof that the photon belt is real, as is claimed. It may or may not be real, but high-energy particles in the heliosphere don't prove it.

The photon belt is also a good example of how urban legends develop in metaphysics. The photon belt theory began as one article written by two people with no background in astrophysics. It was reprinted in a popular, and usually better researched, international magazine, *Nexus*. From there it was repeated so many times that it became a fixture in the 2012 literature. If you ask people who follow 2012 whether they have heard of the photon belt, they will not only say yes, they will be sure it's a scientific fact. They will agree that what will happen when we move through the photon belt may be channeled information, but its existence is considered a fact.

Pole Shift

The theory of a pole shift or pole reversal is another application of bad science. First of all, these are often used as interchangeable terms. They're not interchangeable. As we discussed in Chapter 10, a pole reversal is the reversal, or flipping, of the magnetic poles so that north pole becomes south and south pole becomes north. This has happened many times in the history of the planet and is recorded in the layers of magnetic rock. Pole reversals seem to be organic to the earth's process. It's associated with a weakening of the magnetic field and may be impacted by severe solar sunspot activity. It generally is a slow process, building up over time.

The pole shift is the hypothesis that the axis or rotation of the planet has not always been the same and the physical poles have shifted position. The anomalies of the axis of Uranus, which seems to make Uranus lie on its side, and the counter-rotation of Venus make this a plausible theory. However, shifting the axis of the planet requires a catastrophic event. What could do this? Being hit with a high-velocity asteroid or comet is a possibility. Scientists believe a pole shift may have happened 800 million years ago in the Precambrian era. A pole shift would happen quickly and be devastating in outcome, possibly destroying all life.

The second problem with the science of pole reversal versus pole shift is that people interchange the consequences. A pole shift is much less likely to happen and the consequences would be much more severe. People often use the proof that a pole reversal is coming based on the weakened magnetic field and strong upcoming solar cycle, but use the catastrophic results of a pole shift as the outcome. The truth is we don't really know what the effects of a reversal might be. They could be benign, they could be severe; but they are not the same as the results of being hit by a high-velocity asteroid.

End Times of the Past

Let's get some perspective by looking at the many end-time prophecies that have already passed without producing the end of the planet. Some of these predictions have had tragic outcomes, such as the mass suicide associated with the Heaven's Gate Community and the arrival of the Hale-Bopp comet. Others simply come and go and people shift their focus to the next cycle of dates.

 Cosmic Caution

Heaven's Gate was a religious group in the 1990s whose 38 members committed mass suicide when the comet Hale-Bopp appeared in 1997. The group believed the earth was going to be "recycled" and their only chance to survive was to hitch a ride on the spaceship they believed was hiding behind Hale-Bopp. Be careful what you buy in to!

In truth, the end times have been predicted for centuries. The original disciples of Christ expected to see the end times in their lifetimes. At the end of the first millennium, people also expected to see the return of Christ as they did in the year 2000. The list of end-time predictions that haven't occurred is long. Here's a sample:

◆ **500 C.E.** Math has frequently been used to predict the end times. In 234 C.E., theologian Hippolytus promoted his belief that the world had a life span of only 6,000 years. He estimated that Adam and Eve were born about 5,500 years before Christ, meaning the world would end in 500 C.E. Mass panic ensued.

◆ **989 C.E: Halley's Comet and beyond.** Comets, eclipses, and other celestial events are often believed to be heralds of the end times. Both Halley's Comet in 989 C.E. and a supernova in 1006 C.E. were interpreted as signs of the end times. In present times, Hale-Bopp in 1997 was believed to start the end times, and in 2003 we were supposed to pass through the tail of a comet, provoking the end-time Earth changes. And of course, alignment with the galactic center in 2012 ….

◆ **1000 C.E: The Second Coming.** The approach of the first millennium created mass hysteria. Everyone believed the return of Christ was imminent, complete with the apocalypse, Armageddon, and Ascension. Some took it to extremes, and as the millennium approached people abandoned their crops and journeyed to Jerusalem. It was a good time to become a good Christian, and in the year 999 people sold their belongings, gave the money to the poor, and awaited redemption.

◆ **1260 C.E.** The Franciscan order of the Catholic Church was based on the belief in an "Age of Spirit" when God's revelations would be sent directly to individuals. Citing the writings of Italian monk Joachim of Fiore (ca. 1132–1202) people believed the end of the Age of Grace was near and the Age of Spirit was approaching. They believed the date was 1260 C.E.

◆ **1666: The year of the beast.** The number 666 is declared in the Book of Revelations to be the number of the beast, or the number of the antichrist. Any time the number 666, or multiples of 666, or years whose numbers add up to 666 arrive, predictions of Armageddon follow. It heralds the beginning of the apocalypse with disease, plague, and famine. Considering that in 1666 600,000 people died in the bubonic plague, it was perhaps understandable that this was believed to be the year of the end times. For 600,000 people, it was!

◆ **Nuclear war: 2000, 2003, 2008.** War is another common end-time prediction. You will be happy to know that not only have we lived through the Bible Code's prediction of a nuclear war in 2000, we have also lived through a nuclear war in

2003, predicted by the Aum Shinri Kyo cult. The most recent one, prophesized to destroy the earth in March 2008, was predicted by the British group the Lord's Witnesses.

A Self-Fulfilling Prophecy?

We all need to apply healthy skepticism to the information about 2012. Otherwise we can get so caught up in the theories that we stop seeing events objectively. The loss of objectivity can cause poor decision-making or close our minds to information that can clarify and help our understanding. Take a quick check; is there anyplace where you do not want to hear any other view than your own? You may be filtering reality to fit your own ideas. Something we all have to watch out for.

Don't forget, prophecies can become self-fulfilling. When a child spills his milk and is told he is prone to accidents, he starts to think of himself that way. His new self-image damages his self-confidence and creates more accidents. The prophecy is fulfilled.

Codex Cues

A great website for more information on defeating self-fulfilling prophecy is www. terrybragg.com/ Article_Self-fulfillingProphecies.htm.

Here's how self-fulfilling prophecy works: you automatically change the way you act and what you do based on your expectations. Here's an example: you own stock in a company. You hear on the news that the stock market is going into a slump or the stock you hold is going down, and you decide to sell your stock. If everyone who heard the news report does the same, the stock crashes and the prophecy is fulfilled.

This process, like so many we have been talking about, is a cycle. It starts with your forming an expectation, then interpreting events based on what you expect, then changing your behavior, and creating the effect. It's important to remember that self-fulfilling prophecies are fulfilled not because the prophecies are true but because we expect them to be true.

If you believe the world is going to end, how much energy will you put into finding solutions to problems like global warming? How committed will you be to energy conservation? If our thoughts create reality and everyone is thinking we are doomed, what are we attracting?

We need to use the prophecies of 2012 to create the reality we want. How do we do this? Stay grounded, stay focused, keep your mind open, work toward positive expectations, and be a problem solver, not a problem maker.

The Least You Need to Know

◆ There are many objections to the interpretations of the Mayan prophecies, including the lack of native Mayan input and the reliance on inspiration over established interpretations.

◆ Predictions are usually too vague to be useful and can only be recognized after the fact.

◆ Many of the prophecies of channels and intuits have been outright wrong. Often when this happens the person making the predictions moves the date further into the future.

◆ Science can be used inaccurately to support people's theories. Always evaluate the science and look to the source.

◆ Be careful of self-fulfilling prophecy; keep your critical thinking skills intact and examine all the ideas regarding 2012.

Voices of Today's Elders

In This Chapter

- ◆ The meeting of the Mayan Council
- ◆ Three Mayan Elder viewpoints
- ◆ Aztec perspective
- ◆ Kogi message
- ◆ Hopi address to the United Nations

Theories about the Mayan calendar abound. Everyone has his or her own idea of what it means and what will happen. However, you may have noticed that the Maya themselves have not been saying much. Don't let this give you the impression that the Mayan tradition is dead. The Mayan culture is alive and well, and Mayan Elders today still keep the calendars. In some ways, their calendar tradition has been hijacked with the interest in 2012. Researchers interpreting the calendars and the end date have elicited little input from the Elders themselves.

In this chapter, we share the views of three Mayan Elders: Don Alejandro, Carlos Barrios, and Hunbatz Men. This is a pivotal time in history, bringing together the traditions of many indigenous people. We also introduce you to Elders from the Aztec, Hopi, and Kogi nations. We offer the words of the Elders with respect to their tradition and voice.

The Mayan Council

Today there are 440 Mayan tribes. Each tribe is represented by an Elder. The 440 Elders meet each year as the Mayan Council of Elders, which is comprised of 265 grandfathers and 175 grandmothers. The elected president of the Council is Grandfather Don Alejandro Cirilo Perez Oxlaj. Don Alejandro is a thirteenth-generation Quiche Mayan high priest also known as Wandering Wolf.

Glyph Interpretation

In 2007, the Council agreed to create a committee of 25 Elders to interpret the Mayan glyphs according to traditional understanding. The currently published glyph meanings have all been interpreted by archeologists and anthropologists. The Council elected to interpret the glyphs with traditional insight in an attempt to preserve the knowledge they hold from the past for the future generations.

According to Grandfather Alejandro, it has been 526 years since the Maya have released information about their prophetic calendars. All the information we have is from the calculations and interpretations of scientists and researchers. This year the Council has decided to release this much awaited information. They intend to illuminate existing calendar prophecies and also release new information from the five calendars that have never been seen publicly.

Publishing the Traditional Perspective

The Council invited Drunvalo Melchizedek, a consciousness researcher, to join them. Colin has known Drunvalo, a respected and trusted conveyor of spiritual and Native perspectives, for many years. Drunvalo was invited by the Mayan Council of Elders to become the vehicle for the publication of their information. He spent many months in Guatemala filming and dialoguing with the Council for this long-awaited announcement. The release will be in the form of a book, signed by all 440 council members, and possibly a film. The book is expected sometime this year.

Codex Cues

You can learn more about Don Alejandro and this important project on Drunvalo's website: www.spiritofmaat.com/support_an_elder.html.

The Views of Don Alejandro

Many Mayan Elders have made statements about the importance of these times and of maintaining the traditional ways. The following views of Grandfather Don Alejandro are derived from a speech he made in 1999 in Santa Fe, New Mexico. You can read Don Alejandro's entire 1999 speech in New Mexico at www.commonpassion.org.

Don Alejandro reads the prophecies in a positive light. His message for people is one of peace and unity—peace not only with each other, something sorely needed, but also peace with the earth and the plants and animals of the earth. He asks people to see the forest trees, the rocks, the streams, and rivers as Elders of the planet, and to hold true with their right to be here.

He says that the prophecies are here to awaken us to a new and better way of living on the earth, a way that was known and practiced by Native cultures. Like all Native Elders, he mourns the destruction of nature that our culture and time period has created. He sees this time as a time to correct our relationship with the earth. He says, "The Mayan prophecies tell us it is time to awaken, time for the dawn, so that the people will have peace and will be happy."

Don Alejandro does not speak of the destruction of the old age, only the dawning of the New Age. In fact, he doesn't use the term "end times" at all. Rather he uses the term "Day Zero," which refers to the first day of the New Age. He denounces those who frighten people with visions of destruction. "I have come in fulfillment of the prophecies; that we may all walk together, no group shall be left behind. I am here in fulfillment of this prophecy, carrying this message to all that hear me and to all who love the Earth, to all who love peace, and who love themselves."

Don Alejandro also has a completely different end-time date than we have seen so far. Whether this date is accepted by the entire Mayan Council of Elders, and how he derives it, we don't know. The date he uses is March 31, 2013, when he says the sun will be hidden for 60 to 70 hours and we will enter the next age. We expect further information to be released with Drunvalo's future book.

He goes on to say the next age may be another dimension where the wisdom of the Maya will be revealed. "I come to say that we should love one another. Let us walk together. We are all children and we pray that our Father be with us."

The Views of Carlos Barrios

We've mentioned Carlos Barrios several times in earlier chapters. Of the Mam lineage, he was born into a Spanish family in El Altiplano in the Guatemala highlands. He's an historian, anthropologist, and researcher. Carlos and his brother Gerardo undertook a detailed investigation into the Mayan calendars. Carlos studied with many traditional Elders to learn the shamanic path, and after 25 years became a ceremonial priest and spiritual guide of the Eagle clan. Gerardo interviewed nearly 600 traditional Mayan timekeepers in villages throughout the Maya region regarding the calendars.

> ### Celestial Connection
>
> The Mam are a Mayan tribe from Huehuetenango in the highlands of Guatemala. Like other Mayan tribes, the Mam hold ancient knowledge and traditions. They are one of the timekeepers and authorities on the calendars.

In keeping with Don Alejandro, Carlos is not happy with the way researchers have interpreted the Mayan calendars and prophecies. He states that researchers reading the inscriptions on steles and temple sites are inaccurate in their translations. Perhaps he is saying that they read them from the context of our biases and worldview rather than from the Mayan worldview. In any case, he believes the interpretations are incorrect. Specifically, as with Don Alejandro, he does not see the end of the calendar as meaning the world will end. He claims that, "Other people write the prophecies in the name of the Maya. They say the world will end in December 2012. The Mayan Elders are angry with this. The world will not end; it will be transformed."

Carlos has said that the date of 2012 has attracted people's fears and influenced how they see the calendar prophecies. He does, however, acknowledge that the calendars foresee a difficult transition that may involve environmental collapse, war, and earth changes. The difference is that he does not call this the end of the world and it's not the focus of the calendar; rather, the transformation to come is the focus.

Like José Argüelles, who we talked about in Chapter 12, Carlos seems to agree that 1987 was a turning point and from that date Barrios says, "We have been in a time when the right arm of the materialistic world is disappearing, slowly but inexorably. We are at the cusp of the era when peace begins, and people live in harmony with Mother Earth. We are no longer in the World of the Fourth Sun, but we are not yet in the World of the Fifth Sun. This is the time in-between, the time of transition."

Codex Cues

You can read the words of Carlos Barrios directly at www.mayanmajix.com.

According to Carlos, the Mayan Day Keepers view the December 21, 2012, date as a rebirth, the start of the World of the Fifth Sun. "It will be the start of a new era resulting from, and signified by, the solar meridian crossing the galactic equator, and the earth aligning itself with the center of the galaxy." With these words he seems to agree with the research of John Major Jenkins, discussed in Chapter 7. However, the final words are these: "The indigenous have the calendars, and know how to accurately interpret them, not others."

The Views of Hunbatz Men

We introduced Hunbatz Men, a Mayan Elder, shaman, and Day Keeper, in Chapter 9. He lives in Mérida, Mexico, and is an authority on the history, chronology, and calendars of Mayan civilization. He wrote a book titled *Secrets of Mayan Science/Religion* (see Resources appendix).

He's a teacher of traditional Mayan wisdom and has founded a mystery school to lead modern people into cosmic consciousness. Hunbatz leads ceremonies at the sacred sites and teaches Mayan breathing and exercise techniques to help people develop energy awareness. He carries the tradition of the X Wenk'al Mayan ceremonial center from his uncle Don Beto.

Hunbatz teaches about the 2012 prophecies from the place of transformation. He quotes the katun prophecies we discussed in Chapter 9 and talks about the return to the sacred Mayan pyramids of the initiates and masters "to continue the work of the Great Spirit." In accordance with the katuns he claims people will be drawn to the sites to reawaken their spiritual awareness.

He looks to the illumination and wisdom of the Maya to light the way into the New Age. Do you remember the mural at San Bartolo, mentioned in Chapter 8? The final fifth age shows people of all colors working together. Hunbatz goes on to say, "These masters will come from many places. They will be of many colors."

Codex Cues

You can read a speech from Hunbatz Men titled "Living on the Edge of a New World" at www.labyrinthina.com/mayan.htm.

Hunbatz joins the other Native Elders in honoring the earth and creatures of the earth and in decrying the current environmental situation. More than any of the other Elders, Hunbatz talks of the essence and spirit within matter. His is essentially a spiritual message.

In his speeches and writings, Hunbatz says the roots of the Maya are in the pyramids. He leads ceremonies at sacred sites, which he says "honor the laws of all that is visible and all that is invisible." These ceremonies are used to awaken people to their own sacred centers (see Chapters 22 and 23).

Celestial Connection

The land of the Maya holds many mysteries beyond the pyramids. English explorer Mitchell Hedges discovered an incredible quartz crystal skull in 1924 in a Mayan pyramid at Lubaantun, Belize. According to Hedges it's at least 3,600 years old, and according to legend was used by the High Priest of the Maya when performing esoteric rites. Hedges's daughter Anna lived with the Maya and was told by Mayan priests that the crystal skull is over 100,000 years old. Scientists at the British Museum in London say that making the skull exceeds the ability of modern diamond-tipped cutting tools and lathes. Mystics say the crystal skull has the ability to open people's psychic centers.

Aztec Wisdom of the Tlakaelel

The Aztec Nation had close ties to the Maya. They came from the same Mesoamerican roots and share many of the same legends and traditions. The Aztec version of the Mayan Tzolk'in calendar is called the tonalpohualli. The 365-day Haab calendar has a counterpart as well, called the xiuhpohualli. The tonalpohualli and the xiuhpohualli relate to each other in the Aztec version of the Calendar round (see Chapter 5).

We can see the two systems developed from each other. One of the biggest differences between the two is the placement by the Aztecs of the current world as the fifth age rather than the fourth age of the Maya.

In 1947, Tlakaelel was commissioned by the Aztec Council of Anahuac with a spiritual mission. He was given the name and spiritual title of "Tlakaelel," which means "Counselor to the Council." In each generation, one person carries this title. The current Tlakaelel is the first indigenous leader in the history of Mexico to have achieved official government recognition of Native Religious Tradition. His success marks the conclusion of 500 years of indigenous effort!

Tlakaelel is most revered for his "rainbow" approach to planetary healing; that is, he is known for pulling people of many cultures together. Working with a consortium of indigenous leaders from North America including Slow Turtle, Wildcat, Big Toe, and Chief Windsong, Tlakaelel developed the Four Colors Ceremony. This is a unifying ceremony honoring the four directions and the four colors of humanity. Tlakaelel has brought the ceremony to many parts of the United States and Canada and has led the Sacred Sundance ceremony in Mexico for the past 13 years.

Tlakaelel has also created the first spiritual pyramid in Mexico in over 500 years. The "Peace Pyramid" began in 1999 and echoes ancient Mexican tradition.

The Views of Tlakaelel

We include the words of Tlakaelel in this important time because he holds the knowledge passed down by the Aztec people. He's both a trained scientist and a man in touch with nature, as his teachings show. His words speak to the heart as we close the current age of both the Maya and Aztec calendars.

Tlakaelel speaks to the spiritual power within. We've heard said from the prophecies that people will be transformed with the return of Kukulkan. Here's what Tlakaelel has to say about what the transformed person will be like: "Perfection will arrive when man is capable of creating all that he is capable of conceiving. Here is the superior being of the future: able to create all that we conceive."

Tlakaelel believes we are here to fulfill our destiny and that destiny is more than fulfilling our desires for pleasure, fame, and fortune. He himself has a strong, abiding social mission. He is a tireless individual who works constantly for the betterment of the earth. We met him when he was well over 80 and he kept a pace we were hardpressed to keep up with (see Chapter 18). He says, "We didn't come to this world just to eat, sleep, reproduce, and die. We have a great destiny. This destiny is possible when we achieve our worth and when we transcend. We live for just a little bit of time. That which continues living after us is the community, the Earth."

Codex Cues

A presentation by Tlakaelel can be seen at www.spiritofmaat.com.

This is his message: "I am an integral part of the universe, of the creation of all. And I continue being part of a great plan of creation. When we are all able to feel this just a little bit, when we identify with All That Exists, we will be planetary citizens, cosmic citizens. And peace will come. The truth will be known."

In relation to 2012 he has told us, "The world will not end in 2012. The world will end when the sun goes out."

Tlakaelel visited England in 1994 to find "the place of the last ceremonial dance." Here are Colin (left) and Tlakaelel (right).

The Kogi: Heart of the World

The Kogi people are the last continuously surviving high civilization of preconquest America. They live in the Sierra Nevada Mountains in northern Colombia, South America. Like so many tribes, they were nearly annihilated by the Spanish conquistadores. After the Spanish invasion, the Kogi and other tribes of the Sierra Nevada retreated. High in the mountains, they have created a community with intricate networks of cities interwoven in the heart of the forest. They farm, live in harmony with the land, and maintain continual prayer for the well-being of the planet.

Sending a Message to the "Younger Brother"

So completely have the Kogi cut themselves off from society that for centuries it was thought that they had not survived the Spanish invasion. Then in 1991 they sent a message down the mountain to the "younger brother." The Kogi people consider themselves the "Elder Brothers" of humanity. We are the "younger brothers," or the newcomers to the planet. They believe it's their job to maintain the Sierra Nevada Mountains where they live, which is the "Heart of the World." If the mountains die, so does the planet. This message rings prophetic in today's world. Wise Elders of the community, known as the Mamas, hold the responsibility of maintaining continual spiritual efforts to this end.

Alan Ereira, a BBC TV journalist, met with a delegation of Kogi who came down from the mountain with a message for the "younger brother." The message was internationally televised in a 1991 BBC documentary called *From the Heart of the World: The Elder Brothers' Warning*. The Kogi broke their retreat from the world because the mountain was sick, which meant the world was sick and they needed to intervene.

The program is riveting and heartfelt, with much significance for this time. Colin watched the message in 1991. It impacted his research into the crop circles, which you'll read about in Chapter 18. It moved him into opening dialogue with indigenous people to understand the symbols in the fields that he was researching.

According to the Kogi, "The snow has stopped falling on the mountain top, it's not there to melt and fill the rivers below. The (Earth) Mother's waters are disappearing. Younger brother is destroying her. Look at the leaves on the trees, they are withering and falling, her lungs are dying." The Kogi talk of "younger brother" as children, "looting the planet, tearing at its flesh without respect." The Elder Brothers say, "If we fail to respond, all life will be destroyed."

The chilling message from Colombia's isolated Kogi tribe led Alan Ereira to travel to the top of the mountain with the Kogi. He documented the melted glaciers and stark, snowless peaks. This was the first empirical evidence of global warming. The Kogi warned there was a brief window to act. In light of the signs of change you will read about in Part 4 of this book, we might have been well advised to have acted on that warning.

> **Codex Cues**
>
> The Kogi story can be read in the book *The Elder Brothers* by Alan Ereira (Knopf, 1992) or can be seen in the 1991 documentary *From the Heart of the World: The Elder Brothers' Warning* (BBC, 1991). Both are available at www.amazon.com.

Washington Meeting

In September 2006, we were invited to a symposium in Washington, D.C., with leaders of the Kogi, Wiwa, Arhuaco, and Kankuamo indigenous communities from the Sierra

Nevada. For the first time in history, the Kogi Mamas had come down from their mountain and entered a modern U.S. city. They repeated the same message, this time with much greater urgency. Things are much worse and the future of the planet is at stake.

Thomas Banyacya and the Hopi Prophecy

You've already read about the Hopi prophecy in Chapter 11. The prophecy was held by the Parrot clan and passed to Thomas Banyacya from the Wolf, Fox, and Coyote clans. Banyacya was the interpreter for the Hopi Traditional Elders and the Hopi Council of Elders. In 1948, he was charged with the job of fulfilling aspects of the Hopi prophecy.

Colin Meets with Banyacya

Thomas Banyacya spoke to the General Assembly at the United Nations in December 1992 about the Hopi prophecy. The prophecy states that sacred offerings were to be made to the "House of Mica." The Hopi word for "peace" is *Mica* and "the House of Mica" is believed by the Hopi to be the United Nations. Thomas gave those offerings and words in December 1992, when he delivered a stern warning for the world and humanity.

Colin also spoke to a subgroup at the United Nations, the United Nations Society for Enlightenment and Transformation (S.E.A.T.). He spoke in October 1993 about the crop circles, also emphasizing the need to curtail the environmental crises underway.

In November 1994, Colin was asked by Thomas Banyacya to meet at a conference they were both speaking at in Atlanta. When Colin and Banyacya met, Thomas stated that giving his statement to the UN was his final responsibility to the Hopi prophecy. He explained to Colin the importance of the prophecy and the signs that had already come to pass. He further stated that the lack of response of the United Nations to his speech marked the point where we could no longer turn from the black road to the red road.

Address to the UN

Thomas Banyacya gave a moving and important speech to the U.N., one that was largely if not completely ignored. Many of the things he said have similarities to predictions for 2012.

Thomas Banyacya stood before the United Nations General Assembly on December 4, 1992. He told them that the Hopi prophecy predicted a Hopi representative would one day speak to the United Nations, or House of Mica. He spoke about the mission of the United Nations to carry out justice in the world and noted that Native Americans have never before been heard or had representation at the United Nations.

Banyacya carried to the United Nations a message of peace from the Hopi and a warning from the prophecies. He warned of the dangerous environmental crisis we are in. His warning was ignored.

Codex Cues

You can read Thomas Banyacya's full statement to the General Assembly at www.alphacdc.com/banyacya/un92.html.

This picture of Thomas Banyacya was taken during Colin's visit with him in 1994.

On April 26, 1993, Thomas sent a final letter to Boutros Boutros-Ghali, the Secretary General of the United Nations. The letter read in part: "The Hopi elders in 1948 accurately foretold that the whole world would be in terrible crisis at this point in time and many peoples would need guidance as to how to survive these crisis times. This is what we offer. I, Banyacya, am just an interpreter, I am not a spiritual leader or medicine man. I am a member of the Wolf, Fox, and Coyote clans come to warn you on behalf of the Hopi elders. I have come to warn all the peoples of the world that this purification is coming. … We need your help. We must join hands together acting as one people to save this Earth."

He asked for a formal response from the United Nations to his message. It never came. Thomas Banyacya passed away on February 6, 1999.

The Least You Need to Know

- Mayan Elders seem to agree that the end of the Long Count calendar will consist of a time of difficulty followed by a transformation.

- Tlakaelel, an Aztec Elder, gives a message of brotherhood of all mankind and creating a better world for the generations to come.

- The message from the Kogi is simple: Mother Earth is dying. Can we learn from the Elder Brothers and change our ways?

- Thomas Banyacya fulfilled the Hopi prophecy when he addressed the United Nations General Assembly. They did not respond, indicating there is no turning off the "black road" we are on.

Part 4

2012: Signs of Change

We are coming to the end of an epoch. The cycle that's ending developed a split between the material and spiritual. The result has been technical and material growth with a loss of connection to the sacred essence residing within matter.

The predictions from the prophets of all ages, past and present, describe a difficult passage. There are declarations of super storms, volcanoes, earthquakes, floods, and changing landmasses. There are predictions of pole reversals, pole shifts, and even massive asteroid strikes. There's talk of lack of food and water and increased social friction. The changing of the ages brings something else as well: the return of the masters and the awakening of spirit.

Looking around the world today, can we find evidence of these changes? This is the mission of this part: to look to the conditions of today for evidence of the predictions for 2012.

Global Warming and Climate Change

In This Chapter

- ◆ What the prophecies say about global warming
- ◆ The reality of global warming
- ◆ Natural and human input
- ◆ The widespread effects of global warming
- ◆ Choices for the future

You've certainly heard about global warming. It's the raising of the earth's temperature. Specifically, it's the warming of the oceans and the layer of the atmosphere closest to the earth. But what does this have to do with 2012?

In fact, if the projections of global warming are real, this may be a mechanism creating the earth changes in the period leading into 2012. As always, we have a choice. As with the Hopi prophecy discussed in Chapter 11, there are markers along the way. We can add to the problem pushing us past the point of no return or we can choose change. We can move to the red road of spirituality and harmony with the earth. In this chapter, we'll look at how the 2012 prophecies relate to global warming and how real global warming is.

The 2012 Connection

The trends of global warming sound alarmingly like the earth change predictions for 2012. From the katuns to the New Age prophets, we have heard the story of extreme weather, flooding, and loss of landmass. The katuns are clear that we're not facing a single moment of change but an *era* of change and that we are already in that era. We are in the katun of transition right now. Maybe the Maya and the New Age predictions didn't name global warming as the mechanism, but they certainly described to perfection the effects.

So what do we do? Do we give in to the inevitability of climate change and say it's all too late? Or do we find the place within that knows that we are a powerful part of the future, powerful creators in the events to come? There are two roads that we can walk. You will see in this chapter what path we are on. The question many are asking is this: Is it too late to change direction?

Path of Destruction or Enlightenment?

When you read this chapter, you may be tempted to say it's all too late. We have traveled too far down the black road of the Hopi prophecy and are experiencing the edge of disaster. While this is totally understandable, it neglects the power of k'ul, the power of the planet itself, and the power of united human spirit. The katuns and the Mayan prophecy reveal that this is the time when the masters will return to teach what has been lost. You may be asking what it is that has been lost. As we have reached unprecedented heights in technological advancement and understanding, what has been lost?

Mayan Wisdom

According to the Mayan writings, we have lost the knowledge of the earth as a living system. We have lost connection to the pulse of energy that surges through celestial alignments activating energy centers on the earth. We have lost connection to our own inner reserve or k'ul that connects us to the universe through the day-signs, the sacred sites, and the opening of portals. We have lost our sacred center. Or have we?

People are now experiencing a tremendous growth in awareness. If we activate this awareness, anything is possible. Reversing the effects of global warming may require awakening parts of ourselves as well as awakening the sacred sites on the planet, allowing the flow of k'ul to revitalize and rebalance the system.

Is Global Warming Real?

You may already know that this topic creates a lot of controversy. For a while, people didn't believe the earth's temperatures were raising. Now pretty much everyone accepts that global warming is real, but they disagree on the causes and need for action. Before we can decide if global warming is "real," we need to define things. Many people think global warming means "human-induced" temperature change on the planet. However, that's not what it really means. Global warming is just one aspect of global climate change; global cooling is another. Climate change is caused both by natural phenomenon and by man-made activity.

Celestial Connection

Natural processes record climate change in "natural libraries," such as tree rings, ice cores, coral beds, fossil records, and lake and ocean sediment. Ice cores and tree rings form in layers; in addition to providing climate data, they provide a timeline so that scientists can track climate change. This helps to illuminate the extreme changes we are currently facing. Evaluating our future becomes clearer by looking at our past.

As for global warming, temperatures have been steadily rising over the last century. You might be surprised that the total rise is only about one degree. However, even a one-degree change in temperature creates big problems! Original models for global warming showed a more gradual rise in temperatures. Scientists are shocked and dismayed at how much faster warming is occurring than they expected.

Global Climate Controls

The earth, like your body, needs to stay within a pretty strict temperature range to maintain life. Also like your body, it has many natural mechanisms that keep temperatures in check. This is called *homeostasis*. To understand how the earth maintains the level of warmth needed for life, we must look to the sun and the earth.

Ultraviolet radiation from the sun enters the atmosphere, heating it up. Of course, if all the radiation from the sun were allowed to reach the lower atmosphere, we would fry. What keeps that from happening is the ozone layer in the outer atmosphere. Ozone reflects harmful UV radiation and protects the earth from excess sunbeams. The magnetic field of the planet also protects the earth from electromagnetic energy from the sun (see Chapter 10).

Heat from the sun as well as heat generated by the earth is conserved in the earth's atmosphere by the greenhouse effect. Gases in the atmosphere slow the escape of heat back into space, regulating our climate by trapping heat and holding it like a blanket around the planet. Without it, the earth's temperatures would be colder by about 50 degrees Fahrenheit. The greenhouse effect is a natural process that is essential for life on Earth. However, too much of a good thing turns bad. Excess greenhouse gases trap too much heat, contributing to global warming.

Signs of Imbalance

The signs of global warming are irrefutable. The arctic sea ice is melting faster than anyone ever expected. As sea ice melts, sea levels are rising, weather is becoming more extreme, and rain patterns and distribution are changing. Areas of desert are starting to get rain and farming areas are experiencing drought.

Codex Cues

In January 2008, daffodils were in bloom throughout Britain—five months earlier than normal.

As the overall planetary temperature rises, the jet stream is shifting. This is breaking down the barrier between the cold arctic air and warmer southern air. The mixing of air masses is making the northern climates warmer and the southern climates colder. As you may have been noticing yourself, this affects seasons, agriculture, disease outbreaks, species extinction, species relocation, and human health.

Over the past 10 years, all signs of global warming have been increasing at a rapid rate. The controversy now is not whether global warming exists, it's whether humans help create it and whether we can slow it down. As with most things, the answer depends on whom you ask.

Natural Warming

Some corporations and government agencies say that humans have little or no impact on global warming. They say it is caused by natural cycles and that human impact is minimal. They look at solar flares, the weakening magnetic shield of the planet, and even the depletion of the ozone layer as outside of human influence.

One thing is for sure: things like holes in the ozone layer and the weakening of the magnetic field are allowing dangerous levels of UV light and electromagnetic energy to enter the atmosphere, contributing to global warming. Are these natural cycles run amok or are they part of a larger picture we are unaware of?

Solar Cycles

When solar flares burst out from the sun, electromagnetic radiation explodes along the magnetic pathways of the Van Allen Belts. As the solar maximum of 2012 approaches and you start to see the amazing Northern Lights farther and farther south, keep in mind the amount of energy being pushed along these pathways.

There is no question that the solar cycle of 2012 will add energy and therefore heat into the earth's environment. We can certainly look forward to a significant impact on global climate as flares increase, but does that explain global warming over the past 100 years, or the incredible leap in warming over the past 10 years?

> **Cosmic Caution**
>
> The best available evidence indicates that the estimated 3 to 7 degrees change in temperature projected over the next century will be unprecedented.

Some scientists think that radiation from the sun has caused global warming, but not on its own. Not because solar activity has increased but because the earth's magnetic field has decreased, letting electromagnetic radiation from the sun enter the earth's atmosphere. Let's have a look at the impact of anomalies in the magnetic field.

Magnetic Field Anomalies

As we discussed in Chapter 10, the earth's magnetic field has been slowly weakening, letting in more electromagnetic radiation, or solar plasma. At the same time, scientists are finding a hole in the magnetic field over the South Atlantic Ocean called the South Atlantic Anomaly.

The question is, are these really new phenomena? We have only been measuring the earth's magnetic field for 150 years and only with high-tech satellites since the 1960s. Although the magnified fossil record has provided details of 3.2 billion years, we don't really know whether fluxes in the field are part of a natural cycle. Some suggest both the hole and the weakening of the field are homeostatic mechanisms meant to keep balance on the planet. In that case, why would the planet itself be pushing such an extreme envelope?

The Role of Volcanoes

If you've thought about volcanoes and global warming, you might have assumed that because volcanoes produce heat they increase global warming. It's counterintuitive, but

Cosmic Caution _____

Volcanoes that are located under the sea directly add to the heat of the oceans. Because they don't spew debris into the air, they don't add the cooling impact of "nuclear winter."

many people think volcanoes are part of the cooling mechanisms of the planet. Land-based volcanoes put more than heat into the atmosphere. They also spew out a lot of particles, gases, and other debris. Rising on air currents to the upper atmosphere, the debris acts like the ozone layer and deflects the sun's radiation, helping to cool the planet. Many people think that as global warming gets worse, more and more volcanoes will erupt to counteract the heating effect.

Earth Cycles

Another added effect in the heating and cooling of the planet is our position in space. The earth's orbit isn't a circle but an oval, meaning that at certain times we're closer to the sun and other times farther away. In addition, the shape of the oval changes, going through its own 100,000-year cycle called the Milankovitch cycle. In the following figure, orbit B is the path the earth takes in the more circular part of the Milankovitch cycle, and orbit A is the path the earth takes in the most oval part of the cycle. This means that at the most oval shape there are even greater differences between how close and how far away from the sun the earth gets. And that makes even bigger temperature differences.

The variations of the earth's orbit bring the earth closer to the sun and farther away from the sun in 100,000-year cycles.

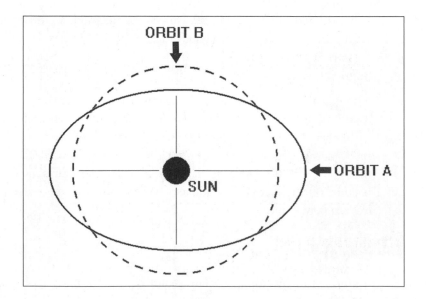

Variations in the Milankovitch cycle are believed to have caused the earth's ice ages and may be part of the current heating cycle. We are now in orbit A, at almost the closest position the earth will get to the sun and its warming effects. But can this 100,000-year cycle explain changes that have happened over the last 100-year period?

The bottom line of the natural cycle theory is that the planet has its own climate controlling mechanisms that are responsible for global warming. While this is obviously true, it's equally true that human activity has an effect as well. What people wonder is whether the homeostatic mechanisms of the planet are capable of overcoming the increasing stress of human impact.

Human Impact

Most climate scientists agree that the main cause of global warming is human activity. Driving your car, using electricity in your house, and using aerosol products all contribute to greenhouse gases.

Trees help reduce greenhouse gases and produce oxygen. Rainforests have been one of the main sources of oxygen in the atmosphere. Right now, the rainforests are being destroyed at an unprecedented rate. Every second we cut down one and a half acres of rainforest. It's estimated that given the current rate of destruction, all the rainforests will be gone within 40 years. That doesn't give us much hope for reversing global warming naturally.

Is global warming related to human activity, and can we reverse it?

Celestial Connection

According to the United Nations Intergovernmental Panel on Climate Change (IPCC), most of the increased temperature in the twentieth century is related to human industrialization. The World Health Organization, the United Nations, and over 60 independent scientists and organizations are looking for ways to slow down the impending disaster by changing human activity. They believe that climate change over the next 20 years will result in "global catastrophe costing millions of lives in natural disaster."

Greenhouse Gases

As you've already learned, the greenhouse effect is essential for life; but you really can have too much of a good thing. Our current lifestyle is accelerating natural processes, possibly throwing them out of balance. So instead of a warming blanket around the earth, we have a heated electric blanket.

It's unquestionable that human activity has increased greenhouse gases like carbon dioxide (CO_2), methane, nitrous oxide, water vapor, and the very important chlorofluorocarbons (CFCs). Although all greenhouse gases have increased due to human activity, let's look at the two most important gases, CO_2 and CFCs.

CO_2 contributes about 50 percent to the greenhouse effect. The concentration of CO_2 has risen by 25 percent in the last century, and half of that has been in the last 30 years. According to the UN special report on emissions, by the end of this century we can see concentrations 75 to 350 percent higher than preindustrial concentrations.

What raises CO_2? Deforestation is a key component. Even more so, burning coal, oil, and fossil fuels has a major impact especially in the face of increased population. We all know that driving our cars increases CO_2 but every time you turn on your television, a light, or your computer, you're using electricity that is created mainly from fossil fuels.

CFCs are man-made chemicals used in refrigerators and air conditioners, fire extinguishers, and propellants in aerosol cans. Although there are lower concentrations of CFCs in the atmosphere than CO_2, they trap more heat, and CFCs last in the atmosphere for 110 years. This is why people want to ban CFCs completely.

Ozone Layer

Ozone in the lower atmosphere is a dangerous pollutant that adds to the greenhouse effect, damages plants, and damages lung tissue. However, ozone is essential in the upper atmosphere for reflecting excess rays from the sun. It's ironic that at ground level ozone is a health hazard, but in the stratosphere we couldn't survive without it.

In the past few decades, chemical reactions involving chlorine and bromine are destroying ozone in the southern polar region. These compounds rise into the atmosphere and are struck by high-energy light waves from the sun, creating reactive compounds that destroy ozone. This depleted region is known as the ozone hole. Scientists believe this is due to the release of man-made chemicals like CFCs.

Resistance to Human Impact

Many businesses and government agencies discredit scientists who are concerned with global warming. You may wonder why anyone would want to cover up a potential problem. The main reason is because facing the human part of global warming requires change. Some companies will lose money even while other companies will find ways to make money creating the needed changes. Most importantly, people will need to change habits and energy-use patterns. Let's face it, change is difficult.

Some governments are taking global warming seriously. European nations are actively working to cap greenhouse gases. Although the United States has resisted acting on global warming, that's now changing. In fact, a secret Pentagon report leaked to the *Observer* newspaper reports that the Pentagon labels global warming as the greatest current threat to national security.

In an article dated February 22, 2004, the *Observer* reports the following: "A secret report, suppressed by U.S. defense chiefs and obtained by the *Observer,* warns that major European cities will be sunk beneath rising seas as Britain is plunged into a 'Siberian' climate by 2020. Nuclear conflict, mega-droughts, famine and widespread rioting will erupt across the world." The *Observer* states that the report was commissioned by Pentagon defense advisor Andrew Marshall.

In the past, governments have discouraged and even repressed scientists who have warned about global warming. Now the tables have turned and new technologies are being explored to reduce dependence on fossil fuels and decrease the human part of the problem.

Consequences of Global Warming

Whether you think humans are impacting global warming, the effects of global warming are real and alarming. Scientists say that the overall rise in temperatures will, in the long run, be greater toward the poles and less in the tropics, there will be more warming in winter than in summer, and the world will be hotter than it has been in 100,000 years. They also say the rise will happen faster than predicted, and by the end of the century the earth will be as hot as during the age of the dinosaurs. So what can we expect as the global warming problem worsens?

Codex Cues _____

Here's an analogy: think of ice cubes in a glass of lemonade. As the ice cube gets warmer, it melts. The melting ice cube makes the lemonade colder. The ice cube is like the ice caps getting warmer and melting as the global temperatures rise. The effect is to cool the oceans, which cools the southern climes keeping them from getting as hot with global warming as you would expect.

Stronger Storms

Storms and hurricanes will become both stronger and more frequent as oceans heat up. In September 1991, Japan was hit by Typhoon Murielle, its worst for 30 years. In September 1993, Japan was again hit—this time by Typhoon Yancy, the thirteenth that year, and the worst for 50 years. In March 1993, the "Storm of the Century" hit America, causing $1.6 billion in damage from Canada to Cuba. In December 1993, hurricane-force storms caused Britain its worst flooding for 40 years. On February 6, 2008, five southern U.S. states were swept by dozens of tornadoes, killing 50 people. Fire erupted at the natural gas pumping station. This was the worst series of tornados in a 24-hour period since May 3, 1999.

More recently, we have seen a tremendous increase in both the number of storms and the strength of storms. In 2004, the hurricane season saw a number of devastating storms causing $40 billion in damages in North America alone. The 2005 hurricane season broke several records, including the highest number of tropical storms (28), the earliest hurricanes in the season, and the most powerful hurricanes.

We all remember the devastation from Hurricane Katrina, whose full damage has yet to be repaired. The annihilation from the tsunami of December 26, 2004, was caused by the second-largest earthquake ever recorded, at 9.3 on the Richter scale. Spring 2008 saw a cyclone ravage Myanmar and another devastating earthquake rip through parts of China. Many are wondering if the extremes in weather are part of global warming and how quickly it will get even worse.

Droughts

Global warming will precipitate worldwide droughts. The farming heartland of the United States will dry out more in summer. We have already begun to see the increase in drought throughout the world. In 1988, the United States suffered its worst heat wave and drought for 50 years. In 2003, extreme heat waves claimed an estimated 35,000 lives in Europe. In France alone, nearly 15,000 people died due to soaring temperatures, which reached a high of 104 degrees Fahrenheit.

2007 witnessed the harshest drought ever in the southeast United States, nearly closing nuclear power plants due to lack of water to cool the reactor cores. This is one example of how many of our modern technologies rely on sustained environmental processes, processes that we are undermining. Officials in the South were concerned that cities like Atlanta, Georgia, were only a few months from running out of drinking water. This extreme drought is entering its second year, and as of this writing, many Southern residents are still under mandatory water use restrictions. Frequent rain is doing little to restore the severely depleted water table.

Melting of the Ice Caps

Sea levels are already rising at a rate of one to two millimeters each year due to the melting of the polar ice caps. The oceans are predicted to rise by 39 inches and storm surges will breach landmasses, eroding the coastal lands of most countries. The Environmental Protection Agency (EPA) projects the United States landmass to lose 22,000 square miles. London and many other British coastal cities will be threatened also. It is now a national priority in England to strengthen Britain's sea defenses.

 Cosmic Caution

It has been pointed out by Associated Press writer Seth Borenstein that as the ice caps melt and the ocean waters rise, the Bushes' Kennebunkport retreat in Maine and John Edwards's Outer Banks estate will be gone. So, too, will the NASA shuttle launchpad in Florida.

Inland Flooding

In addition to the loss of coastal lands, there will be increased flooding in river estuaries such as in Bangladesh and the Nile Delta. Severe flooding is expected in London along the river Thames and in New York along the Hudson. The British government has made it a national-security priority to close down access from a North Sea surge along the river Thames through a system of barriers regulating water flow. It has already been put to the test in the past few years as sea levels have risen and storms have become more intense.

Weather Changes

The El Niño and La Niña weather patterns have always existed. What global warming and solar flares do is increase their frequency and intensity, as we already saw. The 1997 El Niño season caused huge problems all over the world, from droughts to floods. In general there has been an increase in the El Niño weather pattern not seen in the last 120 years of instrument observation.

Another impact you may not have thought of is the lack of snowfall in the mountains. Snow in the mountains feeds streams and rivers and keeps the valley soil fertile. The Northern Hemisphere annual snow cover extent has consistently remained below average since 1987, and has decreased by about 10 percent since 1966.

Social Changes

Here's one to stop and make you think. The United Nations Disaster Preparedness scholars say that by as soon as 2010, 50 million people around the world could be driven from their homes by weather *each year*. Janos Bogardi from the United Nations said in a *Newsweek* interview that "there are absolutely clear signs and compelling statistics showing the situation is getting worse. We now have two to three times as many extreme events of climatic or water related emergencies per year as we did in the 70's. The annual economic loss has increased 6 fold."

According to the World Health Organization's (WHO) own figures, an estimated 150,000 deaths occurred in 2000 due to climate change. An unprecedented heat wave in 2003 left 14,800 people dead in France alone, representing a 60 percent increase in expected mortality. Much of North America experienced a severe heat wave in July 2006, which contributed to the deaths of at least 225 people. Five hundred people died in the European heat wave of July 15–22, 2007. One can readily see that global warming is already happening and is an important threat to human life.

Economic Costs

The economic costs of global warming are astronomical. Just looking at the costs of extreme weather alone is enormous. The loss of personal property is only part of it. Government costs in rescue and restoring infrastructure are crippling. Consider the past few years in the United States. How many Katrina-like storms can any country absorb?

Storms are not the whole story; many aspects of the economy are also impacted, such as health care, agriculture, and energy costs. Consider the increased health risks from the loss of the ozone layer, like skin cancer from increased UV radiation, and asthma. Agriculture is suffering from drought, crop damage, and increased energy requirements to grow crops. The overall effect is skyrocketing prices for food, energy, and other commodities.

Codex Cues

At the same time as we are experiencing huge economic challenges from global warming, there are areas for growth and expansion. The melting of the ice caps has manufacturing and shipping companies increasing production of cargo vessels to take advantage of the opening of new trade routes. Oil exploration into large oil fields is being negotiated among different countries. Tourism into the Artic is expanding. While none of these are good news for the arctic ecosystem, the development of eco-friendly technologies is finally receiving the research and development money they require. There is no doubt that for some, global warming is an economic opportunity. With proper political and social direction, the new technologies can make us all winners.

Environmental Impact

The environmental impact is so severe there is no real way to quantify it. I'm sure you have seen the awful pictures of polar bears trying to adjust to the disappearing ice caps as their habitat is destroyed. They have recently been added to the endangered species list. The way things are going, they will certainly become extinct along with many other species. It's estimated that climate-induced habitat change will push species that are endangered over the edge to extinction. The loss of the rainforest over the next 40 years will remove the cauldron of new species development. And this is a small part of the picture.

Climate change is killing the coral reefs in the Caribbean Sea, the South Pacific Ocean, and parts of the 18-million-year-old barrier reef in Australia. In your lifetime, you will see the loss of these natural resources. There are those who think the death of the coral reefs will bring the death of the oceans. That's how important these natural treasures are to life in the oceans.

As we lose rainforests, ocean ecosystems, and other natural habitats, biodiversity on the planet decreases. The first law of ecology is that diversity increases stability. As we lose diversity on the planet, the global ecosystem becomes more fragile.

Into the Future

Looking at the models and the trends, the future is looking a little bleak. Certainly the United Nations and most worldwide governments see a potential disaster in climate change. However, if the prophecies have taught us anything, they have taught us that we have a choice. The future is what we make it. We can work to shift the trends, or we can be overcome by them.

Lifestyle Change

Maybe you believe that human impact is negligible to the larger picture of global warming. Even so, doesn't it just make sense to work on the levels that we can? Any reduction in the problem has to be helpful. The changes we must make to reduce global warming involve creating better air quality and cleaner water, conserving natural ecosystems, and living healthier lifestyles. Regardless of global warming, aren't these goals worth working for anyway? Change to the next age of the Maya can be traumatic and filled with loss or it can be a creative shift to a new relationship to the earth, nature, and the celestial system we live in. The choice is ours. What shall we do with the future?

Reducing Your Carbon Footprint

You've certainly heard about reducing your carbon footprint, using fewer resources, recycling, and being responsible for your effect on the planet. You may even have gone to workshops sponsored by government or environmental groups. Do you leave feeling this is all too little too late? You're certainly justified in feeling disappointed that it took this long to see the problem, but don't give up! The cumulative impact of each person on the planet is astronomical, and each of us makes a difference. Don't forget, the planet is a living system with its own homeostatic mechanisms. We don't have to do the whole thing alone. We simply have to get out of the way of the planet by reducing our impact. Each of us makes a difference!

Codex Cues _____

Check out the following websites for ideas on how to reduce your carbon footprint:

- The U.S. Environmental Protection Agency: http://epa.gov/climatechange/index.html
- Earth Easy: www.eartheasy.com/article_global_warming.htm
- Climate Crisis: www.climatecrisis.net/takeaction/whatyoucando

Check with your own town or state for local advice.

Maybe you feel that in order to make a difference you must spend a lot of money putting in solar panels, buying hybrid cars, or replacing all of your appliances. Not so! Making a difference is about changing habits, changing the way we think about how we live on the planet. Little things add up to big differences. If you wait until you have the money for big changes, you may wait right past the moment of action. Here is a quick list of simple habits you can easily change to decrease your impact on the planet. These steps may not save the planet but they will show your respect for the earth:

- ◆ Turn the water off while you brush your teeth.

- ◆ Reduce car trips by combining errands.

- ◆ Reuse your take-away coffee cups or get a travel mug.

- ◆ Reuse plastic shopping bags or get canvas bags.

- ◆ Turn off lights when you leave the room.

- ◆ Lower the thermostat on your water heater; most people have it set far hotter than needed.

- ◆ Change air filters and keep your air conditioners and furnace cleaned and tuned.

- ◆ Weatherproof windows in the winter.

- ◆ Reduce, reuse, recycle!

- ◆ In the winter turn your thermostat down three degrees, and in the summer turn it up three degrees.

- ◆ A leaky toilet can waste 200 gallons of water a day; be sure your fixtures are tight.

- ◆ Carpool whenever possible.

- ◆ Keep your car tires properly inflated and drive the speed limit!

Cosmic Caution

Did you know that a five-minute hot shower is equivalent to running a light bulb for 18 hours? You may want to consider that fact when taking extra-long or extra-hot showers!

Changing Relationships

In the end, changing how we act on the planet is one important step in slowing global warming. However, what is truly required is a change in our relationship to the earth. As long as we see ourselves as either masters subjugating nature or victims of cycles we have no control over, we have missed the point. Ironically, people who do not accept the level of human impact on global warming seem to believe that we are both masters and victims simultaneously. What the prophecies show us is that we are neither.

Rather we are part of a living universe—one that is interactive from the celestial level to the cellular level. What we need to do now is relate to the earth as a partner, to respect the natural cycles, and to find a place of balance and harmony in our lifestyles. In the end, what we do is a reflection of what we think. It's time to change how we think of ourselves, of the earth, of the celestial cycles. It's time we return to alignment with the natural cycles and assist the planet in restoring balance.

The Least You Need to Know

◆ Global warming may be one of the mechanisms creating the earth changes predicted for 2012.

◆ Aligning to the celestial pulses of energy and activating sacred sites with k'ul may be part of rebalancing and revitalizing the planet.

◆ Global warming is a real trend and is causing major problems including raising sea levels, flooding, extreme weather, droughts, species extinction and relocation, and loss of human life.

◆ Both natural cycles and human impact are driving global warming.

◆ Simple changes in everyday habits can save energy and reduce your carbon footprint.

◆ To change the direction we are going requires changing the way we think.

Chapter 16

Earth Changes, Epidemics, and Disease

In This Chapter

◆ The activity levels of volcanoes, earthquakes, and tsunamis

◆ The impact of weather and technology on disease

◆ The return of old diseases

◆ The creation of new diseases

◆ Regaining our balance with nature

We are in the end times of the Mayan calendar. Both the destruction of the current age and preparations for the New Age are underway. We are seeing the prophecies come alive as we fast approach 2012. Past ages were destroyed by floods and fire and shakings of the earth. What does the end of this age hold?

According to the book of the *Chilam Balam*, we're in the katun of "total collapse where day will be turned upside down and heaven and Earth will be consumed by fire." What role do volcanoes, earthquakes, and tsunamis play in fulfilling the predictions? Are we seeing a higher incidence of activity?

This chapter will explore the patterns of Earth changes, the incidence of diseases, and the emergence of new diseases in the fulfillment of the predictions.

Forces of the Earth in Turmoil

Volcanoes, earthquakes, and tsunamis are all different aspects of the same Earth forces. The ground under your feet is not as stable as it seems. The earth's crust is made of many plates (called tectonic plates) that move in response to internal pressure from the earth's molten core. As heat and pressure builds, the plates move to release energy.

Earthquakes are the result of these plates grinding against each other. Volcanoes, on the other hand, provide an escape for hot molten rock, ash, and gas formed in the smoldering core. What about tsunamis? When volcanoes and earthquakes happen under the sea, lots of water is moved causing the huge tsunami waves.

The question we're asking is this: Are we seeing more pressure within the earth causing more earthquakes, volcanoes, and tsunamis?

Volcanic Activity

In order to have an increase in volcanic activity, there has to be an increase in pressure deep inside the earth, enough pressure to force an eruption. Right now scientists are wondering about the weakening magnetic field. Is it a sign of changing pressure in the earth's core? Could it result in increased volcanic activity? You may be wondering what the connection is between the magnetic field and volcanoes. The magnetic core creates the magnetic field. If the field is weakening, then something must be changing in the core. If the core is changing, then pressures change, which may cause an increase in volcanic and earthquake activity.

Codex Cues

When a volcano erupts, fiery material can be spewed 25 miles into the air while sizzling lava pours across the countryside. In addition, lightning strikes can be seen in the cloud above the rim. This is due to electrostatic buildup between the rapidly moving particles. What an amazing sight!

According to the Smithsonian there are about 1,511 active volcanoes. This doesn't mean they are actively erupting; it means they have the potential to erupt some day. Volcanoes can sleep for hundreds of years before erupting. Mt. St. Helens is a good example of this.

In 1914, there were about 35 volcano eruptions each year. By 1990 that had grown to 50. Does this indicate an increase in activity? Hold on to that question, we're getting there.

Earthquakes

As you know, earthquakes are measured on the Richter scale; up to a 3 is a small earthquake; over 7 is large one. The really super earthquakes have been over 9. Small earthquakes happen constantly around the world, especially in places like California, Alaska, Peru, Indonesia, Iran, New Zealand, Greece, and Japan. Large earthquakes happen less often. You might be interested to know that the U.S. Geological Survey (USGS) estimates there are several million little earthquakes happening all over the planet each year! In contrast, since the 1900s it's estimated that the earth has one large earthquake per year. This is considered a stable condition.

Earthquakes can happen in clusters, called earthquake storms, which can be misinterpreted as an increase in frequency. Basically it's a lot of small energy releases from the same pressure buildup.

A new NASA study conducted with the USGS predicts that earthquake activity may be increasing. No, they haven't read the Mayan prophecies; they're pointing their finger at global warming! What does global warming have to do with earthquakes?

According to the USGS study, retreating glaciers are changing external versus internal pressures in the earth's crust. Apparently the weight of the glacier stabilizes the plates underneath them. With the rapidly melting ice caps, shifts in weight distribution are increasing the likelihood of earthquakes. This confirms it: the Maya were right and everything is interconnected!

Celestial Connection

It's no accident that volcanoes and earthquakes happen in the same areas, such as the Philippines, Indonesia, or California. The biggest and most active area where tectonic plates meet is the horseshoe-shaped Pacific ridge known as the "Pacific Ring of Fire." It follows the Pacific coast in an arc from the southern tip of South America up along the North American Pacific coast to Alaska, then across the ocean to the entire Pacific coast of China. The Pacific Ring has 452 volcanoes—75 percent of the world's active sites.

Tsunamis

A tsunami is actually a series of waves, some of which can be quite huge. They're often incorrectly called tidal waves. While tidal waves are the result of tidal activity, tsunamis are the result of underwater activity such as underwater earthquakes, landslides, or volcanoes. Tsunamis are also caused by meteor and asteroid impacts in the ocean. Surveys of the ocean floor and examination of shoreline sediment reveal that every few thousand years an asteroid or meteor hits the ocean, causing a mega tsunami.

Increases in tsunamis happen with increased earthquakes and volcanoes. Of course, they happen more frequently along the Pacific Ring of Fire. Several times a year earthquakes measuring over 7 on the Richter scale cause a Pacific tsunami. Japan is reported to be hit by a tsunami at least once a year! Historically, about 1,000 tsunamis have been documented, with only about 100 being large enough to cause damage and loss of life.

The three most recent big tsunamis were:

- *July 17, 2006:* An earthquake measuring 7.7 on the Richter scale occurred south of Java, Indonesia, causing a tsunami that killed 700 people.

- *December 26, 2004:* An earthquake measuring 9.3 on the Richer scale off the island of Sumatra in the Indian Ocean created the worst tsunami disaster in living history. More than 300,000 people were killed in eight Asiatic countries, including Sumatra, Sri Lanka, India, Thailand, Malaysia, and Bangladesh. The flood wave even reached East and Southeast Africa.

- *August 17, 1999:* Northwest Turkey was struck with a large earthquake, 7.8 on the Richter scale, which generated a local tsunami. About 17,000 people lost their lives and thousands more were injured.

If you want to see a record of the tsunamis over the last 1,000 years, check out www.tsunami-alarm-system.com.

Is There an Increase in Earth Activity?

Many people involved with 2012 predictions report there is an alarming and dramatic increase in volcanic and earthquake activity. However, scientists disagree.

Volcanic and earthquake activity goes through cycles of peaks and valleys. Are we approaching a peak? We really don't know. The two biggest valleys in the past coincided with World Wars I and II when people's attention was focused on the war, not

Earth changes. Scientists claim that today's increase in Earth activity is a matter of increased attention, reporting, and technology.

Satellite technology and global communication have dramatically increased our ability to know what's happening all over the planet. You know the phrase that the earth is getting smaller. In addition, more seismographic stations that record earthquake activity are being installed each year. In 1931, around the time your grandparents may have been alive, there were about 350 stations operating world-wide. Today there are over 8,000. Scientists say the increased ability to detect volcanoes and earthquakes is the reason for the "increased" Earth activity.

Celestial Connection
At this writing, there are three earthquake storms occurring along the Pacific Rim from northern Mexico to Alaska. According to Mitch Battros at Earth Changes Media, geologists believe this may be the start of a major event along the Cascadia Subduction Zone or fault line. You can learn more at www. earthchangesmedia.com.

Maybe the question isn't whether there are more earthquakes, volcanoes, and tsunamis, but whether their magnitudes are increasing.

Pestilence and Plagues

As the prophecies foretell, epidemics and disease are definitely on the rise. The past 20 years has shown a dramatic increase in disease activity. We're seeing a return of old diseases we thought were beat, like tuberculosis; as well as new diseases like Sudden Acute Respiratory Syndrome (SARS), West Nile virus, and Morgellons.

What's causing epidemics and new diseases? While there are many factors, we can look at three key ones: environmental changes like global warming, bacterial mutations against antibiotics, and unexpected fallout from new technologies like genetic engineering.

Environmental Change and Disease

The World Health Organization (WHO) is pointing to global warming as the cause not only of new diseases but also of old diseases appearing in new places. Global warming seems to be responsible for many of the 2012 prediction outcomes. In this case, we're looking at how disease spreads.

Many diseases are kept in check by cold weather. Insects that transmit disease, like mosquitoes and ticks, can't survive in really cold areas. Consequently, colder climates

214 Part 4: 2012: Signs of Change

have been immune to diseases like malaria, West Nile virus, and Lyme disease. In fact, these kinds of diseases are on the increase in once-colder climes as global warming changes temperatures.

Another environmental cause of disease growth is extreme weather. As extreme weather and natural disasters increase, infectious disease also increases. Partly this is due to things like flood waters overriding sewage control systems and contaminating local water supplies. It's also due to people being pushed together into higher populations allowing disease to spread more easily.

Here's an example of how environmental extremes can affect disease. In 1993, an explosion of rats in the southwestern United States created an outbreak of a debilitating lung infection. The infection was caused by the hantavirus that is spread by rats. What caused the explosion of rats? A sustained drought killed off the main rat predators. When rain finally came, it increased the rats' food supply allowing the rat population to grow unchecked.

Antibiotic-Resistant Bacteria

Drug-resistant bacteria are on the rise! You may have heard of MRSA, or the methicillin-resistant Staphylococcus aureus bacterium. This is becoming a big problem in hospitals. People come in for routine surgery and leave with an antibiotic-resistant strain of bacteria. Maybe you've also heard of the new stains of tuberculosis (TB) that aren't responding to antibiotic treatment. This has been on the news a lot related to air travel. People with TB traveling on airplanes have put others at risk. The emergence of antibiotic-resistant bacteria is another sure sign we are out of balance with nature.

Bacteria are smart: as we hit them with antibiotics, they mutate to counter the attack. In the past, pharmaceutical companies have kept up with mutations pretty well, but recently the bugs have gotten the upper hand. TB, MRSA, and drug-resistant salmonella and pseudomonas are only a few of the better-known resistant bugs.

Overuse of Antibiotics

Many people think the main overuse of antibiotics happens with doctors. It's true that the Centers for Disease Control (CDC) believes that up to one third of the 150 million prescriptions written each year for antibiotics are unnecessary. However, the biggest problem is the overuse of antibiotics given to food animals such as cows, pigs, and farmed fish. In 1999, a study in the *New England Journal of Medicine* solidified the link between the farm use of antibiotics and difficult-to-treat antibiotic-resistant foodborne bacteria.

You may well wonder why antibiotics are given to the animals you eat. The simple answer is overcrowding. Animals that will become dinner are crowded into small areas with poor sanitation; disease is inevitable. The cure? Feed them daily doses of antibiotics, antibiotics that later affect you. Consider a young boy in Nebraska who contracted antibiotic-resistant salmonella from infected cows that had been given antibiotics. Or the outbreak in Malaysia killing 32 people from encephalitis contracted from antibiotic-fed pigs. If you're not concerned with the suffering of food animals, you should well be concerned with the health implications to you!

Technology-Created Illness

New diseases show signs of having been created by new technologies, specifically genetic engineering. How does this work? Genetic engineering involves the transfer of genes from one species into another species. Using pig genes in apples to give apples stronger skins is one example. Sound like science fiction? It's not!

This is called "horizontal gene transfer" or the transfer of genes between unrelated species of plants or animals. Horizontal gene transfer has been implicated in drug- and antibiotic-resistance bacteria. Think of it: this technology depends on breaking down the natural barriers between species. It designs "gene transfer carriers" that pass genes from one species to another! Certainly the Maya did not predict this mechanism for disease and epidemics, but it's become one of the ingredients in the mix.

 Cosmic Caution

The Third World Network reports that scientific investigation is drawing a correlation between the increase in virulent infections and antibiotic resistance with the commercialization of biotechnology, specifically genetic engineering. Check out www.twnside.org.sg/title/heal-cn.htm for scientific articles.

Recently it's been revealed that microorganisms genetically engineered for "contained use" may not be effectively contained. Could this be the source of some problems to come?

Diseases Old and New

2012 prophecies of increased plagues and epidemics can certainly be seen in the rise and spread of diseases in the past 20 years. Scientists are seeing the spread of diseases happening much faster than they expected. Consider West Nile virus, which was introduced into the United States in 1999 and within four years had spread across the country.

Try not to get depressed as you read on. So far medicine is staying on top of the disease resurgence, and there are tremendous resources being activated to make sure it stays that way! Our job is to look at the trends and see if they fit the 2012 predictions.

Cholera

Cholera was pretty much erased from North and South America by the beginning of the twentieth century. Suddenly in 1991 cholera returned with a vengeance, sweeping down the west coast of South America. Between 1991 and 1995, more than one million people were infected and 11,000 were killed. Africa had a similar surge in 1991, as did India in 1992, and three years later Russia followed.

There's a worry that as the population increases, close living conditions will encourage the spread of cholera. Combined with extreme weather that overloads sewage control, many countries are preparing for cholera epidemics. As we write this book, Myanmar has been hit with a cyclone, leaving at least one million people homeless and surviving in devastating conditions. The world is preparing to respond as cholera is erupting through the population.

Malaria and Dengue Fever

Malaria and dengue fever are tropical diseases spread by mosquitoes. As the climate changes and mosquitoes begin to live in new environments, malaria and dengue fever are spreading into northern climates. Malaria is spreading in Europe, the United States, and Turkey.

Dengue fever was confined to Southeast Asia in the 1960s, but is now widely distributed in Africa and Central and South America. Dengue fever even moved as far north as Florida and Texas, but quickly fizzled out in the face of aggressive measures to fight it.

Severe Acute Respiratory Syndrome (SARS)

In 2003, an outbreak of Severe Acute Respiratory Syndrome (SARS) threatened to become a pandemic, or worldwide epidemic. The SARS virus is a mutated form of "bird flu," the coronavirus that infects birds. The disease spread rapidly throughout Asia, infecting backyard chickens, and then transferring to the families who kept them.

SARS quickly spread to many countries around the world due to infected people traveling on airplanes and transporting the virus to new countries. Maybe you were one of the air passengers caught in the struggle to contain the disease. In a desperate attempt to halt the spread of the disease, airplane companies began screening passengers for fevers or flu-like symptoms. Passengers with symptoms were not allowed to fly. Many passengers began to protect themselves from infection by wearing face masks on airplanes. When the outbreak spread to Toronto, some Toronto residents also began wearing face masks. However, no one could stop the spread of SARS through migrating bird populations.

At the height of the 2003 SARS pandemic, the World Health Organization reported that a total of 8,098 people worldwide became sick. Of these, 774 died. In the United States, only eight people had verified lab evidence of SARS.

Morgellons

You may not have heard of this new disease, but it's starting to get a lot of attention. It was discovered in 2001 and was largely discredited until recently. Here's a brief description: a person will start to itch, get nasty sores on his or her skin, and then feel something alive and moving underneath the skin. At first people with Morgellons were diagnosed as having psychotic parasitosis. In other words, it was all in their heads!

Unfortunately for the people who get it, these moving things under the skin eventually erupt through the skin as multicolored fibers. The fibers have been collected and analyzed from people all over the world. They are all the same. Hard for a psychosis to produce!

Other symptoms of Morgellons include arthritis pain, confusion, memory loss, vision problems, and itching, stinging, and biting sensations. It often occurs in people already diagnosed with Lyme disease.

What's really odd is that the fiber material is unknown. Many suspect it's a type of nanotechnology, or genetically engineered material. The fibers seem to have a component of cellulose, leading some researchers to believe it's caused by a rare infection of Agrobacterium. This is a bacteria that has an ability to transfer DNA between itself and plants, and for this reason has been used extensively in genetic engineering. Is it possible that genetically modified bacteria got out of the lab and is transferring DNA to humans? Hopefully we will know the answer soon. In 2007, under extreme public pressure, the CDC began an investigation into Morgellons. We await the results.

 Cosmic Caution

Morgellons is a very serious disease that everyone will want to stay abreast of. Here's a website where you can get accurate and up-to-date information: www.morgellons.org/newsletters.

Finding Balance

This chapter may have left you feeling a little overwhelmed, as it did us, too. The Maya predicted that life would become more difficult as humans lost balance with nature. In fact, that's really what's going on. We have lost our balance with nature and lost respect for the purpose of natural barriers and design. On the positive side, if we've learned anything from the Mayan calendars, we know that cycles come and go and balance is found and lost repeatedly. As our current imbalance with nature gets more extreme, it will in fact create its own turnaround point that will bring us back to balance. Like the pendulum swinging, nothing stays the same. The question is, will it happen in time to avert total destruction? Let's keep delving into the signs of change for an answer.

The Least You Need to Know

- ◆ At present it's unclear whether increased reports of volcanic activity and earth-quakes are real or the result of the increased detection and reporting.

- ◆ The upsurge of old diseases and the spread of warm-climate diseases are related to global warming.

- ◆ New technologies may be producing bacterial mutations and antibiotic resistance.

- ◆ Genetic engineering may be responsible for new diseases such as Morgellons.

- ◆ The situation we are in is a sure sign that we are out of balance with nature.

Chapter 17

Cutting the Pie

In This Chapter

◆ The impact of population

◆ The human footprint

◆ Finite resources and social tensions

◆ Attitude shift for the coming age

Earth changes and severe weather are not the only warnings of the 2012 predictions. The prophecies warn of social problems, too. In the Mayan *Chilam Balam*, we're told there will be "scarcity of resource, food shortages and many people dying." The katun predicts a time when people lose confidence in both established religion and government.

The Bible says of the end times: "Nation will rise against nation, and kingdom against kingdom. There will be great earthquakes, famines and pestilences in various places, and fearful events and great signs from heaven." (Luke 21:10–11 NIV) Nostradamus predicts that the social upheaval of the times will allow the "antichrist" to come to power. Are you having fun yet?

If you start to feel overwhelmed reading this chapter, we felt overwhelmed writing it, too! Just remember, we have everything required to shift things. How we've done things in the past is part of the old age that is breaking down. The time leading to 2012 may well be the pressure cooker forcing us to evolve our thinking, our relationship to the planet, and our ways of living. As much as this is purification, it's rectification as well.

Population Explosion

The world population is currently about 6.5 billion people. By 2012, this will rise to over 7 billion people. Those are big numbers to grasp! The plain fact is that as people are living longer and more babies are being born, more than twice as many people are being born each day than are dying. The population is growing at a rate of 74,629,207 people per year, which is 2.37 people per second.

Codex Cues

You can watch the numbers of births, deaths, and other statistics changing in real time at the world clock website: www.peterrussell.com/Odds/WorldClock.php.

Many think increasing population is the biggest issue in global health and well-being. Ever-increasing numbers of people are stressing the food supply, air and water quality, resource availability, and our quality of living. It's the single biggest factor in both global warming and the loss of ecosystems. Will population increase stress world resources enough to fulfill the predictions for 2012?

An Increase in Consumption

You may have noticed that the cost of living has skyrocketed as more people compete for land, lumber, fuel, and food in a growing world market. Of course we know that consumption of all resources increases with population, but that's only half the picture. Our demands on the planet also increase with prosperity! Certainly prosperity is a good thing, but let's look at its effect on resources.

Developed nations have multiplied their consumption of product per person exponentially. You consume today over 100 times the resources of your great-grandparent living 200 years ago. During the same time period, the population has increased by a factor of ten. This makes a thousandfold increase in consumption, waste production, and pollution.

Herman Daly, formerly of the World Bank, is an ecological economist. He's often called the unsung hero of ecologically responsible economics. In his book *Beyond*

Growth: The Economics of Sustainable Development (see Resources appendix), Daly outlines the reality that the physical world is finite and we cannot continue to grow forever. Can the earth continue to provide for our growing population or will we, like the early Maya, outgrow our ability to support ourselves?

Resource Limitation

Will resources become more scarce and become the reason for wars and famine? Here's some of the mounting evidence:

◆ In many parts of the world, fresh drinking water is becoming scarce. This will get worse as weather patterns continue to change. What happens when drought leaves populated cites without drinking water?

◆ Electricity and fossil fuels are at a premium. Wars and conflict over energy are increasing. Sustainable energy production is only now gaining widespread attention, years behind the need.

◆ Farming has turned to genetic engineering to produce genetically modified (GM) foods for increased production on less land with decreased needs for fertilizer and pesticides. Sound good? Unfortunate by-products of this technology are increased food allergies, possible new diseases, and corporate control of our legal right to grow our own food.

◆ The destruction of mature forests and the increased demand for lumber and building supplies is overrunning what forests are able to supply.

Codex Cues _____

This may sound extreme, but GM seed companies are getting laws passed that control people's ability to grow food in their own gardens. Don't believe it? Check out these resources:

◆ *Stolen Harvest, The Hijacking of the Global Food Supply* by Vandana Shiva (South End Press, 2000)

◆ *The Future of Food* and *Unnatural Selection* (Lily Films, 2004)

◆ www.organicconsumers.org

The Impact of Today's Lifestyle

Some indigenous people think of modern man as a cancer on the planet. Maybe they have a point. Cancer cells are normal, natural cells that have forgotten the rules. They grow without respect to the space available, they reproduce without respect to the supply of food, they steal food and nutrition from nearby cells, and they try to live forever.

In Native thinking, there's a principle called the "Seventh Generation." This principle requires that every decision is considered in light of the impact it will have seven generations into the future. Now that's long-term planning! Consider the impact just one generation into the future of our present growth and expansion, let alone seven!

Species Extinction

We have used the coats, skins, oil, meat, and blood of animals to sustain us since the beginning of human life. The animal populations and ecosystems we have depended on are struggling. As reported in Chapter 15, we are losing the rainforest, our most important ecosystem, at the rate of one and a half acres per second. In less than two generations it will be gone. The rainforest is the ecosystem that produces the most new species. Would you believe that biologists estimate many thousands of species living on Earth have not yet even been discovered? Many will be extinct before we ever know they existed.

According to the National Wildlife Federation (NWF), the current worldwide rate of extinction is about 27,000 species per year, or three species lost every hour. The main reason is habitat destruction. We are destroying ecosystems at such a rapid rate we have no way to calculate the impact on planetary and human health.

Pollution Fallout

Have you wondered why so many children today have asthma? Or why allergies are on the increase? Have you noticed the bulletins along waterways saying: "Don't eat the shellfish"? It's not new news that we're poisoning the planet and the species living here. As our population grows, pollution gets worse and the planet's ability to clean up the mess decreases. Of course, what we do to the earth we are doing to ourselves.

I hear people say that we don't have to worry about pollution because the planet has mechanisms to clean the environment. So what are these mechanisms? Trees clean the air; they are the lungs of the planet. We've already noted the loss of mature ecosystems that provide trees for this process. Natural environments like swamps, wetlands, and tributaries filter and clean the water; they are the kidneys of the planet. We are fast developing this marginal land despite laws passed in the 1970s to protect them. In reality we're growing exponentially, producing more waste than our planetary lungs and kidneys can process, while at the same time destroying these vital organs.

Nature has no way to clean modern-day hazardous waste. Nuclear waste will survive on this planet a hundred generations into the future. Not such a happy thought when we consider the insufficient storage containers!

More and more people are seeing the planet as a global ecosystem and are beginning to respond to the signs of ecosystem imbalance. The truth is that the planet will survive and recover whatever we do. It's not the long-term health of the planet in question, its human health and survival in the balance.

Plastic Waste

How are we getting rid of the enormous waste we generate each day? Much of it's dumped in the oceans, weighed down to land on the ocean floor. However, huge floating mountains of plastic waste are being reported "growing" in the Pacific Ocean.

Oceanographer Curtis Ebbesmeyer is the world's leading flotsam expert. He refers to the area of plastic collection in the Pacific as "the great Pacific Garbage Patch." The garbage patch is the size of a continent and is composed of plastic fragments that have floated together. Captain Charles Moore reports, "My research has documented six pounds of plastic for every pound of plankton in this area." The plastic waste is entangling sea life, being eaten as food, and destroying ecosystems.

Cosmic Caution

Hazardous waste is defined as any waste that is toxic, infectious, radioactive, or flammable and that poses a hazard to human, animal, and/or environmental health. Worldwide, about 400 million metric tons of hazardous wastes are generated each year.

As problems like this grow, we're challenged to find new solutions. Many solutions come from simply seeing the world through different eyes.

Vote with Your Dollars

We all have choices. You probably already live with an awareness of the impact you have on your local ecosystem. Interestingly, right now in the United States, any state that tries to exceed the federal government's environmental standards is chastised. State air-quality standards are not allowed to exceed federal standards. Why? Because it creates "unfair" economic stress on corporations.

You may be active on environmental or conservation committees, or in local politics, all good ways to influence the direction we're taking. Another point of power is the influence we have as consumers. If economics is the language of political and corporate decision making, then make your dollars count. Every dollar you spend is a vote. If people stop buying energy-inefficient products, choose organic foods, and start demanding new energy technologies, corporations will alter production to fit the new demand. Change happens from the bottom up. We can change the direction we're going, and if we don't, the snake will certainly bite its own tail before long!

Economic Crises

You may not have a lot of background in economic theory, but it doesn't take a financial Einstein to see the worldwide economy is in a mess. Realistically, how could it not be? Isn't it amazing how many factors coming together in this time seem to be driving us toward the 2012 prophecies?

Financial Trends

The U.S. dollar value is at an all-time low. The U.S. trade deficit, the gap between U.S. imports and exports, is $600 billion. That's nothing compared to the national deficit. As of March 2008, the deficit stands at $9,371,626,066,337.15 (keep the change). Each United States citizen shares the national debt, which amounts to $30,871.57 per person. Unfortunately, we are still in a downward trend. Since September 29, 2006, the debt has increased at the rate of $1.65 *billion* per day.

> **Celestial Connection**
>
> President Bush announced in February 2008 that with his new economic plan the United States will have a budget surplus by 2012. This is one of the 2012 predictions we're putting in the category of bad science!

We hear the word billion these days without really being able to visualize what the numbers mean. Let's consider some examples. A billion seconds ago, it was 1960. A billion minutes ago, Jesus was alive, and a billion hours ago we lived in the Stone Age. As far as government expenditure is concerned, a billion dollars ago was only eight hours and twenty minutes in Washington.

When such a major world currency as the U.S. dollar is in this kind of trouble, it's not hard to see the final pieces coming together for the dreaded condition called "World Recession." A look at the volatile New York, London, and Japanese stock markets shows how true this is. And if there's any doubt left, the worldwide credit crunch seals the deal.

Does the trend just keep going down? Is there a bottom? Business cycles are normal in a world of inexact balances between supply and demand. Is this a normal cycle or have we broken the rules and moved into a new arena? Are there financial forecasts for 2012?

Market Models

Market models allow economists to analyze market factors and predict trends in the economy. One market model is called the Elliott Wave theory, developed by Ralph Nelson Elliott in the late 1920s. He noticed that stock markets did not behave in a chaotic manner as was believed. He noticed trading followed repetitive cycles based on the emotions of investors. It was thought investors made their decisions based on logic. Contrary to belief, emotions of investors were often based on intangibles. Market emotions were not necessarily influenced by actual events, like a good strategic move by a company, but were influenced by mass expectation. This is the type of self-fulfilling prophecy we talked about in Chapter 13 that causes runs on banks, fulfilling the fear that the bank isn't solvent.

Elliott stated that the upward and downward swings of "mass psychology" always showed up in the same repetitive patterns. The patterns themselves could be further divided into patterns he termed "waves." The Elliott wave pattern allows current market analysts to predict cycles. Today we know that Elliott had stumbled onto the theory of *fractal* mathematics as expressed in economics—the same fractal mathematics the Maya found in the cycles of time.

The Elliott Wave system predicts that between the years 2012 and 2015 there will be a sharp burst in the economic bubble in response to credit implosion and the lack of credit reserve. In other words, there will be an economic meltdown. The good news? The years 2017–2033 will herald a new era called "The Great Global Re-Balancing."

def•i•ni•tion

A **fractal** is a rough or fragmented geometric shape that can be subdivided into parts, each of which is a smaller copy of the whole. The leaf of a fern is an example of a fractal.

Codex Cues

You can learn more about the Elliott Wave theory at www. elliottwavetechnology.com.

Here's an amazing synchronicity: the first katun of the New Age starts on 2013 and runs to 2033. If you remember from Chapter 9, the first katun brings changes and rebalancing of systems. How interesting that the stock market forecasts so closely match the Mayan katuns!

Social and Religious Tension

As economic pressures build and resources become more limited, competition for resources becomes more intense. The result is an increase in social, religious, and political tension. We're seeing war for oil in the Middle East, and barely contained stress in many parts of the planet. Fishermen have to travel farther for fewer fish, farmers are forced to buy GM seed, and people have lost faith that governments are in place for them.

How much additional stress will it take to push things beyond control? One pandemic? Five massive hurricanes? Three earthquakes? Or a solar flare that knocks out satellite technology and the power grid? Will you be ready? See Chapter 20 for tips on preparedness.

Assessment 2012

This chapter (as well as the previous three) has assessed the unique stress the global community is under as we head toward 2012. We found consistent support in today's world for the prophecies of 2012, but this doesn't mean things have to get worse. We can turn things around with nothing more than a change in attitude.

Population Bottleneck

What the Mayan and New Age predictions describe is what in ecology is called a population bottleneck. This happens when the resources of a system become so narrowed, or conditions become so extreme that the population is massively reduced. Those who get through the neck of the bottle to the next era of growth and expansion have demonstrated an ability to adapt and change.

The bottleneck we are in was predicted by the Mayan prophecies, which say this time eliminates what doesn't work and establishes a better foundation. Our current mindset doesn't work. We can't have unlimited growth with finite resources. We can't take whatever we want without paying back. The new behaviors we need to adopt may be spiritual. In the creation stories, the earlier ages created the material world. Each time, what was missing in creation was the "people's" ability or desire to "worship." We can loosely translate the word worship to mean spiritual awareness. If humanity develops the tools of spiritual awareness, will we make it through the bottleneck? Or more importantly, will the bottleneck be needed at all?

Attitudes for the Fifth Age

It's been suggested that the bottleneck we're going through is creating a change in paradigm, or the way in which we see the world. Right now modern man acts as if the material world is all there is. People act as if we are in competition with each other for our piece of the pie. If you get your piece, I might not get mine. How about this: neither if us gets a piece of the pie unless we both do. Or, even better, there is no pie! It's a myth!

The world is more than matter. Energy flows constantly from one form to another. Imagine money as a flow of energy rather than a piece of a pie. In the pie analogy, once you eat it, it's gone. In the energy analogy, money is in constant flow, coming in and going out. Can you encompass an idea that we effect the direction of flow? Check out Chapter 21 for more on this.

In our travels around the world and our discussions with elders of many traditions, we have come across attitudes that repeat in all traditional cultures. These are attitudes that can assist us all in the transition underway. You will not be surprised; these four cornerstones are things every culture teaches:

- ◆ **Respect:** For self; for others; for all life forms; for the planet itself; for the celestial bodies; for those we walk beside; for our ancestors; for our descendants.

- ◆ **Gratitude:** Everything is a gift, nothing can be taken for granted—not the fruits of the earth, not the ground we walk on, not the people we love or the wealth we aspire to. However much we may deserve something or however hard we've worked for it, what we have is a gift and can be taken at any moment, including life itself.

- ◆ **Harmony/Balance:** The flow of life exists in rhythms and harmonics. All things have their place. All people, all life forms, all events both good and bad have their place in the circle of life. To stay in harmony and balance requires taking no more than we need and giving back equal to what we use. Resonance with the cycles and flow brings great joy and gratitude.

◆ **Interconnectedness:** We are all one, part of the same whole. What affects you affects me. What we do to the earth we do to ourselves.

The Least You Need to Know

◆ Predictions of 2012 seem eerily accurate in the light of current social and environmental stress.

◆ Population growth and increased prosperity has created a tremendous burden on natural resources of the planet.

◆ Earth's ability to cleanse and regenerate has been compromised by the size of the load and the destruction of ecosystems.

◆ We can use consumer choice to drive corporate decision making.

◆ Getting through the bottleneck requires a paradigm shift emphasizing cooperation over competition.

◆ Common traditional attitudes of indigenous cultures are respect, gratitude, harmony/balance, and interconnection.

Chapter 18

Crop Circles and Other Signs from the Meta-Conscious Mind

In This Chapter

- ◆ Crop circles, defined
- ◆ An evolution from simple circles to complex designs
- ◆ Tlakaelel's quest
- ◆ Astronomical relationships
- ◆ Mayan and Aztec connections
- ◆ Other signs from meta-consciousness

The term meta-consciousness means the part of our awareness that is beyond the ordinary. Swiss psychologist Carl Jung spoke of this as the collective unconscious, the part of our self that is connected to everything on the planet. Meta-consciousness can be activated through signs and symbols opening the door to the deeper awareness within. In fact, the signs and symbols are said to be coming from our meta-consciousness and manifesting in the material world to jolt our conscious mind. In other words, communication from self to self!

In Chapter 9, we learned from the *Chilam Balam* that in the last katun of the Long Count calendar the Mayan masters would return to awaken humans. It's said that humans will be awakened by signs and symbols that stimulate our memory and inner awareness. There is no doubt the crop circles fit the criteria of meta-conscious messages. In this chapter, we'll explore the crop circles as well as other signs of the times.

Colin has researched crop circles since 1983 and wrote the first book on the subject, *Circular Evidence* (see Resources appendix), with co-author Pat Delgado in 1989. This chapter is written in Colin's voice, telling his journey into the mysterious astronomy of the Maya and their connection to the crop circles.

Mysterious Crop Circles

Crop circles are designs found in corn and other cereal crops. Despite what you may have thought, they're not mowed into the crop; they're laid down with the stalk bent at a 90-degree angle to the earth. The genuine circles are not broken over, or damaged in any way. The stalk is simply bent, as you can see in the following photo. The plants are swirled down into designs with no damage to the plant, no marks in the soil, and no signs of human involvement. Along with the rest of the field, crop circles are harvested at the end of the year and the plants become part of the cereal and bread we eat.

def•i•ni•tion

Crop circles are circular areas of flattened plants, normally flattened in a spiraled fashion. The term *crop circle* was coined by Colin in 1985. It was added to the *Oxford English Dictionary* in 1997 to describe the areas of flattened crops. Although the formations in the field moved beyond simple circles, the term stuck and is now a household word around the world.

Although the first formations were simple circles, hence the name, they quickly evolved into dramatic and intricate designs. Some of the formations have been hundreds of feet long and across!

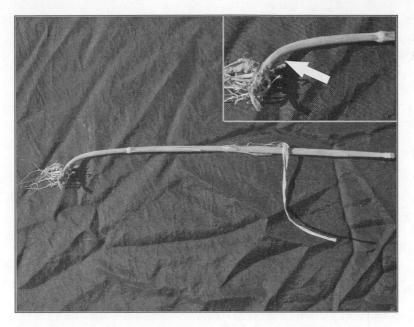

This is a typical bent stalk that can be seen in the plants in genuine crop formations.

Reports from the Fields

Crop circles have existed for decades, but the first documented and photographed crop circle appeared in 1976 in a wheat field on an English farm. Since 1976 there have been well over 11,000 reported crop circles. Although most of them have appeared in England, they've been found in 30 different countries from all over the world.

I started researching in 1983 after seeing a crop design from my car as I drove over the crest of a hill, looking down into a field of wheat. The formation was composed of five circles with one in the center and four "satellites" surrounding the central circle. I was hooked on first sight. How were they made? What force could do this? Were people involved? At this point I have personally visited, measured, photographed, and experimented with approximately 2,500 crop-circle formations.

Knowing what I know now, on seeing my first five circles I might have immediately thought of the Tree of Life with a central pole and four corner posts; or of a medicine wheel with the four directions. It also has the central elements of the Sunstone Calendar; the fifth age is in the center surrounded by the four previous ages (look back to the illustration of the sunstone calendar in Chapter 8 to compare the images). Coming from my own background, I saw the elements of a Celtic cross. In actuality, the evolution of the designs shows all the astronomical elements of the Maya celestial vision, which we'll examine more closely in a few moments.

Ancient Evidence

There are many reports in local folklore of circles arriving in the crops. The oldest documented crop circle–type report was of a circle that occurred on August 8, 1590, and can still be read about in the 1686 book *The Natural History of Stafford-shire* by Robert Plott. (This book is out of print but can sometimes be found in rare bookstores. Amazon.com has one copy available at $3,567! Any takers?) The crop was swirled to the ground in the shape of a circle. Another such circle was drawn and reported in the local paper in 1678 and was known as the Hertfordshire Mowing Devil.

Codex Cues

You can see a picture of the Hertfordshire Mowing Devil in Colin's third book, *Crop Circles: Signs of Contact*, written with Steve Spignesi (see Resources appendix). The book also explores the crop-circle mystery in great detail.

During the course of my investigations, I have talked to many farmers about the designs in their fields. They report that the formations have appeared for years and are always in the same fields. The earliest eyewitness account I received was from a farmer who saw circles in the field as a child in the 1920s. Circles still arrive in his and surrounding fields today; many of the formations link the crop circles to the prophecies of 2012 by displaying intricate Mayan designs.

Circular Anomalies

While researching crop circles, I experienced a number of anomalies when inside the formations. Magnetic compasses would rotate wildly, electronic equipment would stop working, and strange objects that I hadn't seen at the time would show up later in the photographs. These types of anomalies happen to many people visiting the formations.

The most startling anomaly was an electrostatic chirping sound that I and others have heard on at least three occasions. On two occasions I was able to record the sound, which has undergone extensive analysis. Its source is still unidentified. Who or what is making these noises, and why?

The Artist's Hand

How and why crop circles are made remains a mystery. Some are human-made, and I'll talk about those in the next section. Others are unknown. Many theories exist but none have been proven. We have looked to find natural magnetic fluxes, have explored the idea of extraterrestrials, and have looked at military technology. We have not found the artist's hand.

We know that the formations occur quickly, in some cases within a few seconds. Eyewitnesses report the plants suddenly oscillate, moving back and forth wildly, then simply collapse to the earth. Dowsing, a technique used to detect earth energy, demonstrates the formations are linked to ley lines, or lines of k'ul, as the Maya would say. Ley lines is the term used by modern people for the lines of energy across the planet. For anyone who wants to know more about this, I highly recommend a book written by one of the first modern-day pioneers, *Principles of Dowsing* by Dennis Wheatley (Thorsons, 2000).

Interestingly, the ley lines also link the formations to ancient sacred sites such as Stonehenge and Avebury. The following photo shows a simple circle located in front of the ancient sacred site of Silbury Hill. Are the circles activating these ancient sites as Mayan Elder Hunbatz Men says will happen?

This single circle was found in a barley crop on the morning of July 15, 1988. In the background is Silbury Hill, the largest ancient manmade mound in the world and one of Britain's sacred sites.

Human Involvement

Since crop circles became a public fascination in the late 1980s, people began trying their hand at making them. Like the genuine phenomenon, human-made circles, often called hoaxes, are large, intricate, and beautiful. They also exhibit anomalies; people who make crop circles have strange things happen to them in the fields. They report feeling compelled to create circles and are often surprised at the patterns they make. Human-made circles often produce magnetic anomalies as do the genuine circles. When I first started to explore crop circles, I thought that if people were making them it would put an end to the mystery. Instead it creates more of a mystery. Is there something special about the geometries themselves regardless of how they arrive? Why do people feel compelled to make them? Is this really just us sending messages to ourselves? Part of the meta-consciousness?

The Power of Intention

Let me share an experience I had one night, September 9, 1988. I lived near Stonehenge at the time of this experience and was deep into my crop-circle research. One night I focused my intention on the design of a Celtic cross. At this point the Celtic cross pattern had not been seen in a crop circle before. I saw the formation in my mind's eye in a field as close to my home as possible. Some might call the process I used prayer, and I won't disagree. What's important is not the name, but the fact that we can use the power of our hearts and minds together to manifest a physical outcome.

You won't be surprised when I tell you that in the morning I received a phone call from a farmer who lived nearby, in fact the closest farm to my house. "There's a new one but you'll have to be quick," he stated. "We're harvesting and it will be gone in an hour." I was awed to see it was a Celtic cross, exactly as I had visualized it. This event has taught me the power of our developed intent, a concept the Maya teach as well.

Interaction with Something Larger

For me, the most intriguing aspect of the crop circles is the sense of interaction people feel. Those who have researched the circles and those who have made them report the same thing: we feel we are interacting with something larger than ourselves. People making the circles report feeling they have been compelled not only to make them but to make certain designs and even to place them in certain locations. That sounds far fetched, doesn't it? But nonetheless, it seems we are all part of a larger design that is now unfolding. At face value, it seems like intelligence is interacting with the minds of those close to the "drawing board." The interaction not only manifests sincerely held intentions but also acts in reverse by placing thoughts into people's minds, thoughts that appear to be their own. A sudden intuition, taken on board and accepted as your own, may have been such an interaction.

Are we playing someone else's game; are we players in someone else's prophecy? As life moves unabated toward 2012, the story is far from over. I wait to see if prophecy brings an abrupt end or if time will morph into a new, much more exciting and wonderful age, the Mayans' fifth world, which I think is likely.

The Impact of Crop Circles

Like me, people who see crop circles are moved in some unidentifiable way. The images evoke deep emotions, an overwhelming sense of awe, and a vague feeling of remembering something locked in the back of your mind. People are brought to tears for no known reason. Many feel they are being communicated with. I have given lectures around the world, showing people aerial photographs of the formations. My experience is that people from all cultures and beliefs are affected. What better way to awaken people than with designs from the meta-consciousness scribed into nature?

> **Celestial Connection**
>
> An interesting thought: since the crop circle designs are harvested with the rest of the fields, many of us have been eating these plants in our cereal, bread, and other products. Is this another way of awakening humanity?

The Evolution of Design

The crop circles began, as the name implies, as simple circles. They quickly evolved through a series of steps into complex, beautiful designs. The designs continued to evolve in groups that we've called "design families." Some have been astronomical families including galaxies, comets, and solar systems; others have been mathematical fractals; others have been religious symbolism from many cultures.

Let's take an evolutionary journey through the fields via the family of astronomical formations. This journey spans nearly a quarter of a century and evolves to reflect the astronomical focus of the Maya.

The first crop circles, swirled into the cereal plants, created a three-dimensional impression of a sphere. They could have represented many things; however, most people were immediately reminded of a planetary body or perhaps even the sun. In the following illustration, you can follow the progression we saw in the fields:

1976: Single circles in the field (#1 in the following illustration).

1983: A single circle was surrounded by four satellites, positioned in the four directions; it could be suggestive of orbiting bodies (#2 in the following illustration).

1986: A single circle arrived with a single concentric ring around it (#3 in the following illustration). Was this intended to represent the atmosphere around planet Earth? Or an orbit around the sun?

1988: The four satellites of 1983 arrive connected by a concentric ring (#4 in the following illustration). Now this does seem to symbolize an orbit around a central body. Someone or something seemed to be talking "astronomy," like a Mayan astronomer's spirit, drawing his chart and using the cereal crops as his canvas.

1992: The first crescent arrived in the fields (#5 in the following illustration). Synthia and I were flying a reconnaissance flight over southern England with pilot and researcher Busty Taylor. Synthia spotted this beautiful sliver peeping out of the shimmering field. Of course we thought of a crescent moon.

1994: Two galaxy designs arrive (#6 in the following illustration). It was as if we had already been shown our place in the solar system and now we were being shown our place in the larger picture, the galaxy.

1994: A simple design appeared looking like a drawing of a massive solar flare leaving the sun (#7 in the following illustration).

Here are the crop-circle designs as they evolved from 1976 to 1994.

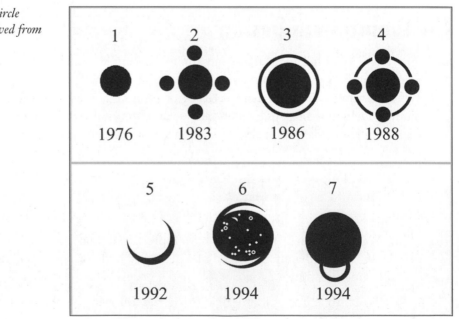

By this time, many people were looking at the circles and getting involved in researching them. The formations continued to evolve, getting more and more elaborate each year. To everyone, it began to feel like something was trying to tell us something. Was this a coincidence, one big hoax, or was this the fulfillment of prophecy?

My Journey with Tlakaelel

Let's take a break from the design evolution for a moment (we'll return later) and let me tell you about my meeting with Aztec Elder Tlakaelel. You may remember Tlakaelel from Chapter 14.

You probably remember from Part 1 that the Aztec Nation is closely aligned and related to the Maya. In fact, the creation stories and calendars are clearly built on each other. What you are about to read is classified as "high strangeness," but it's all true and verified by many witnesses.

Tlakaelel's Request

Synthia and I were working in the Circles Phenomenon Research International (CPRI) office in Guilford, Connecticut. Out of the blue we received a visit from the 87-year-old Aztec Elder with his interpreter/guide, Burt Gunn, and two friends. Synthia knew Tlakaelel and Burt from the past, having participated with them in sacred ceremony and sweat lodge. They arrived on May 23, 1994, with a story and a request for help with an important question.

Tlakaelel told us about an unexpected experience he had while being driven across Mexico. He was sitting in the rear seat, letting his mind wander with the passing scenes. Suddenly, he had a vision of a series of symbols in his head and heard the request: "Find the place of the last ceremonial dance." He did not know what the symbols were until he was later shown pictures of crop circles. This is why he sought me out.

Sitting in my office with pictures of crop circles on all the walls, Tlakaelel asked for a pencil and paper. He sketched an intricate symbol consisting of a crescent abutting the side of a large circle with satellites around it and with a tail of ever smaller abutting circles. The line of circles formed an arc. At the end of the arc was another, smaller crescent. It looked to me something like a scorpion. After drawing the symbol he became silent, looking with deep meaning into my eyes. "Have you seen this," he asked, "and where?"

The CPRI Catalogue of Images contains the most comprehensive record of crop patterns from around the world. I felt how important this was to Tlakaelel but had to respond, "No, I have not, but let me show you those that I have knowledge of and have recorded in the data." I was able to show them many designs, some that were composed of pieces from Tlakaelel's sketch. You've seen some already in the previous illustration.

Of the many hundreds of different designs in the database, some repeating many times and in many countries, there were none with all the elements assembled in his vision. I could see he was disappointed and I hoped his long journey had not been wasted. I had no idea what a shock awaited us within seconds of the departure of this Aztec Elder from our office.

Arrival of Tlakaelel's Design

We walked Tlakaelel and his party to their car and watched them climb in and drive slowly out of the parking lot. We returned to the office to hear the fax machine starting up. It was a message from my friend Reg Presley (lead singer of the music group The Troggs) in England. He was reporting a newly found crop circle in the field under Silbury Hill.

Codex Cues

Crop circles often frequent the same places year after year. They have been found by farmers within sight of Stonehenge since the 1940s but only since 1988 have they been found within sight of the ancient mound of Silbury Hill, England. The circles now appear every year in the same fields around Silbury Hill, forming one of the most prolific hot spots in the world.

The crop formation Reg faxed was of an exciting and unusual new design. As you might be guessing, the second page coming out of the fax machine provided a shock. Here in front of my eyes was the very design Tlakaelel had been asking about. You can see the crop-circle design in the first image in the following illustration. I was so shocked my heart was pounding! It took a few moments to register that the field the formation was discovered in was an archeological site where ancient ceremonial dancing occurred.

Of course we faxed the information immediately to Burt Gunn, Tlakaelel's interpreter and guide. Why was this design so important? What was the intention for the Aztec Elder?

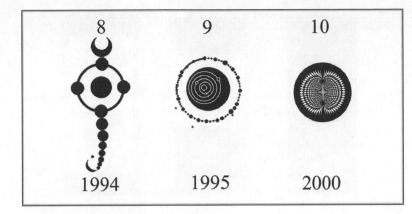

Here are three designs of Mayan significance.

Tlakaelel Visits Silbury Hill

Although Tlakaelel and Burt were deeply moved by the pictures I sent of the formation, it was one full year before they were able to join us in England. Synthia and I escorted Tlakaelel and Burt to Silbury Hill and to the field where the scorpion design, now long gone, had appeared. A whole book could be written about the series of strange things that happened surrounding this one crop circle, but I will conclude with this last synchronicity.

We climbed the ancient mound of Silbury Hill and gazed out across the fields. Tlakaelel stood and felt the energy flows along the landscape. He pointed to several locations, implying they were important energy spots. I was the only person there who could confirm he was correct; all the places he pointed to had indeed been the sites of past crop circles. Across the road from Silbury Hill is another ancient sacred site called West Kennett Long Barrow. While standing on Silbury, Tlakaelel was drawn to West Kennett and we trekked down the mound and across the fields to the long barrow.

It was a sunny, clear day with a wonderful sense of peace and well-being penetrating the scene. As Synthia and I walked with Tlakaelel and Burt toward the barrow, a young man, perhaps 18 or 19 years old, advanced across the open fields on a bicycle. We hadn't heard his approach and he seemed to materialize out of thin air. The young man's eyes did not touch on anyone in the group except Tlakaelel. He stopped, straddling his bicycle, and looked directly into the Elder's eyes. They both behaved as if they had been expecting the meeting. The young man said "My ancestors respect and welcome you and thank you for coming." A meeting lasting some minutes ensued as Tlakaelel shared some ancient knowledge from Mexico and the young man talked about the spiritual significance of the land we were on. Both agreed that respect for the land was of paramount importance. It was a poignant and emotional meeting for all.

Celestial Connection

There's an interesting and very important side story related to Tlakaelel's design. It involves my U.K. research field team and their experience investigating this pattern. One of the team was a nuclear scientist working at high levels in the British government and a very reliable witness to events. The team was harassed the entire time they were in the formation by a black helicopter hovering just feet above their heads. We have no idea what the point was, but a full account of all the unusual events of this day can been found on my website: www.cropcircleinfo.com.

Evolution Continued

After Tlakaelel's visit to England the crop circles continued to evolve into ever more complex and related designs. Designs that related to the ancient Aztec and Maya seemed to escalate. We were soon to see exact replicas of the solar system and a multitude of Mesoamerican patterns. Patterns reflective of 2012 predictions arrived as well. Let's take a look at three of the most significant.

Solar System

On June 22, 1995, a large pattern appeared near the location of the first circle back in 1976. This design was an accurate representation of the inner planets of our solar system, the planets that played such a large part in the ancient Mayan calendar system. The accuracy of the orbits and placement of planets was verified by my colleagues, astronomer Prof. Gerald Hawkins, now deceased, and astrophysicist Prof. Robert Hadley. You can see an image of the solar system in image #9 of the previous illustration.

This huge accurate replica of the solar system showed the placement of the planets on their respective orbits around the sun. Even the asteroid belt that separates the inner planets from the outer planets was present. But there was a problem with the design. Although all the inner orbits were in place and all were equipped with their corresponding planets, the orbit for the earth, third from the sun, was missing its planet. The earth was not present. Lots of coffee and concerned discussion surrounded this information. You can see the analysis in the following illustration.

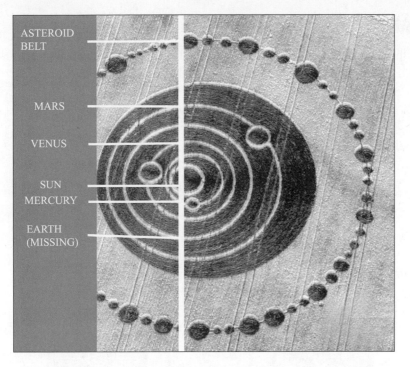

ASTEROID
BELT

MARS

VENUS

SUN
MERCURY

EARTH
(MISSING)

*This details the individual
orbits and their planets.*

Gerald Hawkins and Bob Hadley went to work. Was the loss of the earth to happen at a particular date? Could we discern the date from the information in the design? Using the planetary positioning of the other planets around the sun, a list of dates was developed. These dates are times when the other planets would be in the same position around the sun as in this design. The list contained three dates. One of the dates was the day the crop circle formed, June 22, 1995. The second date was earlier, July 11, 1971. The third date is in the future, not 2012 but September 1, 2033.

At the time, this future date meant nothing to me and we decided the significance of the design was due to the fact that the planetary positioning matched the day of its arrival in the fields. Writing this book, I realize the true significance: 2033 is the last year of the first katun of the new fifth age. That is, the first katun of the fifth age starts in 2013 and ends in 2033. If you remember, this isn't the only reference to 2033. The Elliott Wave theory from Chapter 17 also points to this year. It predicts this year will be the end of the economic rebalancing that begins in 2017. It will be the start of a new period of prosperity after the economic crash. I am left with two questions: Why is the earth missing from its orbit? Is this date giving us hope that the Golden Age of the Maya is still to come?

Magnetic Field Formation

Avebury is an incredible megalithic stone circle in England that dates to the time of Stonehenge. It's located about 25 miles away. Millions of people visit it each year. In the summer of 2000, in a nearby field another amazing formation arrived. This formation appeared to be a replica of the earth and its magnetic field (see illustration #10 in the earlier figure). I couldn't help but think this was drawing our attention to the weakening magnetic field of the earth.

Mayan and Aztec Crop Designs

New and impressive Aztec and Mayan artwork has arrived in the fields since Tlakaelel's visit in 1994. Take a look at the following illustration to see some of the crop circles that look like they could have been drawn by the Maya themselves. These formations occurred between 2001 and 2005. More continue to arrive to this day.

Here are some Mayan- and Aztec-type designs that arrived between 2001 and 2005.

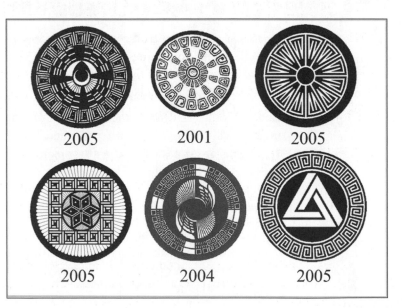

2005   2001   2005

2005   2004   2005

Crop Conclusions

If crop circles are expressions of meta-consciousness, they represent themes in our own collective unconscious. Like the Mayan calendars and 2012 prophets, the crop designs draw attention to the sky; to planetary cycles, orbits, solar flares, comets, galaxies, and even changes in the solar system. I find it very interesting that the date shown by the solar system crop design is the end date of the first katun of the fifth age. The designs speak to multiple stories; this was one of them.

> **Codex Cues** _____
>
> In the positive spirit of this book, here is a quotation from Chief Dave, Oglala Lakota, about "The Circle": "The Circle has healing power. In the Circle, we are all equal. When in the Circle, no one is in front of you. No one is behind you. No one is above you. No one is below you. The Sacred Circle is designed to create unity. The Hoop of Life is also a circle. On this hoop there is a place for every species, every race, every tree and every plant. It is this completeness of Life that must be respected in order to bring about health on this planet."

More Signs from the Meta-Consciousness

Crop circles are not the only sign from the meta-conscious. Meta-conscious states of awareness seem to be linked to avenues of perception. We are finding there are more ways to perceive the world than our five senses. In fact, we're waking up to senses moving beyond even the idea of the sixth sense. In these times approaching 2012, more and more people are experiencing meta-conscious states. Let's look at a few.

Synchronicity: An Expression of Meta-Consciousness

The Mayan calendar shows the importance of timing and the flow of energy through matter. An expression of this is synchronicity. Have you been experiencing more synchronicity in your life? More and more people are experiencing this intensified level of timing. (We'll discuss synchronicity in more detail in Chapter 19.)

We have experienced an unprecedented level of synchronicity while writing this book. Many times we have just come to the point of needing a piece of information or a contact and immediately it would arrive. We would open the e-mail or check the phone messages and the answer or person we needed would be there. This type of connection is available to all of us in bigger and bigger ways.

Telepathy and ESP

The ability to know things outside of the rational intellect is a keystone of meta-consciousness. It implies the breakdown of the barriers between time and space allowing us to bridge both with our minds. If you look back to Chapter 12, we talked about some of the ways people received information, like remote viewing or channeling. In the past, people either had a gift or had to train themselves to access these levels of awareness. What's different now is that many people are simply "awakening" to their own ability, like it's been asleep in all of us, waiting to be called into action.

Astral Projection

We're all said to have energy bodies that are the template for our physical bodies. Reports throughout history talk of the ability of some to move their awareness into their energy body and use it as a vehicle to travel outside of the physical body. This is called astral projection. Astral projection can be triggered due to extreme shock where you suddenly find yourself outside of your body. If you don't know what's going on, this can be really frightening!

You can also be trained to achieve astral projection naturally. Today more and more people are awakening to their ability to travel in their energy body, easily and without fear.

Energy Awareness

Everything is made of a matrix of energy, and all form has an energy radiation or field around it. We measure this field when measuring the electrical output of the heart in an EKG or the brain in an EEG. Some healers and psychics have been able to see the fields of energy and manipulate them to create better health. Again, people are finding themselves able to see and feel energy fields naturally as we approach 2012.

A Word of Caution

All the states of awareness we're talking about are natural abilities that have great power. Power can have both beneficial and harmful effects. It can be like playing with fire. When these abilities develop organically, it's because we're ready for them. On the other hand, trying to force these abilities can be very harmful, overwhelming the nervous system and burning out your body.

The Least You Need to Know

◆ Crop circles are areas of flattened crops where the plants are undamaged, fall in elaborate designs, and are accompanied by strange happenings.

◆ Crop circles evolved from simple circles to elaborate designs. The astronomical family of designs synchronically relates to information in the Mayan prophecies.

◆ Aztec Elder Tlakaelel saw a pattern in his mind that then appeared in the fields. His visit to the circles in England was profound for all involved.

◆ A formation representing the solar system left Earth out of its orbit. The date the formation depicts based on positions of the other planets is 2033. This is the last year of the first katun of the New Age.

◆ There have been a number of elaborate crop-circle designs of Mayan and Aztec origin.

◆ Other aspects of meta-consciousness such as developing altered states of awareness have been spontaneously increasing for many people.

Part 5

Transition

As 2012 approaches, you may be wondering what this means to you personally. Although all of us are affected by global change, 2012 has an individual impact as well. This part will help you negotiate the transitional period, clueing you in to changes you may experience in your personal life and the growth and expansion underway for you.

This part will also help you prepare for potential weather events and earth activity. Even if super storms or earthquakes aren't brought on with 2012, it's always a good idea to be prepared.

Finally, this part will help you prepare internally. It will support your inner guru and help you find balance and inner awareness, being alert and prepared as the journey to 2012 unfolds.

Chapter 19

Your Personal Journey

In This Chapter

- ◆ What to expect personally in the time leading up to 2012
- ◆ Signs of developing awareness
- ◆ How your thoughts create your reality
- ◆ Challenges in lifestyle, goals, and relationships
- ◆ Tips and tools for adjustment
- ◆ Your own personal purification

The approach of 2012 is bringing personal changes into all aspects of your life. Relationships, careers, interests, goals, and even your belief system are undergoing radical change. What do the two key words purification and awakening mean in your life? How will this time period affect you?

Maybe you're noticing signs of heightened awareness or are having thoughts and feelings you never expected. This chapter helps you chart your way through the personal challenges and revelations you may be experiencing and provides tips and tools to help you adjust.

2012 Awakening

According to the 2012 prophecies, we are in the midst of both the death of the old and the birth of something new. Whichever way you look at it, there's no question that uncertainty is stressful. It requires that you learn new ideas, skills, and behaviors. Just as science and society are developing creative insights and problem-solving abilities, you, too, may be called on to change at a deeper level.

The Mayan prophecy predicts the coming of a Golden Age. (We don't think they're referring to the cost of gold reaching $1,000!) According to the mystics, it signifies a time when humans undergo an evolution of consciousness. This means you can experience your higher spiritual and human potential. You can outgrow ingrained habits and belief systems and live a happier, more fulfilling life. It means that by experiencing more of yourself you can develop a deeper relationship with life. Often personal growth and changes in consciousness coincide with overcoming big challenges. In that case, this is a golden opportunity!

Increased Sensitivity

Maybe you're already becoming more sensitive to the approaching changes. Are you finding yourself feeling events of the evening news more poignantly or wanting to spend more time with friends and neighbors? You may be feeling the effects of the coming fifth age. Here are some indicators that you are tuning in to the times:

◆ Becoming interested in new, unusual ideas and activities

◆ Having shifts in attitudes

◆ Approaching problems in new ways

◆ Wanting to spend more time outside in nature

◆ Feeling an urgency to get things done

◆ Noticing increased synchronicity

◆ Being drawn toward a simple, natural lifestyle

◆ Feeling more connected to people and animals

◆ Experiencing strange sensations in your body such as vibrations, electric currents, or shock-like jolts

◆ Standing up for yourself when confronted

- Having unexpected opportunities fall into your lap

- Feeling emotions more deeply and having more empathy for others

- Desiring to be of service to others

- Noticing quick results from positive thinking

Increased Stress

As exciting as new growth is, you may also be experiencing the challenging aspects of change. Remember, this is the death of the old as well as the birth of the new! People grow at different speeds, and what we like at one stage in life doesn't always fit another. If you're experiencing more friction than usual, don't take it personally; it could just be the shock waves of change. On the other hand, you may want to pay particular attention to the tips in the upcoming chapters and avoid as much unneeded stress as possible. Here are some of the more difficult indicators of the times:

- Feeling that many of your relationships are strained as the old doesn't fit anymore

- Feeling that long-standing goals are falling apart

- Feeling a sense of agitation and unrest

- Losing and breaking things due to lack of attention

- Having trouble staying focused on mundane matters

- Losing interest in activities you always enjoyed

- Feeling polarized with family members and friends over politics or worldviews

- Feeling the magnification of your fears

- Feeling overly sensitive to others

- Having mood swings

- Having difficulty with your financial and material needs

- Experiencing immediate consequences to untruths or bad behavior

 Cosmic Caution

If you're experiencing the challenging side of the 2012 shift, it's perfectly normal to feel these things, but remember that they can also be signs of more serious medical or psychological stress. You may want to get professional support as we head into these demanding times.

Increasing Synchronicity

Everyone experiences some form of synchronicity. Synchronicity is coincidence that happens with meaningful events, like when you're walking through a park thinking of a person you want to talk to and as you round the corner that person is walking toward you. Or you sit down in your airplane seat to find the person sitting next to you is someone who holds the key to a problem you've been working on. Synchronicity lets us know that more than random chance is working in the universe.

Synchronicity is a great indicator that you're on track. When people, events, and opportunities fall into your lap at just the right moment you know you're in "sync" with your higher purpose. Although most synchronicities are meaningful and validating, they can also be uncomfortable. Sometimes the people who pop up aren't the ones you want to see. The magic job or relationship you stumbled into doesn't work out as you thought.

Synchronicity is a sign you're on the path, not a promise that the path is easy! When synchronicity brings challenge into your life it's an opportunity for growth. You're being asked to look at what you need to change in your attitudes, beliefs, or lifestyle. Welcome these opportunities with open arms. As you clear the old, the birth of the new begins.

Increasing Awareness

We've said before that awareness relates to how you perceive the world. Becoming more aware implies perceiving the world in more ways, or perceiving more of the world. This is true, but what we're really saying is that increasing awareness means using more of your self in how you perceive.

Here's an example: someone is telling you a story. You're listening with your ears and examining it with your mind. But a lot of other things are happening, too. You're feeling the emotion of the story in your heart, your body is reflecting the body language of the other person, and your energy sensors are monitoring the person's energy field. Some part of you measures all these things and they become the basis for your gut reaction. Increasing awareness is not about finding new senses, it's about being conscious of the ones you already have.

As we head toward 2012, you may become more aware of other ways of perceiving. You may start having an inner sense of knowing, or start feeling the truth behind events and words. You might start seeing or feeling the energy field around people.

You may break through the barriers of space and have sudden visions. For example, you might be talking to your friend about his or her new house and suddenly see the view out the back window in your mind's eye.

Opening awareness is exciting and fun, but it also carries a certain amount of responsibility. As awareness awakens, it's easy to start feeling overly confident. Don't let your ego take you out of balance and allow you to act high-handedly. It's never a good idea to think that because you have a new perception you know what's best for other people. Only they know what's best for them; only you know what's best for you.

Time Acceleration

Researcher Carl Johan Calleman says the information from the pyramids indicates time is accelerating as we approach 2012. What does that really mean? One of the attributes of time is that it creates space between cause and effect. This allows us to learn the impact of consequences. As time accelerates, the space between what we think or do and its results becomes less. You may remember this concept from the section on Barbara Marciniak in Chapter 12.

Thoughts Are Things

You may have heard the expression "thoughts are things." What exactly does it mean? Every thought you have creates an effect. In its most basic form, when you think fearful thoughts your shoulders tighten, your stomach produces acid, you feel stressed. Your thought has created a physical reaction. What you think changes your behavior, too. Your fearful thoughts affect how you treat people and in return how they treat you. Your body language, word use, choices, and energy transmission all reflect your fear. This affects whether you get the job or the raise, or attract the right relationship.

In the world of metaphysics, what you think creates the experiences you have. Your thoughts act like magnets attracting people and events into your life. Like attracts like and your fear brings toward you what you're afraid of. Limiting emotions come from deeply held and often unconscious attitudes and beliefs. Now is the time to explore what they are and change the ones that don't serve your higher good.

Changing Attitudes

With time acceleration, each of us has to choose our thoughts wisely. There's no time to counteract the effects of bad thinking. What you think returns as fast as you think it.

This is a great time to start using your mind to manifest better conditions for yourself. You can start with a vision board, affirmations, and energy-building exercises. We'll show you how in Chapter 21.

Equally, it's time to ferret out the beliefs and attitudes that hold you to old ways of thinking. This is a powerful time to change those patterns! Again, we'll give you tips in Chapter 21, but right now, practice consciously choosing the thoughts you have, right at this moment. Your thoughts aren't random; they're a choice. Ask yourself whether the thought you're having this minute helps you or hinders you. Does it add something positive to the world? If you don't like the answer, choose a different thought!

Codex Cues

There are many great books on the power of positive thinking. Here are three favorites. *The Game of Life and How to Play It* by Florence Scovil Shinn (bnpublishing.com, 2007) is a classic! Originally published in 1925, it has inspired millions of readers. A more recent and equally excellent book is *Excuse Me, Your Life Is Waiting: The Astonishing Power of Feelings* by Lynn Grabhorn (Hampton Roads Publishing, 2003). The most recent and hugely popular book is Eckhart Tolle's *A New Earth: Awakening to Your Life's Purpose* (Penguin, 2008).

Heading Toward 2012

Even positive change brings unexpected difficulties. Remember when you got that promotion you were after and suddenly your co-workers were less friendly; or you finally bought your dream house and your friends said bad things about it?

As you change with the new energies coming in and begin to access deeper parts of yourself, your identity may change. This can put you at odds with different aspects of your life. On the other hand, as you live by your inner light and work toward harmony, you may find unexpected changes in your friends and family, or people you have overlooked in the past suddenly come popping out of the woodwork.

Who Are You?

Your identity is based on many things. It's based on your beliefs about the universe, spirituality, and religions—who you are in the spiritual world. It's based on how you have behaved in the past, what your failings and successes have been. It's based on the expectations of your family and how well you've lived up to them. As 2012 approaches, many people are drawn to live more authentic lives that reflect their inner truth. Maybe in the past you saw yourself as a victim and spent time with friends sharing your feelings and experiences. While there's nothing wrong with this, when you stop feeling like a victim you may find yourself uncomfortable or even bored as the role of victim no longer reflects your new self-image.

Maybe you've always seen yourself as a rescuer, helping people with their problems, being the good listener and fix-it friend. Once your attitude changes, you may see people in a higher light and know they are not really broken and don't really need to be fixed. You may become someone who empowers your friends rather than fixing them. While this will make some friends very happy, others will start looking for someone else to fix them. It's okay to let some people go as others arrive.

Changes in Goals, Interests, and Careers

Your new sense of self and new awareness will most certainly change your interests. You might find goals you have held for a long time no longer matter. New goals and interests may become more exciting and intriguing. Don't hesitate—jump right in to the areas you're fascinated with. Take the trip to Peru you're being drawn to; learn about herbs and energy healing. Follow where the energy leads. What does this mean? In every decision, ask yourself this: does thinking about this give you energy or take it away? When you think of it, do you feel energized and motivated? Or do you feel tired, depleted, or drained? Consider each decision as a net sum balance. In other words, is the energy you get more than the energy you will need to expend?

This is a great time of excitement and expansion, but you do need to be cautious. Some people get so excited they make decisions that don't serve them well. For example, a client of Synthia's had been in a job for 20 years. She was set to retire with a good pension and benefits within two years. She was so excited about her new path and interests she wanted to immediately leave her job. When looking at her situation in the short term, quitting her job certainly brought her more energy. But when she imagined life without an income, she suddenly felt drained. Instead of rashly leaving, she worked out a deal with the company where she took a cut in hours and pay. This allowed her to keep her pension and have the time and freedom she wanted to pursue her new goals without going bankrupt.

Relationship Stress

Whenever one person changes, it puts stress on the relationship. Even positive change does this. For example, when one spouse loses a lot of weight, it makes him feel great but it might make his partner insecure, bringing all sorts of strange new stress to the relationship.

Partnership stress can be a great opportunity to explore some of the attitudes and beliefs within the partnership and allow a real opportunity for growth. On the other hand, your partner might not want to grow. She might be comfortable where she is. You may have to face what this means to you. There are no easy answers, and only you know what's best for you.

With luck, you and your partner might discover new territory together. Even so, renegotiating roles and rules with changing identities might not be so easy! The most important tool you have is communication. Here's a tip: when you communicate about an issue, be on the same side. Couples often take sides *over* an issue; putting the issue in the middle and themselves at odds with each other over it. Try instead to take sides *against* an issue; put yourself and your partner on the same side against the offending item. This little shift in perspective can save you lots of unnecessary tears.

The final tip when experiencing relationship stress: don't rule out miracles. Your partner might not respect your new ideas and direction in life. This may be causing great unhappiness. Then out of the blue your partner wants to go to a yoga class, or read one of your books. Just remember, synchronicity is happening in his or her life, too, and many things might bring your experiences together. All things are possible; don't rule anything out.

Encountering Anger and Resentment

We've said a hundred times that change isn't easy. It's harder for some than others. As 2012 approaches and new energies come in, not everyone will be able to adjust easily. People who are deeply invested mentally and emotionally in the structures of the old age will have the hardest time. You may know some of these people; they may be family members, co-workers, or spouses. Unfortunately, you may take the brunt of their stress.

If people are overreacting to the changes in your life, the new ideas you're expressing, or shifts in your behavior, don't take it personally. Anger and division are the result of frustration felt by those having trouble letting go of the old. The more apparent these shifts become, the harder it will be for these folks to understand them. Be careful, though, as anger and resentment can lead to violence, in word if not deed.

In this changing age, no soul is left behind. Tolerating different views requires respect for others and patience with the process of change. Being calm and grounded, or being panicked and volatile, are nothing more than choices. "Reality" is what is shifting, and not all of us will shift with grace and ease!

New Circles, New Friends

For your own well-being, you may steer away from old associations as new ones enter your life. Welcome new friends, interests, and activities with open arms. Be patient with those you no longer see eye to eye with. Who knows who is right or wrong? The truth is, everyone is free to chart their own path.

Rule of thumb: go through the door, but don't close it. Keep it open for any of your friends and family who may decide to come along. Like a recovering alcoholic, you may need to leave friends who engage in destructive patterns. But also be willing to accept them as they are and know they may decide to change, too. You never know, they may have been waiting for the opportunity to shift all along and were afraid to leave you behind!

Decision Making

It's often said that we act out of either fear or love. Fear-based decisions are ones you make out of scarcity thinking; out of fear of lack or loss. Love-based decisions are ones that contribute to growth. Here's the thing: all of your emotions have a purpose, even fear. When fear pops up in your decision making, ask yourself what message your subconscious is sending. It could be sending a message that you're letting lack of confidence run your life; it could be saying danger lies ahead; it could be telling you about old wounds that need healing or beliefs that need changing.

Bottom line, it isn't wrong to feel limiting emotions; it's wrong not to find out what they mean. Here's an analogy. It would be silly to be afraid to cross a street with no

Codex Cues

Having trouble making a decision? The ancient Maya made all major decisions by consulting the Day Keeper. With the help of our modern version, the computer, you can do this, too. There are many Mayan day-sign consultation websites. You might want to try www.alabe. com/mayan.html.

cars to be seen. It would be equally silly not to be afraid when crossing a street in front of a bus! Maybe you were hit by a car before and the subconscious fear keeps you from crossing the street even though it's empty. Whatever the situation, your fear is telling you something. Don't make decisions based on fear or limiting emotions, but don't ignore them, either. Expand your awareness by finding out what your emotions are telling you and let them become your guides.

Lifestyle Purification

If you're a typical citizen of the twenty-first century, you've probably taken advantage of the many opportunities of the past 10 years. There's been unprecedented access to financing for your dreams and ambitions. Maybe you went all out, banking on your ability to succeed as you followed your dreams. The problem is, you might have thought you had more time to make your dreams come true and pay back the piper. Unfortunately, time is running out.

The point of this chapter isn't to problem-solve for you, it's to look at the problems through the lens of the process underway: purification. The definition of purification is "The act or instance of cleansing; the act or process of removing impurities." As the challenges mount in your life, what areas are being hit hardest? These are the areas that you're being asked to cleanse. Purification is getting rid of everything that isn't your true self.

In addition, purification is cleaning up your lifestyle for better health. Difficult times require all our faculties, and health is key. Besides, you want to keep your health so you can enjoy the new interests and ideas you have!

Are Your Priorities Serving You or Hindering You?

We don't need to tell you how much the cost of living is rising. You're living with the effects every day. Let's take a creative approach. Purification is essentially getting rid of what isn't working, isn't needed, or is just plain taking your energy. It's an opportunity to look at your priorities and evaluate whether they serve your better good or not. Everyone needs food, clothing, and water, but do you need the most expensive restaurants, the best house, and designer clothes? What will you have to change in your self-identity to feel good about yourself with less?

Making choices around spending is tough. You can't just "disappear" your credit card debt, but you can cut costs. When you come home at night, do you turn on the lights in all the rooms in the house? Keep them on only in the rooms you go in and out of? Or do you turn the lights on and off as you go in and out of rooms? Do you heat the whole house or turn it off in the rooms you're not using? These things sound too simple to count, but consider the difference between how we live and how our grandparents lived. What we waste every day is more than they lived on in a month.

How you spend money is a reflection of your self-identity. Your financial picture reflects to the world who you are. Is this a picture of who you want to be or who you really are? If not, what choices are you making that don't reflect your true self?

Pure Water

Finding pure water will likely get harder in the days to come. However, it's essential for good health to drink pure water. You're probably making good choices, but here are a few things you might need to know.

Chapter 17 already talked about pollution and poor water quality. Many people are drinking bottled water instead. The number of water bottles sold went from 3.3 billion in 1997 to 15 billion in 2002. Unfortunately, bottled water is one of the worst choices you can make. Why? Because the plastic bottle is leaching poisons into the water that you're drinking. This is especially true when you leave your water out in a hot car, or worse yet, microwave it. The type of bottle you're using determines the type of poison you're ingesting. You may be getting bisphenol A, which is a xenoestrogen, or estrogen-mimicking substance. It's linked to breast and uterine cancer in women, low testosterone in men, Type II diabetes, and many hormone-related diseases.

Another sad but true fact is the cost to the environment of water bottle waste. Remember that mountain of plastic floating in the Pacific Ocean? Not only does this clog the guts of sea birds and fish, it also adds estrogens into the environment. Getting rid of plastic water bottles is high on the list of personal priority!

Your best choice for pure water is filtered tap water. You want more than an activated charcoal filter system, though. Other choices include ozonators or UV systems along with activated charcoal filters. These usually get

> **Codex Cues**
>
> Here are some websites for good water purification systems. Be sure to pick the type of system that's best for you. After you filter your water, use glass or ceramic water bottles for carrying or storing your drinking water. Check out www.tersano.com, www.costpluswater.com, and www.freedrinkingwater.com.

the majority of chemicals and bacteria out. If you're worried about the pharmaceuticals in the water supply, you need to clean your water with reverse-osmosis machines. What system you want to use will depend on whether you have a well or city water; what city or state you're in; and obviously how clean your water already is.

Pure Food

Finding pure food is also a pretty big challenge. Animal products are rife with added hormones and antibiotics. Plant foods are subject to genetic modification, pesticides, and toxic fertilizer. It seems like our food is under attack! Eating organic is the best choice you can make short of growing your own food, something you might want to consider. But be aware, the FDA has changed the labeling laws so that not everything that says organic is organic! Another good choice is buying locally grown produce from local farmers. There are many organic farm associations in most states, so you can pick local organic farms.

Codex Cues

Here are two great websites for finding good-quality organic food and for participating in food legislation. Check out www.organicconsumers.org and www.localharvest.org.

One more thought on food: we've heard in the 2012 predictions that part of what's happening is our frequency is being raised. It's interesting to think of frequency in terms of emotions. Some emotions physically lower your energy level; other emotions raise your energy level. You probably wouldn't choose to keep your emotions in a lower state of frequency.

Native Americans believe that when you eat an animal you're taking in the animal's spirit. They honor the animals they kill and give thanks for the gift of life. Eating animals that have been raised in feed lots, force-fed, and tortured before death is eating the frequency of fear. You might want to consider whether eating that frequency raises your energy or lowers it. Organic, pasture-fed meats are a good alternative.

Personal Purification

As we head toward 2012, everything of the old frequency is being challenged. The old age is destroyed to make a new and better world. Not only is the earth going through purification, but so are you and everyone else. We're all going through an internal cleansing.

Each of us has our shadow side, that part of us that holds our fear, hurt, disappointment, pain, greed, lust, and all the other emotions and beliefs that keep us in a state of limitation. This side unconsciously directs our thoughts and actions, creating limiting behaviors. To free ourselves of limitation requires integrating the shadow. The shadow side only has power when we try to submerge it. Like trying to keep a ball underwater, it can pop up at just the wrong time. When we can accept our imperfections and stop trying to hide them, we are free to begin the process of change.

Facing Your Demons

This is not easy work. If it were you'd already have done it. Of course, many of us have done a lot of self-reflection, maybe using self-help books, meditation, therapy, religious practice, or going to human potential workshops. However, there will always be areas still to work on. How do you know what needs resolution? Don't worry; you won't be able to hide from it. As new frequencies are coming into the earth, your cells and energy structures begin to vibrate. The vibration literally shakes loose everything inside that's creating resistance to spiritual growth. What needs to change will show up in your life as a challenge to be overcome.

Here's an example: a man decides he wants to pursue a business opportunity. He's afraid his wife will stop him, so he lies to her. He justifies it as an innocent lie since he's not really doing anything wrong or hurting anyone. Any other time in history this would have just gone by, perhaps with only a mark on his heart as residue. But this isn't just any time in history, it's the approach of 2012 and cleansing is underway. The wife finds out and believes the lie is covering an affair. The couple faces tremendous difficulty and the marriage nearly fails. It only survives because each faces the inner demon that created the situation. His demon turned out to be fear of punishment; hers was fear of betrayal. You could just brush this off and say it happened because he made a mistake. Or you could say the parts of themselves that needed healing were activated and they attracted the conditions they needed to grow.

Clearing Your Shadow

Clearing your shadow means facing the old hurts, low self-esteem, and inner fear. It means looking at the beliefs you hold and how they affect your life. Some of the Mayan Elders say that 2012 is magnifying everyone's fear. If that's true, and it seems so, then the reason must be to clear the old beliefs that are creating the fear.

You can never erase the past or completely get rid of pain. You can stop pushing it down and trying to hide it by being extra good or extra strong or extra powerful. These behaviors don't fool anyone and they don't get you what you want, which is healing. The only way healing happens is through embracing your feelings and accepting yourself. In this time leading to 2012, you will be given ample opportunity to find the hidden beliefs that dictate your life. Welcome the opportunity to grow!

The Least You Need to Know

- The period of 2012 represents more than cataclysmic events, it's a transition from the old to the new. It represents internal changes resulting from personal growth.

- You may be experiencing increased sensitivity as 2012 approaches.

- You may be experiencing personal growth while at the same time having more friction with old friends, family, and relationships. You may be outgrowing your career, past goals, and interests.

- The importance of time acceleration is that the consequences of thoughts and actions happen more quickly.

- The process of purification shows us what in our life needs cleansing, including personal habits, foods, and thought patterns.

- Now is the time to work on our inner limitations and the shadow side as we head toward 2012.

Chapter 20

A Sensible Approach to Storms and Crises

In This Chapter

- ◆ Why stay informed?
- ◆ Preparedness planning
- ◆ Emergency and evacuation kits
- ◆ Community building
- ◆ Learning basic skills

Let's be clear: talking about survival doesn't mean we believe there'll be a disaster of huge proportions on December 21, 2012. Almost certainly, though, the year 2012 will witness storms or disasters of many kinds—just like every other year does. Somewhere, at some time, there will be problems that will be easier to manage if you're prepared.

In this book, we've discussed different trends that could be leading toward some level of disaster. Humans have created many environmental problems all on our own. Now with the help of a few extreme natural cycles, we may be headed for some larger-scale super-storms or other earth activity. This seems to have been foreseen by the Maya and is now confirmed by science.

In this chapter, we'll discuss some common-sense steps you can take to plan for storms and other disasters. Of course, you can't plan for everything, but a little preparedness goes a long way.

Stay Informed

Staying informed on all the areas we have covered in Part 4 of this book is a good idea. Before disaster hits, this will keep you ahead of the pack and as things unfold it will allow you to know where resources are and how best to adapt to developments.

Keeping informed ahead of time enables you to budget and plan for any equipment you might need, tells you where to go for emergency help, allows you to store provisions and medical supplies, and allows you to adjust your plans in accordance with the situation and the timeline foreseen. Whether you're planning for a severe hurricane that's approaching the local coastline or a tornado outbreak moving into your area, you will need to take precautions. Knowing what to expect and what to do may be the difference between getting hurt and staying safe.

> **Celestial Connection**
>
> Nostradamus admonishes in his quatrains about the end times that people "should be prepared spiritually and intellectually and be more aware of survival abilities."

What Could Happen in Your Area?

One thing you'll want to know is what kind of natural disasters are more likely in your area. Obviously you wouldn't prepare for a blizzard in the tropics or a volcano eruption in Oklahoma. Find out what types of disasters are more likely in your region before you make your personal preparedness plan.

Also, be sure you know what your community's warning signals are. Some communities have a special sequencing of the fire siren, others use church bells, others have an independent siren system. What does yours sound like and what should you do when you hear it? Your community is probably part of the Emergency Broadcast System so turning on your TV or radio should hook you into emergency information.

You'll also want to consider the special needs of your family in different events. Find out how to help elderly and disabled family members. Have a plan for your animals: what will happen to them after an emergency? Of course, every parent knows the disaster plans for their kids' schools, but you also need to know the disaster plans of your own workplace. You may be surprised by what you find. Is there a lockdown procedure that will keep you from getting your kids? These are answers you need to know *before* disaster hits.

National and Local Disasters

Consider different regional scenarios. Your electricity is cut off; your home damaged or destroyed; your water and sewage system disrupted; food stores and medical supplies depleted; and transportation impossible. Maybe someone is hurt and needs medical care. Now you have major challenges.

As awful as this scenario is, it's nothing compared to a national disaster. Consider if satellite technology is disabled, the national power grid down, and transportation countrywide disrupted. The help you would find in the first scenario doesn't exist in the second. You will need to find and give support in community and neighborhood connections.

Planning for the worst possible disaster is not really possible unless you're a government official whose job it is to think and plan for such contingencies. So let's break it down and apply common sense to what you can and can't do for yourself.

Know Your Local Services and Procedures

Staying informed as events unfold is a must for you and your family. You need to know not only what's going on but also where to find help. Do you have a family plan in the event of disaster? Do members of your family know who or where to call for help?

Check out your local government emergency plans. You can find this information from your local Department of Civil Emergency Planning. Take notes of all the local emergency telephone numbers. Keep a copy of this list near the phone and in your wallet or purse. Make sure every member of the family has a copy. Find out where all the nearby police stations are. Do the same for ambulance, doctors, hospitals, and emergency evacuation centers. Don't just look up the address; drive by and make note of alternative routes as well. Don't leave this important information until the last moment; getting lost can be the difference between life and death.

In the case of evacuation, where should you go? How will you get there? This is something everyone in your family needs to know. It's the role of government to provide a civil emergency plan, to practice its effectiveness and make it available to the public. It's your job to know what the plan is and what you should do.

Federal Resources

It's fair to say that some towns and states are better than others at civil and emergency planning. As we all saw during Hurricane Katrina, local disaster response in New

Orleans and along the Gulf Coast didn't work. In addition, federal agencies such as the Federal Emergency Management Agency (FEMA) and the National Guard failed. In the end, one result of the Katrina fiasco was the federal government telling the public that people need to be prepared to take care of themselves and their pets in an emergency. While this is always good advice, it's not what you expect to hear from the people in charge!

U.S. Resources

If you live in the United States, there are municipal and federal agencies to help with preparedness planning. Some places to look are your local and state Public Safety or Emergency Planning Department. At a federal level, check the Department of Homeland Security, The Municipal Research & Services Center of Washington, Federal Emergency Management Agency (FEMA), and the American Red Cross. For up-to-date weather warnings, check the website for N.O.A.A. See the "Preparedness" section in the Resources appendix for these websites and more.

It's a good idea for all U.S. residents to download a copy of the FEMA publication "Are You Ready? An In-depth Guide to Citizen Preparedness (IS-22)." This is FEMA's most comprehensive source on individual, family, and community preparedness. "Are You Ready?" provides a step-by-step approach to disaster preparedness. It will help you get informed about local emergency plans and how to identify hazards that affect your local area. It will also give you instructions on how to develop and maintain an emergency communications plan and disaster supplies kit. Other topics covered include evacuation, emergency public shelters, animals in disaster, and information specific to people with disabilities.

Canadian Resources

The Canadian government's approach to preparedness and emergency planning seems to focus more on coordination between government agencies and emergency responders. Canadian websites are more orientated toward agency response during events than toward providing information to the public about what to do, where to go, or who to contact. Be sure to check with your local town and province authorities. See the Canadian websites in the "Preparedness" section of the Resources appendix.

United Kingdom Resources

In the United Kingdom, it appears to us that the county level offers useful information, while the central government websites give you the run-around.

The UK counties provide detailed emergency plans with information on where to go and what to do. They provide evacuation routes and emergency information channels. They also help with the practical matters of creating and sustaining an emergency kit and an evacuation kit, and share information on how often to check batteries or change water and food supplies. An emergency can happen at any time with a variety of outcomes. A ready-made emergency pack in your home, stored in an accessible area, is essential. You can download instructions from the local county websites. See the "Preparedness" section of the Resources appendix for some UK websites, including one for Hampshire County Council, a good general resource for emergency planning.

International Red Cross

Being prepared beforehand might help save your life. Knowing where to get help afterward may keep you alive. The Red Cross helps people affected by situations ranging from house fires to floods to disasters. Be sure the Red Cross help line is one of the numbers on your list.

In addition to helping with the basic needs of survival like food, water, and medical help, the Red Cross provides both information and support for helping children cope with disaster, for helping people with disabilities and special needs, and for animal safety. The Red Cross website (see Resources appendix) provides great preparedness information.

Family Preparedness

Knowing where to go and who to call is essential but do you know what to do? Do you have a family plan? Does everyone know what his or her specific role is? Do you check in with your family members and reinforce the plan, changing it as needed? Do you have a preparedness kit? Let's break these down into useable steps.

Making a Plan

The first thing you need to do is talk to your family. Everyone should know what kinds of events could take place. Even though you may be preparing for a weather event like a hurricane, be sure to talk about offshoot problems, too, like fires and floods. Explain the dangers and create a plan where everyone has a job and works as a team member. It's natural to be afraid, but handling fear is easier when you have a job and know how to do it.

You can't always plan to all be together when disaster hits. Have two places where people should go to meet. If the emergency is specific to your house, like a fire, your meeting place can be right outside your house. If the event is larger and you can't return home, have a second meeting place outside your neighborhood that everyone can get to. Be sure everyone knows the details of the plan and what to do. Don't forget to include your pets in your planning!

Cosmic Caution

In local disasters, phone services may be disrupted locally but not nationally. It's sometimes easier to call long distance. Have an out-of-town friend or family member be the contact person for family members. Family members should all check in through this person and tell them where they are.

Safety Precautions

If you have warning that a disaster is going to hit, there are several things you need to do. If you have propane gas cylinders in your home, remove them and make sure they are all turned off. Turning off the water supply, electric supply, gas supply, and oil burners may save both your house and possibly your life. Do you know where the main taps for these are and how to shut them off? Ask your plumber and oil or gas supplier to show you. Don't be embarrassed to ask; these things have gotten so complicated many people don't know where they are.

If you have time, tie down large moveable objects, like picnic tables and chairs. It's always a good idea to put boards over windows to protect them. If you don't have boards, make a huge "X" across the window with duct tape to contain flying glass if a tree branch or something else hits it.

Emergency Kit

After a hurricane, tornado, or flood, you could be stranded in your house without electricity for days. Having an emergency kit is essential. The kit should be kept in an easy-access area, and should be checked regularly to be sure that batteries still work and medicines and supplies are still within the use-by dates. Any time you use this kit, you need to replace whatever is used up.

Here's a commonsense emergency kit checklist:

❏ Battery-powered radio with local radio frequencies marked. A radio with solar cell capability and or a wind-up handle is an excellent choice. Check it from time to time to make sure it still works.

❏ Several high-powered flashlights.

❏ Candles: get plenty of them and be sure you have fireproof containers to light them in. The last thing you want is a secondary fire started from a tipped-over candle!

❏ Matches or other fire lighters. Be sure they are in a waterproof zipper-top bag.

❏ Spare batteries, also in a waterproof bag.

❏ First-aid kit.

❏ Common over-the-counter medicines such as Benadryl or other allergy medications in the event of a bee sting, etc.; anti-inflammatories such as aspirin, also good to keep on hand for heart conditions; antibiotics if possible.

❏ A copy of your up-to-date emergency phone list, laminated if possible. Include the numbers of relatives and friends.

❏ Two-way walkie-talkie radios can be very useful (don't overlook spare batteries for these also).

Codex Cues

Allicin, the active ingredient in garlic, is one of the best antimicrobials around. It kills bacteria, fungi, and viruses. Keep some concentrated garlic oil capsules in your emergency kit and replace them when you replace other medicines. You can swallow the capsules to fight colds and infections. You can also use a pin to pop the capsule and squeeze the garlic oil directly onto a bacterial or fungal skin infection. Be prepared, it may sting!

In addition to an emergency kit, there are other things you'll want to have readily available. Keep a supply of bottled drinks and water. Water can be kept safely in gallon-size or larger containers. You can put a few drops of bleach in the water to stop the growth of algae or bacteria. (Don't worry about the ill effects of a few drops of bleach in a gallon of water; your water authority puts a lot more than that into the municipal water supply.) You should still replace the water often. Be sure to consider water needs for sanitation as well as drinking.

You'll also want canned foods (don't forget the hand-operated can opener!), nonperishable foods, and staples such as beans, rice, flour, powdered milk, and sugar. Think about a supply of firewood, cooking pots, and toiletries. Be sure you have an extra supply of needed medications. Also, keep some bleach on hand for disinfecting items and water.

If you own a generator, be sure to test it regularly, place it safely outside while in use, and store petroleum in a safe place, well away from living quarters. Remember, your gas will only last so long.

You'll need some basic materials like ground sheets, plastic ties, rope, string, duct tape, heavy-gauge chain, a handsaw, and a basic tool kit. All these are normal parts of most households, so the trick is to be sure you know where they are and have them readily available when a storm is approaching. Of course, depending on where you live, you may want some very specific items on hand. For example, if flooding is a possibility you'll certainly want an inflatable safety raft, row boat, or some other means to stay afloat if that becomes necessary.

Evacuation Checklist

In the case of evacuation, things get tricky. You don't know how long you'll be gone or what will be available at the shelter. You'll probably want an evacuation kit. Remember, it has to be small enough to be easily carried. An evacuation backpack for every family member is a good idea. Here are some ideas of what you should include:

❑ Warm clothing, underwear, and socks, and protective shoes for each family member.

❑ A blanket or sleeping bag for each person.

❑ Personal items such as glasses or contact lenses.

❑ Things you'll need for your baby: food, medication, diapers, clothing, toys.

❑ Wallet, purse, bank cards, and cash. Access to cash might be difficult if electricity is disrupted and ATMs are down. Keeping extra cash in the house for emergencies is good thinking.

❑ Mobile phone and charger.

❑ Home and car keys.

❑ Toiletries and sanitary supplies.

Codex Cues

It's good practice to keep your car's fuel tank filled. Certainly if you know a storm is coming, filling your tank should be high on the list of things to do.

❏ Regularly prescribed medication.

❏ Pet supplies, including food, dishes, medication, carrier, collar, and leash. (If you absolutely can't take your pets with you, make sure you have made proper provisions for them!)

❏ Flashlight and fresh batteries.

❏ First-aid kit.

❏ Insurance information, including your policy number and the agency's emergency contact information. This number should be on your list of phone numbers.

Special Training

Everyone in your family should be trained in basic life support. CPR and lifesaving techniques save lives every day. Even without the possibility of a natural disaster, you should be prepared to help someone in need. Training is inexpensive and can be obtained through your local fire station or Red Cross. If you have a group of people, you can arrange a special training session in your home.

If you live in a flood zone, everyone in your family should know how to swim. Consider lifesaving lessons as well. Look in your local YMCA or school system class extracurricular schedule. One more important training is first-aid skills. In a first-aid class you'll learn how to splint a broken bone, use butterfly bandages for deep cuts, and wrap a sprained ankle. You'll also learn techniques for safely carrying an injured person.

Don't think of this as hard work. The classes are really fun and are great family-building exercises. Everyone in the family will feel like they can contribute when they learn these basic skills.

Forming a Community

Knowing your neighbors is one of the most important aspects of preparedness. If disaster strikes, you may be cut off from help for days or even longer. It will be natural and necessary for you and your neighbors to work together helping each other through. Of course, you may not live in a traditional neighborhood or even know the people around you. Now's the time to change that. Let's look at some simple steps you can start to take.

Knowing Your Neighbors

Start introducing yourself to the people on your street, in your condo complex, or in your apartment building. Put up flyers and invite people to meet and participate in a preparedness plan. Many communities did this as the year 2000 approached. (Fortunately, no disasters happened.) You can usually get someone from local government, the fire department, or the Red Cross to facilitate community planning meetings. You may be surprised that other people around you are concerned as well.

Assessing Resources

Some things that are useful in an emergency don't have to be owned by everyone. One person may have a big truck, and someone else has a generator, someone else may have a gas-powered chain saw, while someone else has a propane stove, and so on. Each person brings his or her own skill level, too. Someone might be a plumber; someone else a carpenter, medical person, or electrician—all needed skills in an emergency. Everyone has something to contribute, and when the chips are down you'll be relying on each other far more than you might think. Part of community building might be to assess the resources available to the whole group.

Also assess the special needs of people in the neighborhood. Know where elderly people live who might need your help. Prepare yourself to be someone else's lifesaver. What can you offer your community, in personal knowledge, expertise, as well as material goods, tools, and food?

> **Celestial Connection**
>
> Colin's parents were married with a baby during World War II. His dad was in the armed forces, away fighting the war. His mom was left within a small village community in England hiding from the nightly raids overhead. The food they ate came from community gardens; the comforts they had were shared with each other. The experience of this generation alone should reinforce in all of us the importance of community.

Finding Your Inner Scout

Being able to take care of yourself and others is a gift. Inside or outside of community, the single greatest support system is you. Finding your own inner Boy (or Girl!) Scout is what this is all about. Each of us needs to learn basic skills, and it's fun! Here are some skills you may want to develop.

Using Tools

If you grew up in a hands-on family, you might be surprised that many people have never used a hammer, a screwdriver, or a saw. Sad but true, most kids today know more about how to get around a video game than how to get around the tool shed. Basic home repair is an essential skill. When you can pick up the phone and call a handyman, you forget the importance of being able to help yourself.

If you don't have basic tools, get some. An important one for managing after a bad storm is a one- or two-person saw. You can use this for cutting branches out of the road, or for cutting trees off your car. A good knife is another handy tool.

Tying Knots

Every Scout gets trained in tying knots. Why? Well, tying that tarp you have on hand over the hole in the roof you got in the storm is only useful if the tarp will stay on. You don't want to be out on that roof in dark, windy, and wet conditions trying to recapture the freed end.

Do you know the best knots for different situations? If you're a sailor you probably do. A reef knot, clove hitch, and surgeon's knot will allow you to use string or rope in ways you had not imagined. A knot that does not hold can be fatal or at the least inconvenient. Take a look at www.folsoms.net/knots to learn a few of the basics.

Codex Cues

Consider getting a Boy Scout manual. They are chock-full of really great survival information that is useful in many aspects of life. Go to www.scouting.org for more information.

Mastering Outdoor Skills

Managing post disaster may require knowing a few outdoor skills. Once your house no longer provides you with everything you need, you may be looking outside for many resources. Can you light a fire without a match? Well, neither can we! On the easier side, you may need to collect firewood, cut trees away from power lines, remove limbs from the road, find water and pour it through filters to make it drinkable. Who knows, you may even need to wash your clothes in a stream. Seriously, take time to consider the many challenges you could be faced with and think about how you would overcome them. If you don't have the skills you need, don't wait; now's the time to prepare.

Get the kids involved and remember the Boy Scout motto: "Be prepared."

The Least You Need to Know

◆ You can be in a good position to weather the storms by simply being prepared. Know your community resources, warning systems, and evacuation plans, and make your own plan ahead of time.

◆ Everyone needs an emergency and evacuation kit. More information can be found at most national emergency agencies and the Red Cross website.

◆ You can get training in basic life support and first-aid skills through your local fire department or Red Cross.

◆ You can get training in lifesaving skills at your local YMCA.

◆ Get to know your neighbors now. Learn what each of you has to offer and who will need extra help.

◆ Learning basic Boy Scout skills is handy for everyone.

21

Inner Tools for Transition

In This Chapter

- ◆ You have what you need
- ◆ Techniques for centering and grounding
- ◆ Develop your energy perception
- ◆ Feeling the flows of k'ul

Old structures and ways of doing things are being broken down as the next age comes into alignment. What will happen energetically on 2012? Old patterns are getting more and more stressed as the alignment with the galactic center comes into tighter and tighter focus. As stress increases, the old ways of responding just don't work. New models have to be created and new methods employed.

In this chapter, we'll explore the new models and methods coming into focus with the 2012 alignment. We'll explore inner preparedness and simple-to-follow exercises for centering and grounding. We'll explore energy perception and other awareness tools.

Finding Your Inner Guru

Hunbatz Men and other Mayan Elders point to the prophecies and the return of Kukulkan as being a spiritual awakening; an awakening of each individual's connection to inner spiritual dimensions. The old models of accessing wisdom are evolving. In the past you may have looked to someone else, a guru or spiritual teacher, to tell you how to interpret the world. The new models are about accessing your own inner wisdom and authority. We call this finding your inner guru.

There's a part of you that knows exactly what to do in any situation. This part of you is in touch with your higher self, with the flows of energy around you, and with your clear and focused center. This part knows the world is an expression of energy. Interpreting events as flows of energy helps to determine right action. All you need to do is make sure energy keeps flowing.

Your Authentic Self

The first step in finding your inner guru is living from your authentic self. This concept is being talked about a lot these days. Your authentic self is the part of you that knows you're not your physical body. Your physical body is a wonderful expression and extension of yourself, but it's not who you are. You're something much bigger and more complete. In the words of empowerment speakers Robert Burney and Wayne Dwyer, "We are not humans seeking a spiritual experience; we are spiritual beings having a human experience."

Accessing the inner guru may require you to change. You may find yourself embracing new attitudes and releasing self-imposed limitations. You limit yourself every time you base your identity on fear; every time you see yourself as not being enough, or having enough, or feeling enough to be successful. As we discussed in Chapter 19, fear is a natural and necessary emotion, one you want to acknowledge and learn from. However, every time you let fear take you out of your place of inner knowing, you have linked your identity in limitation. In our example in Chapter 19, your inner guru knows it's safe to cross the empty street. Only your fear keeps you standing still.

> **Celestial Connection**
>
> Living from your authentic self includes acknowledging spirit as it moves through your life. The Mayan calendars, in all their intricate interactions, demonstrate one truth very clearly: there's a cosmic design to life, a plan that's unfolding with the movement of the spheres. Whatever direction 2012 is taking, there's a plan and purpose with a higher level of nature at work.

Developing Awareness

Developing tools of awareness is another means to finding your inner guru. Just as you are more than your body, your awareness is more than the sum of your senses. It includes the ability to access intuition. Your body is an extraordinary instrument. It's equipped with everything you need to sense and interpret the world, including the world of energy. Through your ears, eyes, nose, skin, and energy sensors, you have the ability to perceive minute changes in the environment around you. Keep in mind that the "environment" encompasses everything. Your intuition tells you what it all means. Similar to a radio set or television, you have the ability to connect to any energy in the universe, or at least the ones you resonate with!

According to the ancient Mayans, our bodies have 13 energy portals that resonate with specific areas of the galaxy. By tuning in and listening to the intuition of your body, you will feel the flow and balance of k'ul.

Inner Confidence

To be confident in the changing world, in facing the challenges of 2012, requires you to be confident within your self. The ability to stay calm in a crisis, to approach difficulty with a flexible mind, to look in the direction of solutions, to stay connected to the body and spirit simultaneously, is called "presence."

There's no question that you will need presence of mind, heart, and person as we move toward 2012. Signs indicate that in accordance with the cycles of the past there'll be storms, earth changes, and social upheaval in the upcoming years. There'll also be unprecedented personal growth and opportunity. The two key qualities in maintaining presence are the ability to be centered and the ability to be grounded.

Centering: Staying Connected to Your Inner Awareness

You've undoubtedly heard the word *centering* a few hundred times in your life. You may even practice it already; most people do, many without knowing it! Centering is about attention: your attention. Having your attention focused internally keeps you connected to flows of information coming from your body and subconscious mind. It keeps your head clear and your body calm. In this state, you make better decisions and are more effective. You can see why this might be important as we adjust to the changing times. Centering will help you develop your awareness as well as help you stay clear and focused in an emergency.

How We Get Uncentered

It's easy to get uncentered when you're excited, angry, or in any strong mental or emotional state and your attention is focused externally. Awareness of your muscle tension, tone of voice, body language, and impact on the people around you may completely disappear. We've all been in a restaurant when a couple has a fight. Any awareness of how they're impacting the rest of the patrons is submerged under the intensity of their feelings. We could say that they were in a "blind rage." This is often referred to as being "outside of your body."

The problem with losing awareness of your body is that your body has lots of good information that you need to know. Your body's constantly monitoring the environment, providing feedback to the brain. If the couple had been paying attention, their bodies would have told them how upset neighboring tables were getting! Their bodies also might have provided information to help resolve their crises.

When you're disconnected from your body, you have less information to work with. As if that isn't enough, your brain gets easily overwhelmed. How effective do you think you would be in an emergency without being able to think clearly or act decisively? This is where centering practice comes in.

Getting Centered

Centering is putting your attention inside. It puts your mind, body, and emotions all in the same container. Centering is about staying connected to your inner awareness regardless of the intensity of the external world. When you're centered, you can maintain a relaxed yet focused state of mind. You can act with urgency and decisiveness, yet be calm and focused.

Even if you never have to go through a crisis or disaster, which we hope you don't, centering practice can enrich your life. It's especially helpful in the midst of strong emotional states, even positive ones such as excitement. It's often used by athletes, public speakers, actors, and anyone else who wants to feel stable and prepared before a potentially stressful event. You may decide to begin a centering practice to prepare for emergencies, but we guarantee you will find it a useful practice for all parts of your life and rewarding all on its own.

The How To's of Centering

Anything that helps you feel tranquil and aware can become your centering practice. All that's really required is bringing your attention inside your body. Some people use sound, movement, or essential oils. Others use meditation, breath, or repetitive prayer, like repeating the rosary. Whatever method you use, be patient. Gently bring yourself back into your body every time you notice you are outside yourself.

Here are some suggestions on creating your own practice:

- ◆ Count numbers, such as counting down from 10. Consciously relax as you number down.

- ◆ Use visualization, imagining yourself in a calm and happy state.

- ◆ Repeat a word or phrase, such as a prayer or affirmation.

- ◆ Smile, sending a message of relaxation into your body.

- ◆ Stretch, focusing your attention on moving with your breath.

- ◆ Close your eyes and breathe deeply; count your breaths.

- ◆ Use a visual reminder such as a quote or image.

- ◆ Use sound such as a bell, chime, or your voice to bring yourself to center.

- ◆ Use essential oils (see "More Ways to Center" later in the chapter).

Codex Cues

There are many health benefits to deep breathing. It can increase oxygen levels, increase energy and vitality levels, promote relaxation, decrease blood pressure, reduce asthma attacks, help with anxiety disorders, and reduce stress. Here are some good references: www. drweil.com, www.healthyplace. com, and www.mindtools.com.

Centered Breathing

Your breath is your direct link between the inside and the outside. Paying attention to your breath can be one of the most calming and centering things you can do. Stop right now and check your breath. Without changing a thing, notice how you're breathing.

Is it shallow and fast? Is it deep and slow? Do you bring air all the way into your lungs, pulling it toward your belly? Do you only breathe with your chest? After you have noticed how you are breathing, you might be astonished to discover that it's changing! Without doing anything, your breath is already becoming deeper and slower. This is an automatic by-product of moving attention internally.

Breathing Exercise

Most of us breathe in reverse. If you watch a baby breathe, their tummy expands as they inhale and contracts as they exhale. Most adults do the opposite and restrict their breath in the process. Try this simple exercise:

1. Sit upright in a chair or on the floor in cross-legged position. Keep your back straight but relaxed; lean against support if you need to.

2. Drop your shoulders and close your eyes. Relax your stomach muscles and let your belly be soft and large, even if it falls over your belt buckle.

3. Exhale and contract your belly muscles and push all the air out of your lungs.

4. Relax your belly, letting it expand and pull air into your lungs.

5. For three breaths continue focusing on your exhalation, squeezing with your belly to get all the air out of your lungs. Don't worry about the inhalation; just relax the muscles and it will take care of itself.

6. Now relax and breathe normally. Keep your attention focused on the gentle in and out of the breath. Notice that your belly expands as you breathe in and contracts as you breathe out. Just by using your stomach muscles, you can inspire a centered state.

You can do this type of breathing anytime, anywhere. You can be standing at the checkout counter using your breath to focus your attention. You can be in the shower, driving your car, or even in a deep disagreement. The point of centering isn't to leave the world you're in; it's to be more fully present.

Meditation

Meditation is the practice of mindfulness, or being self-aware. It requires bringing our attention into the present moment. We're often lost in the past or future, thinking about what we want to do, what we didn't do, what someone said, how angry we are, etc. By residing in the present moment, you become centered in your body, mind, and emotions.

When you think of meditation, you probably see someone sitting silently in cross-legged position. While this is a great way to meditate, it can also be done sitting, standing, moving, or lying down. The point is to bring your mind into your body and into the present moment.

Here's a simple centering meditation. Continue doing whatever you're doing. While you're driving, walking, working, or whatever, pay attention to your breath. Breathe deeply and evenly, letting your belly expand as you breathe in and contract as you breathe out. As you breathe in, imagine light being pulled into your body and collecting in your center, perhaps your heart region. As you do this, say the word "calm" in your head. Then relax and exhale, releasing muscle tension with the exhalation as you say the word "now." Continue breathing in and out while saying "calm, now."

Codex Cues _____

For a comprehensive website with user-friendly meditation "rooms" and a really great energy, check out www. meditationcenter.com/center/ index.html.

More Ways to Center

Moving with awareness can be a great way to center. Yoga, Tai Chi, and Qi Gong are forms of moving meditation, as is mindful walking. Try this for yourself: use the breathing and meditation practice above while you take a walk, stretch, or dance with the wind.

Sound is also a powerful tool to induce a centered state. Sound affects brain waves and calms the mind. Music has been used this way for centuries. You can use sound to help produce a centered state. Hit a chime and focus your awareness on the sound entering your ear and moving inside your body. Every time your attention goes back outside, hit the chime again.

Essential oils stimulate the limbic area of the brain and also induce changes in awareness. Put a very small drop of essential oil on the area above your lip and under your nose. Vanilla and lavender are both calming and can be used alone or with centering exercises.

Keep Your Feet on the Ground

Here's another abstract concept involving the placement of your attention. When you hear the expressions "his feet are on the ground," and "she's a real down-to-earth sort of person," you know exactly what's being described. People who are grounded are connected to their strength. They have their wits about them. Grounding is being completely in your body, aware of your physical sensations, being present mentally and emotionally, with your attention focused on the earth. Connection to the earth fortifies your inner core of strength.

Grounding is something we all do with different levels of success at different times. When we're ungrounded, we're unfocused and our attention is scattered. Can you imagine trying to find your strength when scattered and unfocused? Once you learn grounding techniques such as the exercise we present in a moment, you can apply them instantaneously.

Responding vs. Reacting

You've certainly experienced the difference between responding versus reacting. When you react, it's a reflex, an impulsive response without thought. When you react, you don't take onboard all the available information and you rarely create a positive solution. A response is different. When you respond, you pause and consider all aspects of a situation. When you respond, you're taking the best possible course and acting out of choice. When you react, you are not in control of the direction you are going.

You may not always know when you're in reaction mode, but your body does. When you're in a situation that requires action, take a moment to check in with your body. If you're relaxed but alert and ready to go, able to think through problems, you are responding. If you're breathing shallowly, stressed out, and highly emotional, you're reacting.

The most important step to shifting from reaction to response is awareness. Once you've checked in with your body, you've created the awareness to take control. At that moment it becomes a choice; you can give yourself over to fear or you can open yourself to creative thinking and problem solving.

Grounding Exercise

Here's a short meditation to bring you back into your body when you're feeling overwhelmed:

1. Close your eyes and sit in a comfortable upright position, with your feet on the ground.

2. Let yourself breathe deeply and comfortably.

3. Notice your breath without changing a thing.

4. As you breathe, feel the air flow into your body.

5. Imagine that your feet have become roots, growing deep into the earth.

6. As you breathe, pull energy up from the earth, up through your feet and into your body.

7. As you inhale, let the energy rise into and through your body and out the top of your head.

8. As you exhale, let the energy drop back down into the earth to the source of safety and strength.

9. Allow your body to feel recharged, strong, and free.

Energy Awareness

K'ul flows through planetary alignments and pulses through the universe. K'ul flows along channels in the earth and channels in your body. Your body has sensors that give you the ability to feel the flows of k'ul. Maybe you already do. You can become more aware of k'ul with a few easy exercises.

Energy Exercise

Feeling energy is like any other skill—it takes practice. K'ul can be felt as the field around bodies, as the flow between bodies, and as the essence within bodies. The easiest way to start feeling it is by focusing your attention on the space around bodies and objects.

Try this simple exercise to help you feel the pulse of k'ul. First, rub your hands briskly together to build up some heat. Then hold your hands about twelve inches apart with your palms facing each other. Keep your hands relaxed, fingers separated, and wrists loose. Gently pulse your palms forward and backward, sending k'ul backward and forward. You'll feel it like a gentle push against the center of your palm. You can make the pulse bigger by bringing your hands close together and then separating them rhythmically. Play with the distance and speed. As they come together, k'ul builds between them creating resistance. It feels like trying to push the north poles of two magnets together.

Now let's try feeling the energy of a body or object. You can pick a plant, person, animal, crystal, or anything you feel connected to. Use your hands and float them about six inches above the body. Follow the contour and notice what you feel as you pulse your palms in and out of the energy field.

What to Expect in Energy Work

What did you notice as you played the energy game? Every one is a little different but here are some common experiences. You may feel temperature changes in your hands, either hot or cold. You may feel tingling, pulsing, or waves of sensation. The truth is that your hands are antennae; your radio station is actually located in your solar plexus. As your hand passes over your friend's body, you may notice sensations in your solar plexus. You may also have images in your mind's eye. As you start these experiments, keep a journal and keep track of what you feel.

As you practice, you'll become more sensitive to energy and your body may go through changes as your nervous system gets upgraded. You may have sudden jolts, hot flashes, or feelings of warmth running through your body. Don't worry, this is all a natural part of your developing awareness.

Positive Thinking

K'ul flow is directed by your mind. As you focus your attention, your energy follows. This is the power behind grounding and centering. Positive thinking directs your thoughts like emissaries you send out of your kingdom, into the world. Your emissaries will bring back whatever you send them to find.

As time accelerates, the relationship between your thoughts and what they create is becoming more immediate. This makes it important to be aware of each thought you choose. Here's an experiment for you. Pick an event that happened to you in the past day. Try to follow the thread of causation to the thought or belief that created the event. Do this every day for a week. Are you noticing that your thoughts are creating outcomes faster each time?

Maintaining Integrity

Have you ever done something and later wondered what on earth you were thinking? It's easy to lose your *integrity*, or connection to your wholeness, when you're stressed. The world looks different; solutions look different. What's possible and impossible become confused. You step out of integrity any time you're not responding from your authentic self.

def•i•ni•tion

Integrity is the quality or condition of being whole or undivided; completeness.

Keeping your connection to your inner guru takes practice. It's really easy to jump right out of your body and back into fear and limitation. This is the effect of the old structures that are collapsing clashing with the new structures you're creating. Here's a tip for getting back on track.

Start a practice of stopping several times a day and checking your level of groundedness and centeredness. Just pause with what your doing, bring your awareness inside, and ask on a scale of 1 to 10, how grounded are you at this moment? How centered are you? Just becoming aware that you are not grounded or centered will bring your focus back. As this becomes a habit, when you get stressed and start to jump outside of your self, your inner guru will pull you right back in.

When all else fails, remind yourself that this is all part of a larger cycle with a plan and a purpose.

Remembering Your "Wayeb"

Do you remember your "Wayeb" from Chapter 2? It's your spiritual companion, or co-essence; your spiritual counterpart. Your Wayeb is always available for insight and guidance. You can connect anytime through meditation, journaling, or dream work. Ask for guidance and don't discount the way it arrives. Your Wayeb is working for you in the world of pure energy. Sometimes making changes in the energy world first is the path of least resistance.

The Least You Need to Know

◆ Old structures are breaking down as 2012 approaches and new models are being created.

◆ You have everything you need inside to know exactly what you need to in every situation.

◆ Presence of mind and heart is developed through grounding and centering. These practices can keep you cool and calm in any situation.

◆ Your body is an energy-sensing device, and you can learn to feel the flows of energy in, around, and between people, animals, plants, and objects.

Part 6

After 2012

The current age is ending. The process has been underway for a long time. As it ends, it brings into focus the errors of the past. We can see the wounding of the planet and even our own souls. Lie on your back and look up at the night sky; watch the drama play out in the stars. Go even farther; step out of your body and journey among the stars.

The transformation underway is a return to seeing the essence behind the material, the energy matrix behind matter. 2012 is the end point of all predictions. We have this unique window of opportunity to create something extraordinary. We can clean the wound and we can heal it. It's no longer a matter of being willing to change, because change is upon us, willing or not.

A final message from Toltec Elder Tlakaelel: The world will not end on 2012. It will end when the sun goes out.

Chapter 22

Transformation

In This Chapter

- The rise of civilizations and their end dates
- How the zodiac compares to the Mayan ages
- Arriving where you're meant to be
- Awakening to higher self
- Expanding your mind

Transformation sounds so exciting, doesn't it? Something new and, of course, better. Getting to transformation, however, requires some pretty hard work. We didn't get to the place we're in accidentally. It's the result of a very specific set of attitudes and beliefs about the world. Throughout this book, we've talked about changing those attitudes and beliefs. The act of transformation requires more. It requires a full paradigm shift.

Centuries ago, we stopped believing that the sun revolved around the Earth. We stopped believing the Earth was the center of the universe. The paradigm shift underway is expanding our view still further as to what our position is in the universe. This paradigm shift is called developing cosmic consciousness. In this chapter, you'll see how the predictions culminate in 2012. You'll look at the uniqueness of being born in this time, and the opportunities for growth as the planetary alignment brings in new frequencies.

The Ending Place of All Predictions

Don't you find it a little bit fascinating that civilization erupted on this planet all at the same time? Some 6,000 years ago vast areas of land became more arid, giving rise to the first great civilizations. Suddenly, around 3500 B.C.E., all around the globe, civilizations took hold. And isn't it interesting that the Mayan Long Count calendar starts at 3114 B.C.E.?

Celestial Connection

Mesopotamia gave rise to the Sumerian culture along the Tigris-Euphrates rivers in 3500 B.C.E.; the Egyptians rose along the Nile in 3200 B.C.E.; Stonehenge and other massive megalithic structures were erected in the British Isles around 3000 B.C.E.; civilizations in the Indus Valley and northern China are perhaps the oldest, dating back as far as 4000 B.C.E. And don't forget the Mayans and other Mesoamerican tribes. Our records date to 1200 to 2000 B.C.E., but their own calendar starts civilization at 3114 B.C.E.

What's even more interesting is that so many civilizations have an end date relatively near each other. The Mayan calendar ends in 2012, the Egyptian Phoenix Cycle ends around 2012, the Muslim calendar ends in 2076, and the Jewish calendar ends in 2240. It's as if we are part of a cosmic experiment, started off and given a certain amount of time to run until the results will be calculated.

What's so special about this time? Why is it the focus of so much activity? As so many arrows converge on the bull's-eye, what are they saying about the aftermath?

Age of Aquarius

The zodiac has a lot of similarities to the Mayan ages. Both describe the trip through the precession of the equinox along the ecliptic, a journey that takes approximately 25,700 years. The zodiac divides the ecliptic into 12 stations making 12 zones. Each zone is governed by a constellation. The Mayans, as you remember, divided the ecliptic into five eras or creation ages. As you'll recall from Chapter 6, the precession of the equinox is created by the wobble in the earth's axis. The wobble scribes a circle in the sky, which we call the path of the ecliptic, and one turn around this path is the precession of the equinox.

The zodiac is the first known celestial coordinate system developed by the Babylonians. An astrological age is called a "house" and corresponds to the time taken for the vernal equinox to move from one sign of the zodiac (or station) into another, around 2,150 years. Modern astrology is based on the movement of the planets through the houses of the zodiac.

You may remember the song from the Broadway musical hit *Hair* called "The Age of Aquarius." According to astrology, we're leaving the old age of Pisces, which started around the birth of Christ, and entering the new Age of Aquarius. The New Age, like the Mayan Golden Age (more about this in the next chapter), is marked by the marriage of science and mysticism. It's both scientific and intellectual as well as visionary. Aquarius is the sign of hope, brotherhood, friendship, and humanitarianism. In the Age of Aquarius, the potential exists to achieve world peace and universal harmony.

Like the Mayan researchers, modern astrologers can't agree on when the Age of Aquarius is really supposed to start, or the Age of Pisces end. It's generally agreed that the switchover doesn't happen on a single day, but will be happening around the change of the millennia—which puts it right in the ballpark of 2012.

Phoenix Fire Stone

The first "old world" calendar was invented by the Sumerians and later adopted by the Egyptians. It was based on the meshing together of a 12-lunar-month and a 360-day "floating" solar year. The Egyptians also inherited from the Babylonians the awareness of the precession of the equinox.

The Egyptians called the precession cycle the "Phoenix Cycle." Some say that the "calendar in stone" of the Great Pyramid describes the Phoenix Cycle. Converting dates to the present time period shows the end of the Phoenix Cycle happening in 2012 C.E. Whether the date is contrived to fit the Mayan end date or whether it's an exact conversion is hard to tell. Either way, it's in the ballpark.

If you ever studied Greek mythology, you know the legend of the phoenix, a mythical bird that builds a nest at the end of its lifecycle and ignites it. The nest and bird burn to ashes and a new young phoenix rises from the ashes.

So there you go—another cycle ending that predicts the destruction of the old and the rising from the ashes of the new. The phoenix is still used today to symbolize resiliency, immortality, regeneration, healing, and divinity.

Near-Death Experiences

Remember Dannion Brinkley from Chapter 12? He was struck by lightning in 1975 and was clinically dead for 28 minutes before being revived. His account of this experience was detailed and life altering. He recounts going down a tunnel of light, passing through a life-recall, and then being shown significant earth events. Brinkley was shown that the earth would undergo an electromagnetic polar shift between 2012 and 2014. He went on to say that there would be the "return of an energy system that existed here a long time ago." He claimed the process would be a tremendous spiritual opportunity to raise mankind's consciousness.

Other people who've had a near-death experience also report seeing earth changes and consciousness shifts associated with 2012. As we approach 2012, more and more people are reporting feeling the energy shifts associated with this time period. We described this process in Chapter 19. People are having out-of-body experiences (astral projection), lucid dreams, remote viewing, and trance states.

Codex Cues _____

You can read about the dimethyltryptamine hormone in the book *DMT: The Spirit Molecule* by Dr. Rick Strassman (Park Street Press, 2000).

A newly discovered molecule called dimethyltryptamine (DMT) produced by the pineal gland produces altered states of consciousness, or trance states, indicating that trance states are a natural part of human consciousness. Some think the change in UV light caused by the decreasing ozone layer is activating people's pineal glands causing higher production of DMT, preparing us physically for the times we are in.

You Were Born to Be Here

It's not an accident that you were born at this specific time in history, in the specific place you live. This is a time of immense opportunity. You are here to seize the day; to see the condition the world is in, and act to change it; to see that the world is a reflection of your own inner beliefs and use that reflection to face your own shadow; to use the power of your mind to create a new reality. Just as the power of our collective minds created the suffering we face, we have the power to change. It takes a special individual to effect this change; you are that individual.

The *Chilam Balam* has much to say about this. The "singing Chilam," writer of the *Chilam Balam*, tells us that the ancient Maya had a job to do. They had to listen to the words of wisdom from the "Lords of Light," or masters, and return during the end times to spread awareness. The masters also promise to return and awaken those who have heard the truth in the past, restoring their memory. The same promise is made in many ancient predictions.

How Do You Know?

Some of you might be wondering how you know that you were born for this time. The fact that you're reading this book, or any book on 2012, is your first clue! Look inside yourself right now and ask: Is it an accident? You already know the answer, but here's a list of some of the clues; it's not comprehensive and you don't have to answer yes to every item:

◆ Do you have a love of nature?

◆ Do you feel regenerated in the natural world?

◆ Do you feel drawn to visit the sacred sites of different cultures?

◆ Can you imagine the world at peace?

◆ Do you feel life has purpose and meaning?

◆ Do you feel your life has purpose and meaning?

◆ Are you an irrepressible optimist no matter how bad things look?

◆ Do you watch the stars?

◆ Do you have vivid and meaningful dreams?

◆ Does the destruction of the environment physically hurt you?

◆ Do you feel compelled to make amends with those you are at odds with?

◆ Do you feel angry at the wanton destruction of life?

◆ Does your soul cry for a better world?

You know inside whether you're asleep and living the dream of the material, or whether you yearn for a world of harmony and peace. Consider this: those who are intent on fulfilling personal greed at the expense of others would not be reading this book. You are here because time has carried you here to fulfill your purpose.

It might help to think about this if you are feeling afraid of changes to come, not sure if you are living in the right place or have made the best decisions. If you're feeling unprepared, check in with your inner guru and see what changes you should make. However frightening the changes we're going through seem, it helps to know there's a plan, and that you're part of that plan. Just as each planet is playing its role in the alignment, you, too, are exactly where you're supposed to be. It's not an accident.

Your past thoughts, actions, and beliefs have brought you to this moment in time for a reason. Knowing this deep in your core is part of living from your higher self. There is a Hopi saying: "We are the ones we have been waiting for."

Healing Old Wounds

James O'Dea is president of the Institute of Noetic Sciences (IONS), a nonprofit organization researching the scientific basis of consciousness. Astronaut Edgar Mitchell was one of the founders of the organization. O'Dea says that to be able to envision world peace requires that you let go of your own enmity toward others. This is a profound statement. Many of us hold on to old wounds because we don't know how to heal them. There is an opportunity at this time to heal the wounds of the world. This means your wounds, too. As you work to forgive yourself and others for past mistakes, you are helping clear the lack of forgiveness in the world. Choosing to make yourself available to help the world situation is an opportunity for help with your own healing, too. If you have asked for the masters to come and awaken you, now is the time to let them in.

Changing Self-Identity

Legends from many cultures report the influence in their culture of higher beings. Called the Lords of Light, angels, Quetzalcoatl or Kukulkan, Masters, Shining Ones, and many more names, the higher beings always promise to return. In fact, they promise to return regularly, at the beginning and end of each time cycle. Each cycle seems to be separated by cataclysmic events, as with the changing of the Mayan ages.

The *Chilam Balam* tells us we will become as gods. This promise is repeated in numerous cultures and legends. In his book *The Book of Knowledge: The Keys of Enoch* (see Resources appendix), Dr. J. J. Hurtak tells us that humans are destined to evolve beyond our present "terrestrial" form. It seems the evolutionary bottleneck we're going through may be pushing us into higher realms.

Becoming as Gods

Many cultures have legends of men becoming gods or gods walking among men. In the Old Testament of the Bible, Enoch is visited by angels and is taken to heaven at 365 years old, where he becomes the angel Metatron. In the Mayan tradition, the same happens with Pacal Votan.

Gods, or the sons of gods, come down and walk among people. In the Mayan legends, Kukulkan walked among men and promised to return in the final days. In Christianity, Christ lived on earth spreading the word of God. When he was crucified, he promised to return in the end times.

The Egyptian legends talk of the Shining ones; there's also Lord Krishna, Buddha, Odin, and the Native American Pahana.

The Mayan legends tell us that this time when Kukulkan returns he will return within the people and "you will become as gods."

Language of the Gods

Dr. Hurtak reveals in *The Book of Knowledge: The Keys of Enoch* that the language of the gods is the language of light. He explains that the language is encoded in natural waveform geometries and is a language of harmonics. The language is a combination of sound and light waves whose vibration travels through the nervous system activating higher consciousness. Isn't it interesting that insight is called illumination?

Imagine celestial bodies in the sky, emitting light and sound that resonate through the planetary alignments. Imagine the thirteen portals in your body as keyholes, accepting the keys of light and sound, vibrating with the resonance of the heavens. How can you awaken these portals within your self to better receive the vibration?

Awakening the Light Within

Prophecies say that people will be drawn to sacred sites in the times leading up to 2012. According to Mayan Elder Hunbatz Men, visiting the ancient sites of the Maya will "correct" your DNA so you can more easily experience the awakening. Dr. Hurtak explains that the light harmonics are sonic equations that are coded into the pyramids and sacred structures. Visiting the sacred sites might well awaken your higher consciousness. All the sacred sites around the world are part of an energy grid system you can tap.

You don't have to visit a crop circle or sacred site to get the benefit of this vibration. You can meditate on the symbols, you can visualize the pyramids, you can work with sound and light healing techniques.

In Chapter 9, we talked about the body's energy centers, or chakras. Although the word "chakra" is from the Hindu tradition, depictions of these energy centers can be seen on Mayan murals, figurines, and glyphs. The chakras are places in the body where consciousness is processed. Each has a color, a sound, a balanced and imbalanced emotion, and a development challenge.

Codex Cues

Mathematician and astronomer Dr. Gerald Hawkins used harmonics to decode crop circles. Comparing the measurements of design elements within crop patterns, he found they were composed of diatonic ratios. For example, when decoding a simple circle with a ring around it, he took the diameter of the ring and compared it to the diameter of the circle to find the ratio between the two. Were these ratios part of the language of light? Many think so. Our experience is that the vibration of the patterns, whether human or man-made, is waking up the ancient energy sites and pathways in the land as well as the chakras, or energy centers, in the body. The language of light is speaking.

The Maya have a saying, "You are the pyramid and the pyramid is you." Hunbatz Men claims this relates to the fact that both the human body and the pyramids process energy. Energy is raised from one frequency to another as it travels up your chakras or up the steps of the pyramid. In both, as the frequency rises, cosmic consciousness is awakened. As 2012 approaches, the energy systems in the pyramid and in your body are being awakened.

As this process of awakening is underway, you may experience some challenges. Your nervous system is conditioned to handle the frequency and amplitude of energy in your normal life. To use more energy requires preparation. The sudden rising of frequency can be likened to running 240 volts of the English electrical energy grid through an appliance geared for the American 110-volt system. You may experience some strange sensations as more energy enters your system. You may feel a tingling sensation all over your body, or jolts of energy that cause you to jump. Many people feel a vibration that starts in the sacrum or solar plexus. The vibration can cause restless leg syndrome. You can use the grounding and centering meditations in Chapter 21 to help.

You may want to start training your system to handle larger amounts of energy in preparation for 2012. You can do this with energy awareness exercises. Consider a practice that combines meditation with breathing and visualization. Tai Chi, Qi Gong, and yoga are good ways to start.

Awakening the energy centers of your body will give you added insights, clarity, and perception. It will help you feel the path you should be on and make decisions easier. It will awaken your telepathic and psychic abilities; abilities we all have but that aren't expressed until the chakras are cleared and opened. It will help you empower and activate your goals and choices and establish your connection to the larger universe.

Cosmic Consciousness

Many think that as we move into this next era, the importance of spirituality and spiritual contact with higher forces will be more important than science. We like to think they will be of equal importance as we see science evolving to understand and embrace spiritual concepts.

Cosmic consciousness refers to the ability to perceive yourself as an interconnected part of a larger whole. The idea is that we are alive in a living universe. Everything here is a part of a larger organism; we can call this organism the universe, or life, or creation. The point is that it is alive, conscious, and interconnected. It has a purpose and a plan; it's not random.

This living organism forms a collective consciousness that we can tap into. Just being aware of this concept changes people's behavior in critical ways. It's impossible to seek revenge on another part of yourself, isn't it? The Mayan have a traditional greeting, *In Lak'ech Ala K'in*. The modern-day interpretation means "I am another yourself."

Unlocking the Doors

It has been hard for most people to open themselves to spiritual experiences. Many people try to feel energy and don't succeed or try to meditate but can't calm their mind. Maybe you feel this way yourself. Sometimes it feels like you don't have the necessary equipment, or you're closed down in some important way.

Dr. Hurtak explains that the human body and mind have gotten out of balance with "the neuro-physiological governance and biological providence" in nature. Let's clarify. Our bodies and minds become entrained with the rhythms around us. Entrainment happens when rhythms harmonize. The classic example is when you put a bunch of grandfather clocks together in a room. They all have the same rhythm, the pendulum moves every second, but they are out of step with each other. The pendulums are moving in all different phases of the swing. If you leave them together, within a sort period of time, say a day, all the pendulums will be moving in sync with each other. This is entrainment.

We have rhythms in our body that are governed by rhythms in nature. Unfortunately, we are not exposed to them. We live in cars and houses and offices, walk on streets, and wear shoes. Like the digital clocks of today, there is no pendulum to synchronize. The cure is simple. Spend time in nature, spend time focusing on the energy flowing between all life. Imagine it in your mind as a beautiful multicolored movie with the most wonderful music you've ever heard. When all of our minds and hearts are in sync with the earth, just like the laws that govern the clocks, the new world will have arrived.

Celestial Connection

Many adults have not experienced the love and connection with another species that animals offer. Those fortunate enough to have lived in the extended family with animals know the qualities to which we speak. Animals are very special and show us unconditional love, loyalty, and respect, which should be cherished. They give us an experience beyond humans that we have not found anywhere else. One sees far too often that a lack of respect for animals goes along with a lack of respect for self and others.

The Return of Wisdom

We need more than belief to experience higher consciousness. We need wisdom. Wisdom and belief together inspire awakening. Awakening allows the connection to other realms and intelligence that we seek. The prophecies tell us there will be a return of wisdom. Each of us is a vessel, fully equipped to receive it. You might be a little rusty, but there are cures for that.

Spend time outside, spend time with animals, dance, and develop meditation skills. Listen to music, draw, paint, and be creative. Give back to the community; spend time with people, helping, listening, being present. Listen for your guides and guidance; be opened to new experience. Enjoy each breath. Become the change you want to see.

The Least You Need to Know

- Civilizations arrived within the same period of time all across the globe. Most of these civilizations provide an end date of somewhere around the year 2012.

- Modern astrology has predicted the Age of Aquarius sometime around the year 2000. The Age of Aquarius shares many similarities to the Mayan Golden Age, such as brotherhood and humanitarian and spiritual pursuits.

- There's no accident in your being here now. You're uniquely geared to this time and this challenge.

- Sacred texts from around the world, including the Maya, tell of the gods walking among mankind with promises to return again at the end times. They also say "humans will become as gods."

- The language of the gods is the language of light and sound. It stimulates people's nervous system and awakens cosmic consciousness.

Chapter 23

The Mayan Golden Age

In This Chapter

◆ Preparing for change

◆ Activation of the ancient energy grid and pyramids

◆ Importance of the Schumann Resonance

◆ Reunification with nature and natural time

◆ What the New Age might look like

The prophecies speak of a Golden Age that will follow the devastation and transformation of the present age. Many people wonder how complete the destruction of the old age will be, how the transition will take place, and what to do to prepare for it. You may also be wondering what the new world will be like. Clues in the Mayan texts and ancient legends help us visualize the changes to come.

In this chapter, we explore what to expect with the changing age. We discuss the transition and how to prepare for it. Using the vision of prophecies from the past, the Elders of today, and 2012 visionaries, we'll draw a picture of the transformed future.

Advancing to the New Age

The approach to 2012 is both the destruction of the old and transformation into the new. It's been called a spiritual evolution, awakening people to a higher level of consciousness. But what will this transition entail? Is there total destruction or can we avert it? Will many people die in storms, earthquakes, and famines, leaving a small population to rebuild? And most important, can we somehow make a leap forward in consciousness and avert disaster?

Our actions of the past have set the earth on a course of destruction, but how difficult the rectification is and how many people are caught in the earth changes seems to depend, at least in part, on us. How much we are able to grow right now in this purification process will impact the result. Let's take a look at the possibilities.

Path of Destruction

World conditions leave no doubt that change is required to avoid catastrophe. Forces have been set in motion that are propelling us toward doom. These are not supernatural forces; they are the activation of homeostatic mechanisms of the earth. They are mechanisms that balance the extremes of the atmosphere, the climate, and the instability of the magnetic core. As discussed in Chapters 15, 16, and 17, our actions have brought the earth to the brink of its ability to sustain our relentless demands. Purification is essential.

Purification does not have to mean destruction, however. It can mean we simply change and move into alignment with higher consciousness. Right now earth changes are already happening daily. News reports detail earthquakes, cyclones, hurricanes, global warming, tornadoes, and terrible losses of life. According to many prophecies, this pattern will continue—and grow much worse. Some say it's too late to avoid the consequences of our past actions; others say transformation is underway and bringing with it the knowledge we need to avert destruction.

The more we do right now to cleanse, heal, and rebalance ourselves and the planet, the easier and less destructive the transition will be. It's thought that the technologies of the past might rise to help us through the end of this world, helping to diminish the destruction as the old passes. But no matter how much we heal, averting total destruction may not mean averting *all* destruction. Seismic activity indicates earthquake forces building off the coast of California. The Yellowstone caldera is building pressure. Loss of life is possible. It's time to move to a new paradigm.

We used to think the sun revolved around the earth; the earth was the center of the universe. Now we know our little planet is one among billions and billions. According to the Maya, celestial bodies in the universe are in constant interaction. Our science is learning that we are not isolated from what's happening on those other stars. Right now, we are witnessing solar flares on far distant suns across our galaxy, flares that dwarf those of our own sun. How much is our solar system affected? How much of the imbalance that we have created here is felt in other systems? These questions have no answers. Maybe in the future we will have expanded our awareness enough to know more.

Preparing for Transition

At this moment we are poised to go through the destructive phase of the transformation. Whether we are able to shift enough people and to shift far enough along the path to avert destruction is unknown. So we need to prepare on many levels.

Chapters 19 and 21 discussed what you can do to prepare yourself internally. Clearing yourself of limiting beliefs, clearing your internal energy pathways, and learning centering and grounding techniques will prepare you for challenges ahead. Doing this work will ensure that you are in the right place, at the right time, in the right relation to yourself and to the earth. Does this mean you won't be challenged or caught in a natural disaster? Maybe not, but you will be able to meet the challenge with courage. You will have access to the inner guru that will guide you through, your inner resources will be at maximum, and your integrity will be intact.

External preparation is important, too. Chapter 20 discussed how to prepare for storms and crises. In this time of uncertainty, a sense of community is essential. We will need to rely on each other in the times ahead. Develop community sufficiency as well as self-sufficiency. Start a vegetable garden, or better yet, a community vegetable garden. Even if it's on the roof of your apartment building or in a window box, start to think about ways to take care of yourself and the people around you.

World Transformation

As we've said, we did not arrive at this place of imbalance accidentally. We arrived here as the result of a very specific worldview that didn't account for the spiritual in matter. The work underway is to expand our awareness to acknowledge this. The Maya say that in the end times the masters will return to awaken the knowledge of the past.

What was that knowledge? The Maya not only were aware of spiritual forces in matter, they knew how to activate and use them. This knowledge involves frequency, vibration, and harmonics. It's the basis of the knowledge of the transformed world.

The change that is needed is the simplest change in the world. It requires moving into an age of truth and respect. In truth is clarity. We have seen that the lack of truth in these times has brought about the katun prophecy of people losing their faith in governments, leaders, and religions. This in turn is the catalyst of the change we seek. When we see through the lens of truth, we see the laws within nature. This one simple change would change everything, our behaviors and our thinking. The prophecies of many cultures say we will be as gods, the return of the Kukulkan will be inside each person. The ability to adjust the physical world with vibration and frequency will unlock the doors of resonance and the fifth age will unfold. Don't forget the fact that you are a powerful spiritual being!

Energy Activation

We have hints of what this new world will be like from the Mayan worldview, legends of Atlantis, and present-day visionaries. The first thing we're told is that the ancient energy grid work on the planet will be reactivated. This reactivation is occurring as the alignment of 2012 approaches. It's said that it will be complete as the center of the galaxy aligns with the Sacred Cross.

The land of the early Maya is covered with a highway system of k'ul, or vital life force that flows along channels covering the entire planet, providing vitality and enlivening the earth. (See Chapter 2 to refresh your memory on what k'ul is and how the Maya used it.) K'ul accumulates at intersection points that all ancient cultures referred to as sacred sites. To harness this energy the Maya erected buildings, pyramids, and temples over these sites.

What will it mean if this energy grid work reactivates?

Imagine that you can see k'ul and how it flows and accumulates. Visualize a city designed on the flows of k'ul. Some channels of energy will be wider and faster flowing, and contain larger amounts of k'ul. They will be brighter, more active. The intersection of these lines will overflow with effervescent energy. A pyramid placed on this site would literally light up. Can you see an entire city lit with vital energy the way our cities are lit with electricity? Can you envision aligning with this source of energy for personal empowerment?

The return of this knowledge and restoration of this system may provide the natural energy we need to create a technological society that's in balance with nature. More correctly, we may find a new technology that is earth-friendly—maybe "Gaiaology" would be a good term.

Not only was k'ul important to Mayan city design and buildings, the pulsing flow of k'ul was an integral part of planning the activities of daily living. We may again begin to harmonize our activities with the flow of energy.

Pyramid Activation

The Mayans say that when the energy grid reactivates, the pyramids and sacred sites will activate as well. What will it mean for the pyramids to activate? We've said in Chapter 3 that the Mayan pyramids were coded with information. This was accomplished in two ways. The Maya created a library in stone by encoding information in the pyramid geometries and wiring these geometries into the grid work of the planet. In addition, they were aligned with the movement of celestial bodies and activities. When the grid and the sites are reactivated, the information they code will be transmitted across the planet along the k'ul lines.

Celestial Connection

It may sound strange to you that information can be transmitted on energy. It's the same as using cell phones or radios. In modern technology, information is coded onto microwaves, radio waves, and other frequencies in the electromagnetic spectrum and transmitted. If you have the appropriate receiver, you can receive the information. More recently, frequencies of light are being used as information carriers as multitudes of signals are being sent along fiber optic cables. K'ul, or vital energy, also exists along the electromagnetic spectrum but in a range that's outside of our measuring devices. When we create instruments that measure this frequency, what the Maya did will seem no more like magic than our own technology.

The Maya say their pyramids transmit information using harmonics. Elder Hunbatz Men says that sacred pyramid sites "vibrate at a higher frequency that is more open to cosmic consciousness." He continues to say that visiting the sites opens the nervous system to receive sacred wisdom. It seems the pyramids were never really asleep; we were. The energy system has been quietly doing its work, but it's been functioning with a lot of blockages in the system. The industrial revolution messed up the energy flows and natural systems. The process of removing those blocks has been underway by Elders of many traditions for the past few decades, and sacred sites are being reenergizing. As the pyramids reactivate, people visiting the sites are changed.

J. J. Hurtak, author of *The Book of Knowledge: The Keys of Enoch* (see Resources appendix), has done extensive research with his wife Desiree into the Mayan and Egyptian pyramids. They say that the pyramid sites are advanced harmonic structures. Using ancient chants and vocalizations, they demonstrated the power of the pyramids to produce "visible standing waves of light." The power in the pyramids aligns with the positions of the celestial bodies, pulsing this energy into the planet. The pyramids also activate the corresponding frequencies in the human chakra system that we talked about in Chapter 22.

If you're starting to feel that you want to visit sacred sites, there are some excellent tours to look into. Not all tours are the same, so be sure the one you sign on with is offering what you would like. Here are two groups that offer small, personal tours geared toward energy training:

◆ If you're interested in Mexico, Central America, or Peru, check out One Community Programs at www.onecommunityprograms.com.

◆ If you're interested in England and crop circles, check out Circle Research Tours at www.cropcircles.org/TourSite/Welcome.html.

Schumann Resonance

When the grid work and the sacred sites are activated, the entire harmonic of the planet will be affected. This sounds a little intangible, so let's look at what it means.

The earth actually produces an electromagnetic frequency called the Schumann Resonance (SR), named for the physicist who theorized its existence back in 1952, Dr. Winfried Otto Schumann. The Schumann Resonance is essentially electromagnetic radiation that gets stirred up whenever we have lightning discharge. You'll often hear that the SR is 7.8 hertz (htz.) or cycles per second. Actually, 7.8 htz. is the average frequency; it spikes higher with lightning activity. The general range is between 6 and 50 htz. As long as the earth's lightning activity remains relatively constant, the SR remains the same.

However, the SR has been rising. The new average SR is upwards of 13 htz. And of course the increase in solar sunspot magnitude and activity during the solar maximum in 2012 will further increase the SR. It's hard to imagine that the SR makes much difference to humans, but it does because of entrainment, which we talked about in Chapter 22. All life on the planet is in sync with the SR, specifically human brainwaves; if the SR changes, your brainwave patterns change, too. Since brainwave activity is linked to states of consciousness, changing the SR changes our consciousness.

The SR is changing with increasing earth events leading toward 2012. In addition, many think activating the grid work of the planet will shift the SR (and our consciousness) still further. In effect, the forces that are creating the purification are the same forces providing us with the input needed for transformation and the ability to survive the purification underway.

> **Cosmic Caution**
>
> The Schumann Resonance rises with the increasing incidence of lightning. On March 3, 2008, there was an unprecedented amount of lightning with 14,000 strikes occurring in Mississippi and Alabama over the course of just one hour!

Inspiration from Atlantis

The lost continent of Atlantis is persistent in Mayan legend (check back to Chapter 1 for a reminder). The destruction of the third age occurred with the "earth shaking, fire falling, and a huge flood" which covered their ancient homeland called Aztlan. Mayan murals depict the people fleeing their sinking home in canoes. Other cultures have legends about Atlantis as well. They tell the story of an advanced civilization, based on high technology, which was destroyed because they lost their spiritual compass. The legends tell of survivors fleeing in different directions and founding the Egyptian and Mayan civilizations. The pyramid structures and astronomical understanding of these two cultures are said to have come from Atlantis, or Aztlan, as the Maya would say.

J. J. Hurtak takes this information further. He describes a worldwide pyramid temple system linked together on key energy channels acting like antennae. He says the temple system was activated with harmonics and used to stabilize the tectonic plates. It's been predicted by some that the lost pyramid-temple system will reemerge as we approach 2012, and hidden pyramids will be uncovered as earth changes reveal ancient cities from our past. Could it be that if we successfully move to transformation this system could be reactivated to stabilize events to come?

> **Celestial Connection**
>
> In Visoko, Bosnia, a 2,120-foot hill rising above the town was theorized in 2005 to be a man-made step pyramid. Excavations in 2006 revealed it to be the first pyramid found in Europe. It's larger than the pyramid of Giza, and author and excavator Semir Osmanagicé theorizes there are three pyramids in the area all connected by underground tunnels. This central pyramid is perfectly shaped with a flat top and 45-degree slopes pointing toward the cardinal directions. It's claimed that workers discovered a paved entrance plateau into tunnels marked with large stone blocks. It's estimated to have been constructed around 12000 B.C.E.

Reunification with Nature

We don't need prophecies to tell us we are out of balance with nature. The evidence is all around us. Every indigenous culture on the planet makes a point of saying modern culture can't have a sustainable society without coming back into balance with nature.

Mayan elders state that reunification with nature is one of the outcomes of transformation. What exactly does this mean? You may wonder if it requires giving up technology. It would seem the answer is yes and no. Technology is great, it just may need redesigning. In the end, reunification with nature is simple. Give back more than you take and live as if the earth is your home.

Detoxification

An important part of living in balance with nature is ridding the planet of toxic waste. The cataclysms of the purification process are essentially a massive detox. Reunification with nature will require establishing enough respect for the creator and the creation to keep it clean. Why wait until 2012 to clean up our act? The times leading up to 2012 are as important as the date itself, and transformation is underway now.

People are feeling the higher frequencies coming onto the planet, and you can see the effects of this all around. Many corporations are going green, new technologies are being created to reduce our carbon footprints, and conservation is the new keyword. Partly the reason for this is the cost of fuel. But something else is going on, too. Changes are underway; this higher frequency is opening people's minds and hearts to new ways of perceiving the world. Simply living to fulfill our base desires is no longer the main impulse. Something new has arrived.

You may be wanting to go green yourself. It's a formidable job to rid your house of all toxic materials. Fortunately, there are many great all-natural cleaning and home care products available. You don't have to do it all at once. Just make a commitment when you run out of something to replace it with an all-natural, nontoxic, biodegradable alternative. There are many fantastic new nontoxic products available for the home and office. Even your standard grocery store will have a great supply. Our favorite cleaning products are made by Seaside Naturals. They're the most effective products we've used and they smell great! You can find out more at www.seasidenaturals.com.

Another important thing you can do is be sure you don't spill toxic materials on your driveway or lawn, or flush them into storm drains. For example, the antifreeze in your radiator is toxic. More birds, cats, dogs, and wildlife die each year from drinking antifreeze than you would like to know. Be aware that what you buy becomes your responsibility to properly dispose of.

Cosmic Caution

Don't be tricked into using energy-efficient fluorescent light bulbs. They're full of toxic mercury and are adding to the hazardous waste in the environment. Believe it or not, you can't even throw the bulbs away; they need to be disposed of in a toxic waste site. Proper disposal is turning into a major nightmare. Of course, if you break one, your house becomes a hazardous site! You want to save energy, but these bulbs have too great an environmental cost. The alternative? Conservation. Use less; turn lights off when you leave a room.

Fuel Economy

There's no question that energy plays a major role in the reunification with nature. The cost to the planet of obtaining, refining, and using fossil fuels is one of the largest factors in habitat destruction and pollution. Here, too, change is underway. New technologies are being developed to produce energy from natural earth processes. Geothermal, tidal, wind, hydro, and solar technologies are receiving major new input in dollars and thinking time. The real breakthroughs will come as we learn how to work with frequency and the energy flows of the planet. Legends from Atlantis describe using frequency to levitate giant stones and move them into position when constructing pyramids. Visionaries talk about vehicles that operate on magnetic pulses, pulsing along the lines of k'ul as highways.

The bottleneck we're going through may have many positive aspects. Fresh ideas and new ways of seeing the same problem arise when we are forced to change. Let's face it, we'll always take the course of least resistance. As long as the old way was easier and worked, why change? The current conditions are forcing each of us to think differently. Out of this comes new solutions, new technologies, and new behaviors.

Medicine for the Future

Another shift as we find ourselves in the new era is how we view medicine. New medicine will use light, sound, and other forms of frequency to create health through resonance and harmonics. Conventional medicine of today is great at heroic interventions, which will always be needed as long as we have physical bodies. However, it's often not so effective at basic healing. It relies more on suppression of symptoms than healing of causes. Traditional medicine of the past was not so effective at heroic intervention, but it excelled at supporting the healing power of nature. Of course, no medicine can truly heal. Only your body has the mechanisms and intelligence required to heal. The best medicine can do is optimize the conditions for healing, remove obstacles to cure, and stimulate the healing power of nature. (These are, of course, the tenets of naturopathic medicine.)

Medicine of the future will create the frequency of ideal health; transmit it on light, sound, or thought waves; and allow your body to come into resonance. Learning to work with the k'ul of the planet will energize the "ideal" and help it manifest. A new world of medicine will indeed have arrived.

In the future, people will have more responsibility and more control over their own health. You might want to start this process now. If cataclysmic events do occur as 2012 approaches, you won't be able to just call a doctor when you get sick. Consider the impacts of this! Just as learning CPR and basic lifesaving is important, a basic herbal medicine kit would do everyone well. Herbal medicine, also called botanical medicine, refers to the use of any plant's seeds, berries, roots, leaves, bark, or flowers for medicinal purposes. Herbalism is becoming more mainstream as its historical claims in the treatment and prevention of disease are being validated through analysis and research.

Codex Cues

You can get great information online for learning about herbs and making medicine kits. Two great sites worth checking out are www.learningherbs.com and www.theherbsplace.com.

Return to Natural Time

Chapters 4 and 5 talked about the effect of the Gregorian calendar. You may find, as others have, that returning to natural time restores a sense of balance. A 13-month lunar calendar, for instance, puts you back in sync with the moon. Why does this matter? Let's look at the most basic level. Right now humanity sees itself as above nature. We use nature, we live on the planet, but we act as if we are not "of" the planet and don't have to abide by natural laws. Just simply basing our time on the movement of the sun and moon restores a little connection to the larger world we are in fact a part of.

Here's another piece of the puzzle. Returning to natural time means reconnecting to the cycles of the planets, solar system galaxy, etc. Remember the gears within gears of the Mayan calendar? We've said a number of times that the calendars marked celestial alignments, which allow flows of k'ul from one part of the universe to another. Alignments create portals through the sky.

The pulses of k'ul transmit different frequencies. Different frequencies activate different parts of your body and mind. When you're aligned with natural time, you're open to receiving these alignment transmissions. Frequencies carry information; by being receptive to the alignments, you become available for being inspired with new ideas, new thoughts, and new attitudes. In fact, you may receive inspiration that will make you the person who designs the breakthrough technology we're looking for.

Living with the Sacred in All Life

The bottom line in reunification with nature is changing our relationship with nature. In the last chapter, we mentioned the Mayan phrase *In Lak'ech Ala K'in*, "I am another yourself." What if we extend this to all nature, all life, all creation? If we believe that the same divine fire that lights your heart lights all of creation and we act as if this matters, we will be reunifying with nature.

The place we may see this first is in our agriculture and livestock industries. Humane and ethical animal practice will prevail in a transformed future. Organic farming and nontoxic food supplies are also part of respecting the divine in nature. New and exciting breakthroughs in this direction are underway.

Several organizations around the planet are leading the way in the future world of sustainability. These communities have been aligning with the consciousness of nature and creation for several decades. You may have heard of Findhorn in Scotland or

Codex Cues

For more information about Findhorn and Perelandra and how to visit them, go to www.findhorn.org and www. perelandra-ltd.com.

Perelandra in Virginia. Both of these communities work with nature's intelligence and strive to create sustainable eco-communities. Findhorn has created a sustainable eco-village and even works with the United Nations to share sustainable technology and food-growing techniques. Both of these places provide training and guidance in connecting with the intelligence and spiritual essence of nature.

Into the Future

If we rise to the challenge the future requires of us, all things are possible. We're moving in new innovative directions that will provide greater personal realization and empowerment while connecting with nature and the larger universe. The possibilities of this are endless!

One thing we need to make clear. We're using models from the past Mayan culture and other traditional cultures to envision the future. But the future will be something completely new. It won't be a repeat of the past, nor would we want it to be. Not everything the Maya did was enlightened. They were advanced in some areas, but just like modern culture, they went off-track in other areas. Human sacrifice, for example, is one area we don't want to return to. Evidence also suggests that at the time of the Maya collapse, slash and burn environmental practices were underway. It just goes to show that no matter how high a civilization can get, there's no guarantee of staying there.

In reality, it seems the Maya suffered the same schism we do. An advanced philosophy was in place to guide them, but they still went off in wrong directions. If you read American philosophy, the American constitution, for instance, is incredibly advanced. But we are not always able to enact it to the same high level. It seems to have been the same with the Maya. So we are not going back, we are going forward!

Learning the Lessons of the Past

We're not the only high technology to lose its balance, nor were the Maya. If the stories of Atlantis are true, there may be a long history of this problem. Society is where it is because of our collective thoughts and behaviors. We're basically changing where we're going by changing how we think.

New technologies and new directions can only come about from new values and beliefs. We create from our values. We have some great values: innovation, independence, freedom, human equality. We also have some not-so-great values: valuing the material over the spiritual, the mind over the heart. Transformation will require valuing the essence behind the physical.

The Good Side of Modern Science and Technology

Technology is amazing. When you consider what the Internet has allowed, how the computer has changed our horizons, and the heroics modern medicine is capable of, it's truly amazing. None of us wants to lose this aspect. But science itself goes through paradigm shifts after which nothing looks the same again. This happened in the past when Newtonian physics gave way to Einsteinian physics. Then again when the theory of relatively gave way to quantum mechanics.

The positive side of cataclysm and the bottleneck we're going through is that it forces new paradigms. We're on the verge of a paradigm shift right now. This shift will guide the development of science in the coming next age.

Micro- and Macro-Understanding

Do you remember the first time you saw a picture of what an atom looked like, with its orbiting rings of electrons? Were you blown away by how much it resembled the solar system? The ancients have always said, "As above so below." The more we get inside of the microcosm and the more we go out into space, into the macrocosm, the more this seems to be true.

When we look at the bigger picture, we can see that there will be no easy future. In order to survive, as author J. J. Hurtak says, "we must be placed firmly in touch with our cosmic counterparts." In other words, we must be prepared to consider other intelligence in the universe and what our place will be in this larger context. Whew! A paradigm shift indeed!

The Least You Need to Know

◆ Internal and external preparation will help ease the transition into the New Age.

◆ In the new era, the energy pathways on the planet will be activated, as will the pyramids and sacred sites. This will have the effect of increasing the Schumann Resonance and increasing human consciousness.

◆ Transformation is based on reunification with nature, the return to natural time, and honoring the sacred in all life. It will affect our medicine, agriculture, and technology development.

◆ Our thoughts and behaviors got us here, and changing our thoughts and behaviors are part of the transformation.

◆ We're approaching a paradigm shift that will expand our awareness of how we fit into the larger universe.

Resources

Books

Andrews, Colin, and Pat Delgado. *Circular Evidence*. Bloomsbury Publishing, 1989.

Andrews, Colin, and Stephen J. Spignesi. *Crop Circles: Signs of Contact*. New Page Books, 2003.

Argüelles, José. *The Mayan Factor: Path Beyond Technology*. Bear & Company, 1987.

Aveni, Anthony. *Empires of Time: Calendars, Clocks and Cultures*. University Press of Colorado, 2002.

Braden, Gregg, et. al. *The Mystery of 2012*. Sounds True Inc., 2007.

Calleman, Carl Johan. *Solving the Greatest Mystery of Our Time: The Mayan Calendar*. Merit Publishing, 2001.

———. *The Mayan Calendar and the Transformation of Consciousness*. Inner Tradition, 2004.

Carter, Mary Ellen. *Edgar Cayce, Modern Prophet*. A.R.E., 1967.

Childress, David Hatcher. *Technology of the Gods: The Incredible Science of the Ancients*. Adventures Unlimited Press, 2000.

Clow, Barbara Hand. *The Mayan Code*. Bear & Company, 2007.

Cotterell, Maurice. *The Tutankhamun Prophecies*. Bear & Company, 2001.

Daly, Herman. *Beyond Growth: The Economics of Sustainable Development*. Beacon Press, 1997.

Drosnin, Michael. *The Bible Code*. Simon & Schuster, 1997.

———. *The Bible Code II: The Countdown*. Viking, 2002.

Freidel, David, Linda Schele, and Joy Parker. *Maya Cosmos: Three Thousand Years of the Shaman's Path*. Perennial, 2001.

Geryl, Patrick. *How to Survive 2012*. Adventures Unlimited Press, 2007.

Gilbert, Adrian, and Maurice Cotterell. *The Mayan Prophecies*. Element Books, 1995.

Hatt, Carolyn. *The Maya, Based on the Edgar Cayce Readings*. A.R.E. Press, 1972.

Henderson, John S. *The World of the Ancient Maya*. Cornell University Press, 1997.

Hurtak, J. J. *The Book of Knowledge: The Keys of Enoch*. The Academy for Future Science, 1977.

Jang, Hwee-Yong. *The Gaia Project 2012—The Earth's Coming Great Changes*. Llewellyn Publications, 2007.

Jenkins, John Major. *Maya Cosmogenesis 2012*. Bear & Company, 1998.

Joseph, Lawrence E. *Apocalypse 2012*. Broadway Books, 2007.

Krupp, E. C. *Echoes of the Ancient Skies: The Astronomy of Lost Civilizations*. Harper and Row, 1983.

———. *Skywatchers, Shamans and Kings*. John Wiley and Sons, 1997.

Li, Hans. *Ancient Ones: Sacred Monuments of the Inka, Maya and Cliffdweller*. City of Light Editions, 1994.

Makemson, Maud Worcester. *The Book of the Jaguar Priest, The Chilam Balam*. Henry Schuman, 1951.

Men, Hunbatz. *Secrets of Mayan Science/Religion*. Bear & Company, 1989.

Pond, David. *Chakras for Beginners*. Llewellyn, 1999.

Phillips, Charles. *Aztec & Maya*. Hermes House, 2006.

Roberts, Timothy R. *Myths of the World—Gods of the Maya, Aztecs, and Incas*. Metro Books, 1996.

Sabloff, Jeremy A. *The Cities of Ancient Mexico*. Thames & Hudson, 1997.

Schele, Linda, and David Freidel. *A Forest of Kings: The Untold Story of the Ancient Maya*. Quill/William Morrow, 1990.

Sharer, Robert J. *Daily Life in Maya Civilization*. Greenwood Press, 1996.

Stray, Geoff. *Catastrophe or Ecstasy: Beyond 2012*. Vital Signs Publishing, 2005.

Tompkins, Peter. *Mysteries of the Mexican Pyramids*. Harper and Row Publishers, 1976.

Webster, David. *The Fall of the Ancient Maya*. Thames & Hudson, 2002.

Websites

2012, Nostradamus, and Edgar Cayce

2012 Predictions   www.2012predictions.net

Edgar Cayce's A.R.E.   www.edgarcayce.org

Ellie Crystal's Metaphysical and Science website   www.crystalinks.com

Internet Sacred Text Archive   www.sacred-texts.com/nos/index.htm

Nostradamus and the Hebrew Prophets   www.godswatcher.com/index.htm

Earth Changes and Population

The Global Oneness Commitment   www.experiencefestival.com

Peter Russell   www.peterrussell.com/Odds/WorldClock.php

The Tsunami Institute   www.tsunami-alarm-system.com

Indigenous Information

The Call of Our Ancestors   www.shiftingages.com

Common Passion   www.commonpassion.org

Gaia News   www.fyicomminc.com/Gaia/gaianews32003.htm

Maya Wisdom: Maya Science and Spirituality, from the indigenous and intuitive http://tribes.tribe.net/mayawisdom

Mayan Majix   www.mayanmajix.com

Saq'Be', Organization for Mayan and Indigenous Spiritual Studies   www.sacredroad. org

Mayan Astrology and Date Conversion

Calendar Converter   www.fourmilab.ch/documents/calendar/

Mayan Astrology   www.mayanastrology.com

Mayan Astrology: Consultancy Services based on the Mayan Tree of Life
http://mayandaysigns.blogspot.com

Mayan Calendars

Articles on Mayan Calendars and Mayan Cosmology by Aluna Joy Yaxk'in
www.kachina.net/~alunajoy/calendars.html

Calendar Converter   www.diagnosis2012.co.uk/conv.htm

Earth Wizards and Their Methods   www.holisticwebs.com/earthwizard/hunbatz.html

Mayan Calendar Tools   www.pauahtun.org/Calendar/tools.html

Note on the Mayan Calendar   http://members.shaw.ca/mjfinley/calnote.htm

Mayan Research Groups

2012: The Odyssey   www.2012theodyssey.com/index.html

Alignment 2012: The website of John Major Jenkins   www.alignment2012.com

The Mayan Calendar: The website of Carl Johan Calleman   www.calleman.com

The works of Maurice Cotterell   www.mauricecotterell.com

New Age Visionaries

Dannion Brinkley   www.dannion.com

Drunvalo Melchizedek   www.drunvalo.net

The Pleiadians, channeled by Barbara Marciniak   www.pleiadians.com

Preparedness

American Red Cross   www.redcross.org

British Environment Agency   www.environment-agency.gov.uk

British Meteorological Office—severe weather warnings   www.metoffice.gov.uk/weather/uk/uk_forecast_warnings.html

Canadian Red Cross   www.redcross.ca/article.asp?id=000283&tid=025

Federal Emergency Management Agency (FEMA)   www.fema.gov/areyouready

Hampshire County Council   http://www3.hants.gov.uk/emergencyplanning.htm

Municipal Research & Services Center of Washington   www.mrsc.org/Subjects/PubSafe/emergency/EM-Planning.aspx

Natural Hazards and Emergency Response in Canada   http://ess.nrcan.gc.ca/2002_2006/nher/ep_act_e.php

N.O.A.A. (for up-to-date weather warnings)   www.weather.gov/view/nationalwarnings.php

Public Safety Canada   www.publicsafety.gc.ca/dir/dir08-050-eng.aspx

The United States Department of Homeland Security   www.ready.gov/america/index.html

Pure Foods and Water

Cost Plus Water   www.costpluswater.com

Free Drinking Water   www.freedrinkingwater.com

Local Harvest   www.localharvest.org

Lotus (water)   www.tersano.com

Organic Consumers Association   www.organicconsumers.org

Research Groups and People

The Academy for Future Science (AFFS)   www.affs.org

The Baldy Institute Inc, and Institute for Resonance   www.mountbaldy.com

Circles Phenomenon Research International, Colin Andrews   www.ColinAndrews.net

Global Consciousness Project   http://noosphere.princeton.edu

The Keys of Enoch   www.keysofenoch.org

Lawrence E. Joseph   www.apocalypse2012.com

Peoplenomics, The Web Bot project   www.peoplenomics.com/history.htm

Science Related to 2012

Science at the National Aeronautics and Space Administration (N.A.S.A.) http://science.nasa.gov/headlines/y2001/ast15feb_1.htm

N.A.S.A. Long Range Solar Forecast   http://science.nasa.gov/headlines/y2006/10may_longrange.htm

New Scientist   http://space.newscientist.com/article/dn13153-maverick-sunspot-heralds-new-solar-cycle.html

Paul LaViolette   www.etheric.com/GalacticCenter/GRB.html

The Laser Interferometer Gravitational-Wave Observatory (LIGO)   www.ligo.caltech.edu/LIGO_web/about/factsheet.html

Travel and Awareness Training

Crop Circle Research Tours   www.cropcircles.org/TourSite/Welcome.html

One Community Programs   www.onecommunityprograms.com

Index